TRADITIONAL OJIBWA RELIGION
AND ITS HISTORICAL CHANGES

TRADITIONAL OJIBWA RELIGION
AND ITS HISTORICAL CHANGES

Christopher Vecsey

The American Philosophical Society
Independence Square • Philadelphia

Fourth printing 1993

Copyright © 1983 by the American Philosophical Society
for its *Memoirs* series, Volume 152
Reprinted 1986

Library of Congress Catalog Card No. 83-72209
International Standard Book No.: 0-87169-152-3
US ISSN: 0065-9738

ACKNOWLEDGMENTS

I gratefully acknowledge the aid given me by the following persons and institutions. Their contributions facilitated my research, organization, and writing of this study; I am indebted to them: Edmund Perry, who encouraged, supported, and defended this as a dissertation project; John Fisher and Carol Ann Lorenz, whose advice has helped germinate and winnow many of my plans; Vivian Cloud and John Nichols, who have introduced me to the Ojibwa language; Åke Hultkrantz, who suggested excellent revisions of my thesis; Katherine Gunning McCarthy and Jessica Bullard, who helped in the preparation of the index and proofs.

John Beaver, Simon Fobister, Andy Keewatin, Pat Loon, Steve Loon, Tom Payesh, Kai Erikson, Hiroyuki Miyamatsu and Anastasia Shkilnyk treated me to great hospitality and inspiration at Grassy Narrows Ojibwa Reserve.

Northwestern University's Graduate School and Department of History and Literature of Religions, Colgate University, and Hobart & William Smith Colleges have enabled me to conduct my research through grants of necessary money.

I am grateful to Murphy D. Smith, Chief Archivist, American Philosophical Society; James H. Kellar, Director, Great Lakes - Ohio Valley Archives of the Glenn A. Black Laboratory of Archaeology at Indiana University, Bloomington; Ruby Shields, Chief of Reference, Manuscripts Division of the Minnesota Historical Society; James R. Glenn, Archivist, the Smithsonian Institution; Josephine L. Harper, Reference Archivist at the State Historical Society of Wisconsin; the personnel of these institutions, as well as of the University of Chicago library, Columbia University library, Hobart & William Smith Colleges library, the New York Public Library, Newberry Library, Northwestern University library, the Peabody Museum of American Archaeology and Ethnology at Harvard University, and Union Theological Seminary's Missionary Library, for the use of their resources.

TABLE OF CONTENTS

INTRODUCTION

The following study describes and analyzes traditional Ojibwa religion and the changes it has undergone through the last three centuries, emphasizing the influence of Christian missions to the Ojibwas in effecting religious change, and examining the concomitant changes in Ojibwa culture and environment through the historical period. Taking into account relevant ethnological and historical data, my primary aim has been to understand: 1) (synchronically) aboriginal Ojibwa religion and 2) (diachronically) how it has changed through time.

Review of Sources regarding Ojibwas

I cannot claim that scholars have neglected the Ojibwas and their religious life. Although no religious history of the Ojibwas precedes this one, my research has been enriched by a wealth of informative sources.

Descriptions of Ojibwa life by missionaries and travelers, collections of Ojibwa myths, and autobiographies of Ojibwas have provided me with close-hand views of their heritage. Passages from the seventeenth-century *Jesuit Relations* (Thwaites 1896-1901) depict aboriginal Ojibwa life and responses to the first Christian missions. Later missionaries, such as nineteenth-century Episcopalian bishop Henry Benjamin Whipple, detail the continuing relations between Ojibwas and Christians, reservation conditions, and the effects of government policies and outside intrusions. Travelers like J.G. Kohl present unsophisticated but stunning insights into changing Ojibwa ways. Some whites, particularly John Tanner (James 1956), lived among the Ojibwas long enough to provide an intimate look into Ojibwa customs, supplementing the testimony of acculturated Ojibwas such as George Copway. Henry Rowe Schoolcraft, married to an Ojibwa woman, published the first collection of Ojibwa myths in 1839. His and the dozens of compilations which have followed are invaluable primary documents about Ojibwa religion. Particularly useful have been manuscript collections which include large numbers of hitherto unpublished Ojibwa myths.

In addition, many ethnological and historical works on the Ojibwas have given me the cultural and chronological foun-

1

dations on which to construct this religious history. Ethnologists have conducted wide-ranging fieldwork among numerous Ojibwa communities, reporting on their language,
social structure, and conceptions, often plumbing Ojibwa
personalities in psychological depth. A. Irving Hallowell's
profound studies of the Berens River and Lac du Flambeau
Ojibwas stand out as some of the most enlightened method-
ological contributions to the understanding of American Indian culture. Other ethnologists, including Sister M. Bernard
Coleman, Frances Densmore, Diamond Jenness, Ruth
Landes, Robert E. Ritzenthaler and Edward S. Rogers, have
characterized the cultural life of individual Ojibwa communities vividly and perceptively. Led by Harold Hickerson,
historians have scoured libraries and archives for written
sources on Ojibwa past and have established comprehensive
chronologies regarding Ojibwa migrations, governmental Indian policy, inter-Indian contacts and societal changes. They
have compensated for the limited interest among ethnologists
in historical change among the Ojibwas as a whole.

Furthermore, analyses of American Indian religions have
included references to the Ojibwas and have helped me establish a conceptual framework in which to examine Ojibwa
religion as a systematic unit in all its salient aspects. In particular, Åke Hultkrantz has scrutinized American Indian religious phenomena and developed a sound methodology for
understanding them. The method I use is my own; however, I
am indebted to Hultkrantz and others — many of whom I
have omitted from my bibliography because their works do
not directly concern the Ojibwas — for demonstrating the
usefulness of depicting religious phenomena in religious
terms, as parts of a religious system.

Finally, I have learned a great deal from Ojibwas themselves, from those living in Chicago, and from those with
whom I conducted intensive interviews at Grassy Narrows
Indian Reserve in Ontario in January 1979. In particular the
Grassy Narrows Ojibwas generously and candidly shared their
religious knowledge, history, and stories with me. Their first-
hand testimony was invaluable.

The following work includes a history of Ojibwa-white
contacts and Christian missions, a description of Ojibwa culture and cultural change, and an analysis of changing Ojibwa

religion — in as comprehensive a manner as possible, taking into account Ojibwas from all areas, from the seventeenth century to the present day. I have attempted to write a history of Ojibwa religion, its persistences and transformations through time, concentrating on the religion as a phenomenon in itself, but not divorced from its cultural and historical connections.

Heuristic Definition of Religion

I have used a heuristic definition of religion as my framework for describing Ojibwa religion, but I do not imply that my definition is the only means of characterizing it. The definition serves to organize the Ojibwa data without violating them.

I have tried, as Hallowell once suggested, to overcome any temptation to relegate foreign conceptions and practices to an undifferentiated hodge-podge of customs (Hallowell 1934: 389). Similarly, I have tried to slip out of my perceptual trappings and enter the native Ojibwa habit. I wish to present Ojibwa religious phenomena as convincingly and empathetically as an Ojibwa might, but without eschewing a scholarly method. I describe the religion as a system but try not to oversystematize. I take local and personal Ojibwa variations into consideration, remembering that traditional Ojibwa religion was not dogmatically codified; it allowed for diversity in belief and practice.

My task has been to present Ojibwa religious phenomena in a way intelligible to both my Ojibwa and non-Ojibwa readers. The definition of religion I use may be less useful in describing religious traditions other than the Ojibwas', but I favor a definition which conforms to the structure and content of the particular religion under examination.

For the purpose of this study I define religion as conceptions of, and relations with, the ultimate source(s) of existence. By "conceptions" I mean ideas and beliefs; however, these do not necessarily insure relations. I wish "conceptions" to be as neutral a term as possible, implying neither thoughts that a person or community makes up and which do not correspond to reality, nor perceptions of existing reality. Whether Ojibwa or any other religious conceptions reveal reality is beyond my discernment.

By "relations" I mean the communication, the active affinity, between the subjects and objects of religion, between those persons who hold the conceptions and the embodiments of those conceptions. Community conceptions are necessary for individual "relations." The community passes down its conceptions through myths and other teachings, but it remains for the persons within the community to establish and maintain contacts with the embodiments of their religious conceptions. Religion is both personal and social in scope, since a person may experience private "relations" with the objects of religion, but those "relations" correspond substantially to community conceptions.

By "ultimate source(s)," the objects of religion, I mean the final, fundamental, and conclusive base(s) upon which all existence depends. In many religious traditions, Christianity, for example, there exists one "ultimate source"; in traditional Ojibwa religion there were many. The paradox of a religious tradition which conceives of many "ultimate sources" finds solution in that each "source" is "ultimate" for an aspect of existence or for an individual Ojibwa. The matrix of many "ultimate sources," covering every aspect of existence in relation to the entire Ojibwa community, constitutes one "ultimate source" of existence.

By "existence" I mean life itself. In some religious traditions this may translate as "being," transcending existence; however, traditional Ojibwa religion did not articulate concern for matters beyond "existence," beyond life. Survival in this life, this "existence," was the Ojibwas' ultimate concern. Their conceptions of, and relations with, the ultimate sources of their existence constituted their traditional religion.

Such a definition needs to be more specific and comprehensive. For the subjects of traditional Ojibwa religion, the Ojibwa peoples, the ultimate sources of existence were extremely powerful beings called manitos. The Ojibwas regarded the manitos as the essential prerequisites for the continuance of life. Humans' existence depended ultimately upon their ability to establish and maintain relations with the manitos.

Ojibwas articulated and passed down their conceptions regarding the manitos through myths, especially in a series of narratives concerning the creation of the present world by the Ojibwa Culture-Hero, Nanabozho. Ojibwa relations with the manitos took place through group and individual ritual activity, largely through a conjuring procedure known as the shaking tent ceremony. Ojibwa youths conducted puberty fasts in order to achieve visions of the manitos and establish lifelong, intimate relations with them.

Because Ojibwa religion was concerned with earthly existence, the desire to obtain game for subsistence permeated religious life. Ojibwas viewed the manitos as ultimate providers of food made available through hunting. Manitos also upheld human health and granted medicine in order to secure human longevity. Thus, hunting and medical concerns were integral aspects of traditional Ojibwa religion. So, too, were specialists in establishing contacts between the Ojibwas and their manitos, in helping to assure Ojibwa existence.

Similarly, because Ojibwa religion concerned earthly matters, its deterioration has carried serious implications for daily Ojibwa existence. Particularly in times of crisis, but also in mundane affairs, Ojibwas alienated from the ultimate sources of their existence have suffered from intense bewilderment and lack of direction.

Summary of Chapters

The chapters of my study disclose my definition of Ojibwa religion and its salient aspects. Following three chapters in which I outline Ojibwa culture and history, recount Christian missions, and delineate Ojibwa responses to Christianity, I begin to portray Ojibwa religious phenomena.

First, I convey Ojibwa conceptions of themselves, the human subjects of their religion, both in existence and the afterworld. In succeeding chapters I indicate the vital role of manitos in maintaining Ojibwa existence, the importance of myths in formulating religious conceptions, the ritual means by which Ojibwas communicated with the manitos, the vision quests by which individual Ojibwas established personal relations with the manitos, the centrality of medicine in Ojibwa religion, and the religious functions of leadership in insuring the continuance of Ojibwa existence. Ojibwas' conceptions of themselves and the manitos, myths, rituals, visions, medicine and leadership, all permeated with vital concern for hunting success: these constituted the main aspects of traditional Ojibwa religion.

At the end of each of the chapters describing traditional religious aspects, I relate how the specific aspect in question has deteriorated, changed, or persisted through the historical period since first contacts with whites. I find that each aspect has diminished to the point of disappearance; the cumulative effect is that traditional Ojibwa religion no longer exists.

In my concluding chapters I show how the traditional religious aspects took on new forms and configurations in religious movements among the Ojibwas. I follow the growth of Midewiwin, a revitalizing development which began in the eighteenth century and which continues today as an esoteric society. Then I discuss divergent religious activities in which Ojibwas have participated, movements which have incorporated some of the traditional religious aspects. I conclude that neither the native religious movements nor Christianity has effectively replaced the traditional religion which has disintegrated through the past three centuries.

Finally, I recount the religious history of one small group of Ojibwas at Grassy Narrows Indian Reserve in Ontario. I note the drying up of traditional religious elements and historical religious developments in the twentieth century, not under some vague process of acculturation, but rather under conditions of oppression and persecution from white religious and political hierarchies. The religious decay, I find, has far-reaching effects on contemporary Grassy Narrows existence.

Criteria for Determining What Was Traditional Ojibwa Religion

Throughout the study I attempt to determine what was traditional to Ojibwa religion and what was introduced by Christian contact, new cultural situations, altered environment, and the like. I have used the following criteria in making such a determination, although it is only in the area of questionable or disputed religious aspects — Midewiwin and the Supreme Being Concept — that I have laid out the evidence in a systematic form. In both cases I have argued that they are post-contact developments, based on the criteria I am now describing.

First, I have looked at the earliest accounts of Ojibwa life, specifically the *Jesuit Relations*, in an attempt to find mention of particular religious aspects. If seventeenth-century sources describe a certain aspect — for example, the vision quest — it was undoubtedly aboriginal.

If these early sources do not mention a certain aspect among the Ojibwas, I do not necessarily assume that it did not exist among them. The Jesuits were not ethnologists; they did not try to record every action of every Indian. Moreover, they probably were not privy to all aspects of Ojibwa religious life. In the case of the shaking tent ceremony, there are no seventeenth-century records of its performance among the Ojibwas. However, there are such records among closely related Algonkians, and I assume that the missionaries simply did not see or record Ojibwa shaking tent ceremonies that did exist. No scholar doubts the aboriginal nature of Ojibwa shaking tents, and I see no need to debate a case that requires no further demonstration.

Therefore, as my second criterion, I have tried to learn how widespread the religious aspects are among the Ojibwas and their nearest Algonkian neighbors. The more prevalent the aspects, I assume, the more likely they were traditional.

Next, I have observed the degree to which religious aspects reflect the Ojibwas' traditional concerns, culture, and religious system. Certain aspects which appear incongruous or anachronistic in the context of aboriginal Ojibwa life are likely to be recent additions to the religious structure. A case in point is the hierarchical nature of Midewiwin. It seems unlikely that such a structure could have had a place in the relatively unhierarchical, acephelous society of pre-contact Ojibwas.

Finally, I have taken the recent testimony of modern scholars into consideration, just as I have weighed the opinions of nineteenth- and twentieth-century Ojibwas themselves. This "modern" literature is essential in filling in the many details of Ojibwa religious life, and indeed the description of traditional Ojibwa religion could not exist without these valuable sources.

Nevertheless, I have not refrained from occasional disagreement with recent scholarly and native opinion. Scholars (myself included) are fallible, and most contemporary Ojibwas are tragically remote from their traditions. I have let the words of neither outweigh all other criteria, in order to produce an original, accurate study. I hope that I have succeeded.

OJIBWA HISTORY

First Contact with Europeans

A t the time of their first contact with Europeans in the early seventeenth century, the Ojibwa peoples existed as a cluster of closely related communities, part of the Central Algonkian language group. They and their closest neighbors, the Ottawas, Crees, Potawatomis and Menominis, constituted what anthropologists today call a culture cluster. They were Great Lakes Indians, possessing very similar languages and ways of life, and recognizing their mutual similarities.

Each Ojibwa community, situated between Lakes Huron and Superior (map A, p. 9), consisted of extended family members united by a common totem. Since marriage with a totemic relative was prohibited by custom, the communities maintained regular contact with one another; however, each community held autonomous authority for itself. These Ojibwa peoples were not a nation or even a unified people (Hickerson 1963: 68).

They represented one of a long series of diverse cultural groups to inhabit the Great Lakes region. Five thousand years ago, long after the last Ice Age had receded, a Boreal Archaic culture emerged, which first manufactured copper objects. The Mound Builders followed from 1000 to 500 B.C.; then the Hopewell culture with its widespread trading system inhabited the area until A.D. 700. Due to changes in the environment and climate, these cultures declined. Around A.D. 1200 the hunting culture to which the Ojibwas belonged came into being in the conifer forests around the glacial lakes (Josephy 1968: 81-92). The rocky soil, foggy skies, and short growing season made agriculture practically impossible in the seventeenth century. These Indians hunted, fished, and gathered foodstuffs in order to survive (Hennepin 1683: 99-101; cf. Yarnell 1964: 144).

Estimates of the aboriginal Ojibwa population range from 4,500 (Bishop 1974: 7) to 50,000 (Ritzenthaler and Ritzenthaler 1970: 4). Although the lower figures are the most exacting, it is probable that Quimby's (1960: 108) estimate of 25,000-35,000 is not too high, considering the present-day Ojibwa population. The numerous communities of Ojibwas

8

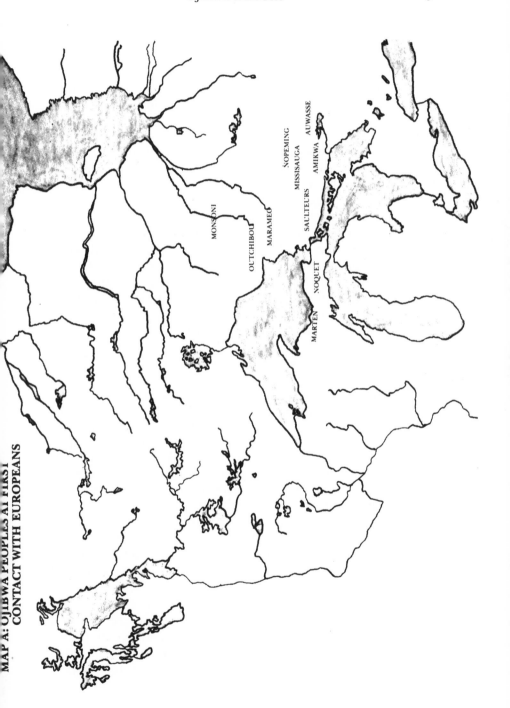

MAP A: OJIBWA PEOPLES AT FIRST
CONTACT WITH EUROPEANS

numbered anywhere from thirty to three hundred persons, depending on the season.

In winter they lived in their smallest units, spread out over large areas in order to survive on the large game, their primary source of food. They hunted deer, moose, bear and beaver, supplemented by occasional lichens, fowl, and fish.

From spring to autumn they regrouped into larger communities, gathering maple sap and greens in the spring, berries and small amounts of wild rice in the summer, and nuts and tubers in the autumn (Yarnell 1964: 144). Even in the warm months, meat and fish composed the bulk of Ojibwa nourishment (Landes 1968: 4-5).

Leadership resided among males but there were no continuing rulers. Those skilled in specific activities led when their expertise was needed; otherwise, they provided for the wants of their immediate family. In particular, the men hunted to keep their family alive; women and children gathered and prepared foods. The family was the basic unit of traditional Ojibwa society (Barnouw 1950: 49-50).

Primary Concern for Hunting

Obtaining food by hunting represented the primary concern of the Ojibwa family, especially in winter when sources of nourishment were relatively limited. Ojibwa cultural continuities revolved around their hunting pursuits, for example, their use of deadfalls and snares, their family hunting grounds (developed in the historical period), and their reliance on animal bone divination and charms for luck in hunting. Their social relationships were colored by hunting concerns also.

Furthermore, European observers found that Ojibwa pride of accomplishment and identity stemmed directly from hunting. Peter Grant, a fur trader for the North West Company in the late eighteenth century, noted that the Ojibwas considered whites inferior to themselves: "They pity our want of skill in hunting and our incapacity of travelling through their immense forests without guides or food" (Grant 1890: 325). Their ability to hunt gave them personal pride; a great hunter was a great person to them, and they considered themselves great hunters. Explorer William Keating commented on their sense of superiority to whites. The Ojibwas, he said, think that they were created to hunt and make medicines (Keating 1824, vol. 1: 168).

Ojibwa preoccupation with hunting showed in their speech and conversation. Activities such as courting were described in hunting terminology and hunting topics predominated discussion. The editor of the narrative of John Tanner, a white American who lived for thirty years among the Ojibwas and Ottawas after having been captured from his parents' home as a child, stated that he had omitted the numerous details of hunting upon which Tanner and the Ojibwas constantly dwelled (James 1956: xix). Despite the omissions, the narrative's major portions dealt with hunting.

The animals which the Ojibwas hunted played the largest part in traditional Ojibwa art. Whites complained that the only thing taught by Ojibwas to their children was hunting technique. Even Ojibwa converts to Christianity in the nineteenth century, educated in white schools, spoke passionately of their hunting accomplishments (Peter Marksman in Pitezel 1901: 165; Enmegabowh to Whipple, 11 November 1893 in Whipple 1833-1934, Box 22). Depending on it for their existence, it was no wonder that hunting was the Ojibwas' primary concern, their preoccupation, the activity which permeated their entire lives when Europeans first encountered them.

French Fur Trade

The earliest contacts between Europeans and the Ojibwa peoples resulted from the French desires for beaver pelts and to convert the Indians to Christianity. Although the Ojibwas felt the first touches of French influence indirectly, through Hurons and other Indians in the latter part of the sixteenth century, they probably did not meet the French directly until around 1610. Earlier trapping of Atlantic coast beavers had depleted the animals' numbers, forcing the French and their native allies to push west into Ojibwa territory.

It was due to this contact that the various Ojibwa peoples became more unified and identified as a people. The *Jesuit Relations* of the seventeenth century mentioned the Mississaugas, the Baouichtigouian or Saulteurs, the Outchibous, the Marameg, the Amikwas, the Monsoni, the Noquet and other Indian communities in the vicinity of Sault Ste. Marie

(Thwaites 1896-1901, vol. 18: 231, 259; vol. 54: 131-133), who in the course of time became the people called Ojibwa.

In 1632 the French fur trade was booming, but the Ojibwas existed at the fringe of the transactions, dealing with the Europeans through the Hurons. In 1649, however, the Iroquois decimated their Huron relatives and the Algonkians filled the bargaining vacuum. By 1641 the Ojibwa peoples had aligned themselves closely enough with the Hurons to attend joint celebrations of the grand Feast of the Dead at Lake Nipissing, a ceremonial made possible by trade wealth and peaceful alliances. Within the decade the Ojibwas and Ottawas replaced their crushed allies as the pivot of the French fur industry at the Sault.

Through the trade — with its central location, its fostering of intercommunity contacts, and its wealth — the Ojibwas came into being by 1670 (Hickerson 1963: 68-70). The Algonkian communities reduced their isolation from one another to join in the trade; they periodically visited the Sault and established villages in its environs. They intermarried with greater frequency and even absorbed many of the French traders into their families and way of life.

In the process they began to adopt French trade goods, items such as axes, knives, metal kettles and other implements which served useful roles in traditional Ojibwa hunting pursuits. By 1670 they obtained firearms to enhance the prospering fur trade. They prospered along with the trade, using their hunting and trapping skills in a new search for profits and goods. In order to protect their enviable position as middlemen, they fought periodically with the Iroquois and Dakotas.

The Ojibwas moved out from Sault Ste. Marie to solidify their trading advantage, first in the 1690s (as the Sault gave way to Mackinac as the French fur and mission center), to Chequamegon (La Pointe) on the southern shore of Lake Superior, which Ottawas and remnant Hurons had abandoned under Dakota and Fox attack in 1670. From Chequamegon they created a commercial beachhead at nearby Keweenaw (L'Anse) by 1710. These proved to be only the beginning of numerous Ojibwa migrations made in the interest of fur trade and conducted along the trading routes. The Ojibwa dependence on commerce during the French regime, until the Capitulation of Canada in 1760 and beyond, colored to a large extent their movements, settlements, alliances and hostilities, in their evolving way of life.

The flourishing fur trade, with its associated mission movement, established a firm union between the French and the Ojibwas, first solidified at a ceremony at the Sault in 1671. Where the tightly controlled voyageurs went in search for the beavers, the Ojibwas followed, contracting new diseases as well as trade arrangements, adopting alcohol as well as guns. Since the Ojibwas continued to use their aboriginal skills, the trade seemed more a blessing than a threat. When the French moved northward and to the west, above Lake Superior to Lake Nipigon, the Ojibwas joined them in the early eighteenth century. They accompanied the Europeans south and east, into Michigan as far as Detroit. By the 1730s they were well north of Lake Superior, pushing the Crees away from a trading station on Lake St. Joseph. To the southwest they settled Lac du Flambeau and Lac Court Oreilles by 1736, clashing violently with the Fox Indians for pelts and profits.

In 1734 French explorer Pierre Gaultier de Verennes de la Vérendrye created a new commercial route from Grand Portage to Lake Winnipeg, and many Ojibwas began their move from the woodlands onto the western prairies. For the southwestern Ojibwas centered at Chequamegon, the new route spelled financial disaster. They had benefited from the previous situation in which they performed trade transactions between the gunless Dakotas (with whom they had formed an alliance in 1679) and the French at the Sault and Mackinac. Now the French met directly with the Dakotas at Fort Pepin, providing them with guns and ending the Dakotas' need to grant the Ojibwas use of the Wisconsin and Minnesota hunting grounds. By 1736 Chequamegon's influence faltered and the Ojibwas migrated along the long portages, forming new alliances with the Cree and Assiniboine Indians to the west, reaching Rainy Lake the following year and Lac Seul in the 1740s (for the period of French contact, see esp. Bishop 1970: 1-6; Bishop 1974: 8-9; Bishop 1976: 44; Hickerson 1956: 289-299; Hickerson 1962b: 12, 69-71; Hickerson 1963: 68-72; Hickerson 1970: 38-40; Kinietz 1940: 318-319; Levi 1956: 15-27; Means 1917: 6-7; Quimby 1960: 147-148; Willford 1951: 4-10, plus numerous other sources in bibliography).

By the end of the French era the Ojibwas were exploring the area east of Lake Winnipeg, having started a base in Minnesota, at Fond du Lac. They had adapted their hunting and trapping skills to European material goods, maintaining traditional subsistence, settlement, and seasonal patterns to a large degree. They had become a cultural unit but were by no means a political entity; they were not a nation with a central organization. Leadership existed on the village level, even for warfare which was taking on a more important role in Ojibwa society as a means of gaining prestige. It appears that population was increasing rapidly and new totems were forming. The Ojibwas were changing, but not rapidly enough to create discomfort.

British Ascension

The French Capitulation of Canada (1760) and the British Royal Proclamation of 1763, which established the bases for subsequent Canadian and United States Indian policies, sent the first waves of shock through the Ojibwa ranks. The following year the British made the first purchase of Ojibwa land, at Fort Niagara, but the Indians were not prepared to accept these newcomers, enemies of their French allies (Henry 1809: 43-44). The Ojibwas participated in Pontiac's battles against the British, destroying Mackinac in 1763.

Only with reluctance did the Ojibwas conduct business with the British traders, who continued to use the French voyageurs for daily contacts with the natives. After Pontiac's defeat, large numbers of British traders entered the Ojibwa territory. The Hudson's Bay Company, which enjoyed a monopoly in the northern British territories, watched as Alexander Henry and his cohorts conducted the fur concession in the Lake Superior area. So many independent trade companies formed that in 1783 the North West Company was founded to incorporate them into an organized venture. In 1805 it subsumed its chief Lake Superior rival, the XY Company, in order to strengthen its competition with the powerful Hudson's Bay Company, which began a southern outpost at Rainy Lake in the 1790s.

During this period the Ojibwas ceased their northern movement and strengthened their hold in Minnesota at Leech and Red Lakes and other inland lakes on the edge of the prairies. Then they began their westward movement past Lake Winnipeg onto the Manitoba plains. In the late 1780s they acquired horses and by 1800 they were hunting large numbers of bison west of Lake Manitoba. By 1820 some traveled to the area of Turtle Mountain, in what is now North Dakota; others continued as far as the Rocky Mountains (Hickerson 1956: 294-299).

Ojibwa prosperity reached its peak during the late eighteenth and early nineteenth centuries. In the rivalry between fur companies the Ojibwas gained favored treatment: they received top prices for their pelts; to win their patronage the competing traders provided them with alcohol and advances of supplies, even setting up their posts to accommodate the Indians.

For their own part, the Ojibwas used the castor of the female beavers to lure the animals into their newly adopted steel traps. In the short run they attained their goal, particularly in the 1790s, when they wore silver brooches, earrings, wampum, scarlet cloth mantles, and other finery which reflected their richness. By 1797, however, they depleted the beaver in the international boundary area between Canada and the United States and were beginning to suffer from a shortage of deer and other game. Some Ojibwas turned to hares, fish, muskrats and other small game (Bishop 1974: 11), others moved farther west (Tyrrell 1916: 204-206).

After years of warfare, the Hudson's Bay Company defeated and enveloped its enemy, the North West Company, in 1821. That date signified the end of Ojibwa wealth. Not only had the Ojibwas exterminated most of the beaver, but they had also lost their trading advantage (Bishop 1974: 255). John Tanner's narrative presented the dilemma. Before the merger he and the Ojibwas obtained gifts and sold their goods at prices of their own choosing. Afterwards, the Indians had to come to the traders: they had lost their power. Furthermore, they had lost many of their traditional belongings which they found hard to replace. Tanner remarked that he had to kill moose now that the trade blankets would no longer be readily available (James 1956: 173).

United States and Canadian Policies

In Canada the Ojibwas became thoroughly dependent upon the Hudson's Bay Company. Their communities came into existence as they gathered around the stationary posts. They needed the company's trade goods because they had ceased their aboriginal manufactures in the boom years that preceded the merger. They had lost many of their skills in the course of a generation or more. Game became so scarce that they vied with one another for the meager rewards of the fur industry. By midcentury they lived under total Hudson's Bay Company control of their economic affairs.

On the United States side they fared no better. John Jacob Astor's trading enterprise began in 1816, with headquarters at Mackinac and Lake Superior posts at the Sault, Chequamegon, and Fond du Lac. Not until the two British companies merged did the Ojibwas consider doing business with the American firm. From 1821 until its liquidation in 1842 the American Fur Company derived wealth from the Ojibwa fur trade, while depleting game and reducing the Wisconsin and Minnesota natives to dependency.

As the western Ojibwa fortunes rose and fell, the Lake Superior Ojibwas entered their decline in relation to the Canadian and United States governments. In 1781 the Mississauga Ojibwas ceded land on the west side of the Niagara River; some of the territory went to loyalist Iroquois three years later. On the American side the first treaty came at Fort McIntosh in 1785 and ten years later at the Treaty of Greenville, Ohio, the Ojibwas and other Indians ceded timber land.

More than twenty years passed before the Ojibwas met the direct threat of the United States and Canadian governments. In 1819 at the Treaty of Saginaw the United States took their lead-rich land in southern Michigan and in 1825 the Treaty of Prairie du Chien created a border between the Ojibwas and Dakotas, who were warring for the plentiful game of the prairies and the broad-leafed forests of Wisconsin (Hickerson 1962: 28-29). The Ojibwas were steadily losing their sovereignty to the United States, which established a Lake Superior Indian agency of the War Department at Sault Ste. Marie in 1822, Henry Rowe Schoolcraft presiding. Two years later the Bureau of Indian Affairs became part of the War Department. The Bureau left the Ojibwas to themselves until 1826, at the Treaty of Fond du Lac, when the United States persuaded them to attest their allegiance, while securing mineral rights from the Indians in return for an annual payment (McKenney 1827: 313-314; 457-458; 480-481).

As the United States inaugurated its removal policies in 1830, the Canadians began the Coldwater Reserve experiment in the southeast corner of Georgian Bay, where the Ojibwas lived in isolation from invading whites, with missionaries and agents to watch over the natives. The reservation system loomed in sight.

In 1833 the Ojibwas were removed from northern Illinois; the following year the U.S. Indian Intercourse Act established a machinery for governing Indians and Indian trade. As the fur trade economy collapsed, as game of all kinds became scarce, as the Feast of the Dead entered its decline in Ontario, as fisheries opened on the Great Lakes and whites entered the Ojibwa areas, the Indians entered the devastating period of land cessions through treaties, losing land for promises of yearly payments and future security.

In 1836 the Ojibwas and Ottawas ceded Manitoulin to make way for Canadians. The following year the Minnesota and Wisconsin Ojibwas made their first land cession at the Treaty of St. Peter's. When copper was discovered in large quantities in 1840 on the south shore of Lake Superior, the American drive to remove the Ojibwas west of the Mississippi began in earnest. In an 1842 treaty the Ojibwas ceded the southern Lake Superior shore in Wisconsin and Michigan, and two other treaties in 1847 took more Ojibwa land in Minnesota, followed by an abortive removal order in 1849. On the Canadian side the two Robinson Treaties of 1850 took Ojibwa land north of Lakes Superior and Huron.

At the Treaty of La Pointe in 1854 the American Ojibwas ceded lands and were reserved territory at Keweenaw and Ontanagon in Michigan, Fond du Lac and Grand Portage in Minnesota, and Bad River (Odanah), Lac Court Oreilles, and Red Cliff in Wisconsin. This represented the first allotment treaty for the Ojibwas. They were divided into two divisions in the United States, the Lake Superior and the Mississippi Ojibwas. Each division had separate treaty rights. The government provided eighty acres to be patented to each full-

or mixed-blood Ojibwa, with the stipulation that the president could survey the land, issue patents, and make rules regarding the disposition of the lands, as well as assign other lands in the case that minerals would be discovered on the allotted plots. The following year another treaty stipulated that the allotted land was exempt from taxation, sale, or forfeiture. Other treaties in 1863-1864 created the Red Lake Reservation and in 1867 the White Earth Reservation began, both with the ex-pressed purposes of making farmers of the Minnesota Ojib-was and removing them from the white population, still wary after the 1862 uprising of Ojibwas and Dakotas. In 1871 the United States ended its treaty policy, during the course of President Grant's four-year Peace Policy which began in 1869. The Ojibwas had lost their sovereignty and all political and economic leverage. They were wards of the state.

The Dominion of Canada formed in 1867. From 1871 to 1875 it conducted five treaties with the Ojibwas of Ontario, Manitoba, and Saskatchewan, where the natives ceded their lands. In 1876 Canada passed its Indian Act and four years later put into motion its paternalistic policies through its Indian Department. In 1905 the Ojibwas and Crees gave up their lands in northern Ontario through Treaty Number 9, and in 1923 the Ojibwas of southeastern Ontario signed the last treaties with Canada, in which they ceded more land and received their last reserves. Their situation approximated that of their American relatives.

From the 1870s the Ojibwas of both countries entered the reservation era, from which they have not yet fully emerged. The policies of both governments aimed at changing Ojibwa culture, from hunting to farming, from pagan to Christian, from sovereign to subject, through coercive education and concentrated control. One of the major tools in the United States was the General Allotment Act of 1887, designed to turn communal Indians into individualistic capitalist-farmers, each working his own plot of cultivated land. It was sup-plemented by the U.S. Indian Service resident staff of physi-cians, and by teachers and missionaries. Many Ojibwas refused to abide by the laws, for example the Red Lakers, and the Leech Lake Pillagers who conducted the last Indian uprising in 1898 against the government policies.

The U.S. Clapp Act of 1906 permitted half-blood Ojibwas to sell their allotted plots, and they found a ready market among the lumber companies. The act also stated that in 1931 the allotted lands would become taxable, and if the taxes were not paid, the land would be forfeited. Only the 1934 Reorganization Act prevented the United States Ojibwas from losing all their land to speculators and the government itself. Approved by most Ojibwas in 1936, the act prohibited future allotments and sales of Indian land, except by the whole tribe, and it authorized land purchases for Indians and allowed individual Indians to return their land to tribal trust (for the history of treaties, land cessions, and laws affecting Ojibwas in Canada and the U.S., see esp. Brown 1952: 57-68; Danziger 1973: 175-185; Hickerson 1962b: 28-29; Hilger 1939: 2-12; Keller 1972: 209-218; Keller 1978: 2-20; League of Women Voters 1971: 14; Levi 1956: 51-62; McKenney 1827: 313-314, 457-458, 480-481; Norton 1830: 4; Winchell 1911: 16-636; Works Progress Administration 1936-1940; 1942: Envelope 1, #11, "Chippewa Treaties," #14, James Arbuckle, "The Removal Order of 1849").

Three and a Half Centuries of Change

Through the past three and a half centuries the Ojibwas have undergone considerable change (Bishop 1976: 43-44; Hickerson 1962b: 88-89; Quimby 1966: 7). Their subsistence patterns have altered; they have migrated from their aboriginal homes; their communities have developed and declined. Their health, leadership, and self-confidence have all deteriorated. As they have participated in the fur trade, met with Christian missionaries, dealt with four different governmental policies; as their intertribal contacts have varied; as they have migrated and suffered from new diseases; as they moved to reservations, intermingled with whites, moved to cities and fought with Dakotas and other Indians, the traditional aspects of their existence have changed.

The first major change was the development of semi-sedentary, and then sedentary, villages from the traditional kin communities. The early fur trade modified but did not radically alter the aboriginal community framework. Even the missionaries, who consciously attempted to form permanent towns around their stations (Thwaites 1896-1901, vol. 54: 139) did not significantly upset the aboriginal organization.

Burgeoning population during the peak trapping years and the rapid depletion of game which followed broke the totemic loyalties of the former period. The game-barren land could not support the large population and the Ojibwas were forced to disperse. In addition, the traders of Hudson's Bay Company preferred dealing with individuals or small families, not extended groupings of many Ojibwas (Bishop 1970: 11-12). Consciously or not, the traders served to weaken tribal communities of large size.

As the Ojibwas migrated in the eighteenth and dispersed further in the nineteenth centuries, their social cohesion and loyalties diminished. Their ties with totem relatives were weakened and in many cases broken. Furthermore, the introduction of liquor disrupted the villages, as drunken violence created and released dangerous tensions, especially in times of starvation. That some Ojibwas intermarried with white traders also helped to debilitate the totem structure.

By the reservation period, factionalism was evident in many of the Ojibwa communities, particularly between full- and mixed-bloods, each of whom accused the other of receiving favored treatment by the governments (Hilger 1939: 18-19). The reservation policies themselves were designed specifically to destroy the extant community cohesion by denying traditional leadership, by altering subsistence patterns, and by removing children from the authority of their parents. In particular, the 1887 General Allotment Act meant to break down the tribal structure by having Ojibwas own their land in private, as individuals isolated from the community. The Ojibwas' situation observed by Ruth Landes at the Manitou Reserve on the Rainy River in southwestern Ontario illustrates the breakdown of community ties in modern Ojibwa life. The reserve is an aggregate of seven villages which, prior to 1914, were scattered and unconnected. In that year the Canadian government joined them together into a single group; they did not develop a sense of unity with their forced neighbors (Landes 1967: 87).

To a large extent the changes in community were brought about by changes in the natural environment. That the object of the large-scale trade, the beaver, was not a migrating animal meant its early demise. The Ojibwas and other Indians were able to trap it easily because they knew precisely where to find it; it was predictable, and vulnerable to the trappers. The increase of Indian population and the adoption of firearms placed too heavy a burden on the large game upon whom the Ojibwas depended for survival. Already by the early nineteenth century, the Ojibwas near Lake of the Woods were forced to live in small family bands of perhaps seven members, each holding between 150 and 180 square miles for the band's hunting pursuits. This large area hardly kept them alive (Tyrrell 1916: 249). By 1821 the Ojibwas were turning to smaller game like rabbits, and fish in the small inland lakes, neither of which supported the Ojibwas adequately. Later they would try to catch bison but would have to fight the Dakotas to reach the large herds. The lack of game turned the Ojibwas to other means of subsistence, first gathering an increased quantity of wild rice (Jenks 1900: 11-13), then planting crops under the insistent tutoring of missionaries and government agents.

The depletion of game forced the Ojibwas to migrate to the prairies and the plains; it caused winter starvation and an apparent increase in cannibalism. Even the fish which were becoming an Ojibwa staple were usurped by the fish industry which began at Sault Ste. Marie by the 1830s. In the reservation period the sedentary Ojibwas were prevented from following game in years of plenty. Whites in Minnesota complained when the Ojibwas left their reservation to hunt deer near Lake Itasca. The *St. Paul Daily Press* on the sixth of January 1864 said that such large game belonged "to white folks," and threatened that the Ojibwa "whelps" would have to be coerced into remaining on their own property, or "else some of them may accidentally be taken for deer by our hunters" (Works Progress Administration Writers' Project 1849-1942, Box 170). In contemporary Michigan, Minnesota, and Wisconsin the Ojibwas are engaged in a running dispute with the state governments over their rights to fish all year round.

Through depletion and later through force the Ojibwas have been alienated from the animals which were traditionally their source of continued subsistence. By the twentieth century one observer at Cass Lake in Minnesota remarked that "some of the present-day Indians have never seen a beaver" (Coleman 1929: 55).

The migrations themselves served to change the Ojibwas, as they came into contact with other Indians as well as with whites, and as new ecological surroundings produced new subsistence patterns. Those who went to the plains adopted the bison economy and many features of plains culture from the Assiniboines. By the 1830s the Ojibwas whom George Catlin met west of Lake Winnipeg knew nothing of the eastern Ojibwas, although they spoke the same language (Catlin 1926, vol. 1: 61). Diversity of culture emerged from the lengthy migrations to the west. Diversity also occurred among a small group of Ojibwas who joined the Mohawk Christian community at Caughnawaga, near Montreal. They, like the Ojibwas who intermarried with the Plains Crees and now live on Rocky Boy's Reservation in Montana, have lost contact with their ancient traditions.

Contemporary Ojibwas

Today the Ojibwas exist as four discretely diverse units (map B, p. 24), sixteen bands in the United States and sixty-seven in Canada (Dunning 1959: 4-8). The Northern Ojibwas, or Saulteaux, live in Ontario and eastern Manitoba, north of Lake Superior and east of Lake Winnipeg. The Plains Ojibwas, or Bungees, live in Manitoba, eastern Saskatchewan, and northeastern North Dakota, west of Lake Winnipeg. The southwestern Ojibwas occupy southwest Ontario, Minnesota, and northern parts of Wisconsin and Michigan. The Southeastern Ojibwas reside in Michigan and southeast Ontario, around Lake Huron. Both southern groups are known officially to United States agencies as Chippewa Indians (for the contemporary Ojibwa units, see Hickerson 1962b: 1-3).

As a whole, the Ojibwas constitute the third largest North American Indian people, numbering around 50,000 in Canada, 30,000 in the United States (Ritzenthaler and Ritzenthaler 1970: 4). In all their diversity they have been set adrift from their traditional moorings; their contemporary culture lies in "shambles" (Hickerson 1970: 17). They possess very little of their former lands. Hunting as a source of food is an activity of the past, although the Canadian Ojibwas in remote areas still do trap, hunt, and fish for some of their nourishment (Bishop 1974: 24-28). They no longer migrate according to seasonal cycles, except for those who work in cities. Most Ojibwas speak their traditional language only falteringly. Many of their towns are indistinguishable from those of their poor white neighbors. They have a high rate of intermarriage with whites and very few full-bloods exist any more. The closest that some Ojibwas come to their traditions is participating in dances of modern creation for white tourists. It is no wonder that many anthropological reports "read like coroners' verdicts" (Danziger 1978: 202) on aboriginal Ojibwas' culture.

Nevertheless, they have not become acculturated Americans (Lurie 1962: 829). Their traditional culture lies moribund but they have not adopted white identity; they have not entered the American ethnic mainstream. They intermingle with whites and white institutions, but they do so as Ojibwas. They distrust whites and white laws; they cling to the remnants of their past, fractured and dimly remembered.

They are not aboriginal Ojibwas; they have changed enormously from the days before contact with Europeans, leading one observer to state that their traditional culture is "for all practical purposes, dead . . ." (James 1970: 439). As a people they stand between their traditions, from which they are removed, and white traditions, which they have not accepted.

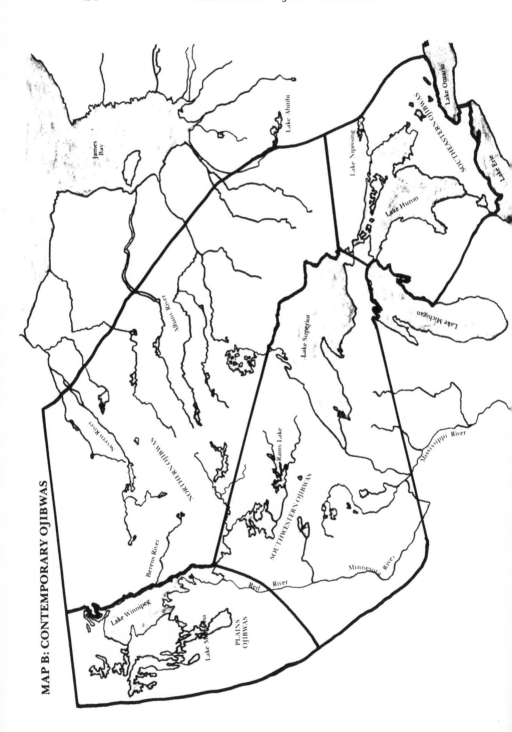

MAP B: CONTEMPORARY OJIBWAS

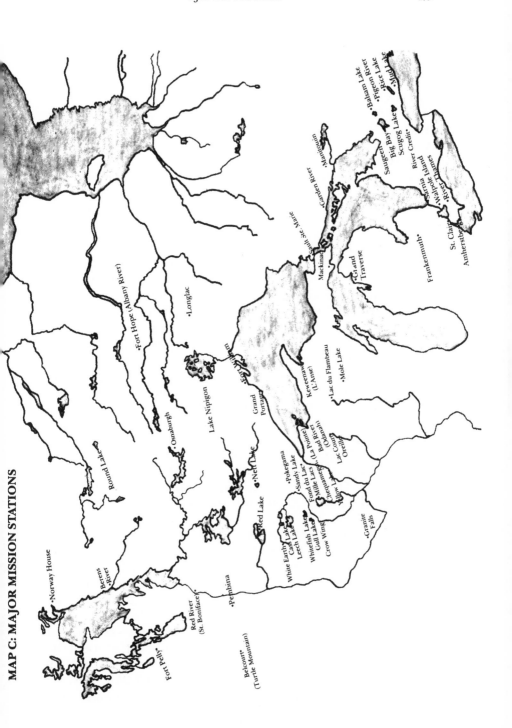

MAP C: MAJOR MISSION STATIONS

Norway House

Berens River

Fort Pelly

Red River (St. Boniface)

Belcourt (Turtle Mountain)

Pembina

Round Lake

Osnaburgh

Lake Nipigon

Fort Hope (Albany River)

Longlac

Grand Portage

Net Lake

Red Lake

White Earth
Cass Lake
Leech Lake
Whitefish Lake
Gull Lake
Crow Wing

Pokegama
Sandy Lake
Fond du Lac
Mille Lacs (La Pointe)
Bad River
Chequamegon (Odanah)
Lac Court Oreilles

Granite Falls

Keweenaw (L'Anse)

Lac du Flambeau

Mole Lake

Mackinac

Sault Ste. Marie

Garden River

Manitoulin

Grand Traverse

Frankenmuth

Saugeen
Big Bay
Scugog Lake
River Credit

Balsam River
Pigeon River
Rice Lake
Mud Lake

Sarnia Island
Walpole Island
River Thames
St. Clair
Amherstburg

CHRISTIAN MISSIONS TO THE OJIBWAS

A major portion of the Ojibwa contact with whites has been with missionaries (map C, p. 25). This chapter surveys the major missionary efforts among the Ojibwas by denomination, and attempts to generalize about missionary interrelationships, goals, motivations, techniques and connections with other white institutions, government and business.

Roman Catholics

The first Roman Catholic evangelist in the Great Lakes region, Franciscan Joseph Le Caron, visited Upper Michigan in 1615 (Craker 1935: 15; Verwyst 1886: 258). Other Franciscans approached the Ojibwa region and probably met the Indians at Lake Nipissing in 1622 (Kennedy 1950: 30-33). But two years later the order ran low on funds and called upon the Jesuits, who had conducted an Acadian mission from 1611 to 1613 and had received official French recognition in 1618. Six Jesuits arrived in Quebec in 1625; however, the English controlled Canada between 1629 and 1632 and deported all the French priests (Verwyst 1886: 259-260).

In 1632 the French regained Canada and the Jesuits received a monopoly on Canadian missions from the French monarchy (Kellogg 1925: 144). Jesuits Jean de Brébeuf and Antoine Daniel first encountered the Ojibwas at Sault Ste. Marie in 1641 (Means 1917: 5), followed by Jesuits Isaac Jogues and Charles Raymbault the next year (Kurath 1959: 211; Levi 1956: 38; Means 1917: 5; Verwyst 1886: 259). Neither of these visits resulted in a lasting Ojibwa mission. Neither did Jesuit René Ménard's ill-fated attempt at Keweenaw in 1661; he died within the year (Levi 1956: 38-40; Means 1917: 6; Neill no date: 1; Nute 1944: 24; Verwyst 1886: 260). Father Claude Allouez lasted two years at Chequamegon, 1665-1667 (Levi 1956: 40-42; Means 1917: 6; Neill no date: 2; Nute 1944: 25; Verwyst 1886: 260), and was replaced by fellow Jesuit Jacques Marquette in 1669, who had spent the previous year at the Sault (Levi 1956: 42; Means 1917: 6; Neill no date: 3; Thwaites 1896-1901, vol. 59: 201-205; Verwyst 1886: 260). The Chequamegon mission ended when Dakota

26

and Fox Indians drove the Ottawas, Hurons, and Ojibwas from the southern shore of Lake Superior in 1670 (Nute 1944: 27).

Mission efforts then shifted to Mackinac and the Sault. Father Gabriel Dreuillettes worked for nine years at the Sault, beginning in 1670, during which time he circuited Lake Superior (Nute 1944: 27-28), planting crosses as did Simon François Sieur de St. Lusson in 1671 at France's formal convocation of its Indian allies (Holland 1933: 159; Nute 1944: 27-28; Verwyst 1886: 261).

But by 1690 the Jesuit expansion ended. France's religious fervor was cooling and the priests fell subservient to the military. The missionaries played parts in political events and their actions depended to a large extent on the political powers with whom they collaborated. When French policy changed regarding the Indians of the Great Lakes, so did the Jesuit policy. The missions retreated steadily until the Capitulation of Canada (Kennedy 1950: 38-39, 50-51, 76; Nute 1944: 31-34). By the time the papacy banned the Jesuits, and the English confiscated the suppressed order's property in 1773, only eleven of the priests resided in Canada, and only Mackinac remained as a regular station in contact with the Ojibwas (Kennedy 1950: 53). Although the last of the old order in Canada did not die until 1800 (Kennedy 1950: 54), over a century had passed since the days of a vigorous Ojibwa mission by the time the second wave of Catholic Ojibwa missions began in the nineteenth century.

That is not to say that the Jesuit presence entirely vanished during the eighteenth century. Priests visited Grand Portage between 1731 and 1741 and Mackinac clerics maintained contact with the Ojibwas throughout the eighteenth century (Woolworth 1965: 301-310). Trader Alexander Henry mentioned the work of a Jesuit there in 1761 and 1763 (Henry 1809: 40, 92) and the Mackinac register of baptisms and marriages recorded the participation of Ojibwas from the Sault and Chequamegon between the years 1713 and 1817 ("The Mackinac Register" 1910: 2-148). The American Catholic priest, Gabriel Richard, made three short visits to Mackinac in 1799 (Craker 1935: 16; Furlan 1952: 62). Thus, a sparse mission effort continued through the eighteenth century.

The nineteenth century Catholic missions to the Ojibwas began in 1815, when the Earl of Selkirk requested that the Bishop of Quebec, Joseph Octave Plessis, provide priests for Selkirk's new colony on the Red River, south of Lake Winnipeg. Plessis first sent one of his diocesan priests on a scouting tour of the Rainy Lake area, but against orders the priest aligned himself with the North West Company against the Hudson's Bay Company, of which Selkirk was a chief stockholder (Norton 1930: 18-30; Nute 1944: xi-xiv, 11-13). The bishop recalled his scout and sent two priests, Joseph Norber Provencher and Sévère Joseph Nicolas Dumoulin, to the Red River Valley to serve primarily the Catholic population of Selkirk's colony. In 1818 they established quarters near present-day Winnipeg but Dumoulin wanted to missionize the Indians and moved his station further south, to Pembina. Even when Selkirk died in 1820 and support for the mission flagged, Dumoulin continued his work, but when the Canada-United States border agreement placed Pembina in Dakota, the heartbroken Dumoulin accepted a transfer to another mission field in 1823 (Blegen 1963: 151-152; Norton 1930: 7-45; Nute 1944: 58-61). In 1848 Father George Anthony Belcourt (who served the Selkirk position, St. Boniface, from 1830 to 1847) revived the Pembina mission, staying there with another priest until 1859. Other Canadian Catholics tried to install a seat in the Fort Pelly region in the 1840s and the 1860s (Aldrich 1927b: 30-33).

As the Pembina mission ended, the Oblates began a more permanent mission station in 1852 at Lake Nipigon; the Jesuits started at Longlac in 1864 and the Oblates opened an Albany River post in 1893 (Majerus 1967: 5-13). In the twentieth century a small number of Oblates, Jesuits, and secular clergy have attempted to continue the effort to the Canadian Ojibwas, including Oblate Joseph-Marie Couture, who covered the 75,000 square miles of his Ontario mission district by airplane, until his death in 1949 (Cadieux 1959: 25-36).

Although Catholic priests were already accustomed to visiting the Chequamegon trading post every two years in the 1820s, the Catholic mission to the Ojibwas in nineteenth century United States received its major impetus from the Ludwig-Missionsverein of Bavaria and the Leopoldine Society of Austria, founded respectively in 1828 and 1829 (Furlan 1952: 9-14, 28). Father Frederic Baraga, presently a candidate for Catholic sainthood, began his work among the Ottawas in 1831. He traveled through Upper Michigan, instructing and baptizing the Ottawas and Ojibwas, but his advice to the Indians against selling their lands resulted in his transfer in 1835 to Chequamegon and Fond du Lac. In 1843 Baraga opened a school at Keweenaw and in 1847 he met with other Catholic missionaries to plan their future positions around Lake Superior. In 1854 he became an itinerant bishop, journeying through Wisconsin, Ontario, and Michigan, almost until his death in 1868 (Cadieux and Comte 1954: 11-16; Fruth 1958: i; Gregorich 1932: 12-98; Hilger 1936; Norton 1930: 46-52; Zaplotnik 1917).

Another participant at the 1847 meeting was Baraga's fellow Slovene, Father Francis Xavier Pierz, whom Baraga persuaded in 1835 to become a missionary to the Ojibwas. He traveled to numerous mission lodgments, from the Sault to Grand Portage. In 1851, when the diocese of St. Paul organized, he moved to Minnesota where he formed posts at Crow Wing, Mille Lacs, and Sandy Lake. In 1862 he helped end the Indian uprising led by Ojibwa Hole in the Day. Pierz died in 1880 (Fruth 1958: 1-3; McDonald 1929: 107-125; Norton 1930: 134-135; Pierz 1947-1948; Winchell 1911: 640; Woolworth 1965: 301-310). The other strategists at the 1847 meeting were Franciscan Otto Skolla, who served at Chequamegon and Sandy Lake between 1845 and 1850, and two Jesuits, Pierre Choné and Nicolas Frémiot, who were stationed at Manitoulin, Grand Portage, Pigeon River, and Fort William through the 1840s (Blegen 1963: 152-153; Norton 1930: 71-73; Woolworth 1965: 308).

The last important wave of Catholic missions began in 1878, when the United States removed a Leopoldine Society preacher, Ignatius Tomazin, from his White Earth post because of his disputes with the Indian agent there (Fruth 1958: 8-18). The Catholic Indian Bureau invited the Benedictines of Collegeville, Minnesota, to replace Tomazin. Father Aloysius Hermanutz and two Benedictine sisters came to White Earth that year, and in 1881 Father Thomas Borgerding and other Benedictines established a permanent base at Red Lake, from which Tomazin was removed in 1883 in another disagreement with the government. Other Benedictines entered the mission field in Wisconsin, at Lac Court Oreilles and Lac du Flambeau, as well as Mole Lake (Maeder 1962: 59).

The Benedictines opened schools for Ojibwas in the 1880s, aided by government contracts. In 1900 the contracts ended but the Benedictines continued until 1938 when the General Council of the Red Lake Band of Ojibwas formally resolved to end the mission school (Fruth 1958: 30-53, 67-70, 87-103). Today the Roman Catholics maintain educational and pastoral contact with Ojibwas in most areas, from Turtle Mountain on the Belcourt Reservation in North Dakota, to Fort Hope, Ontario, but the major effort to convert Ojibwas to Catholicism has passed.

Anglicans in Canada

The Anglican mission to the Ojibwas began in 1820 at Lord Selkirk's Red River settlement, under Rev. John West (Nute 1942: 257, n.; Young 1899: 88-89); however, the major mission effort of the Anglicans centered around Manitoulin. In 1832 Canada's plan to relocate all their eastern Ojibwas and Ottawas to the Manitoulin district included an Anglican depot at Sault Ste. Marie. In 1835 the mission established a Manitoulin colony and persuaded around 400 Indians to move there (Copway 1850: 188-190; Graham 1975). Rev. A. Elliott took charge of the post, to be succeeded by Rev. Frederick O'Meara and Rev. Frederick Frost, who served the area into the twentieth century (History of Manitoulin 1955; O'Meara 1847-1848: 1-3; Frost 1904).

In 1868 Rev. Edward Wilson founded a position at Sarnia but his main work was at Garden River, dating from 1871 (Wilson 1886). Other Anglican installations included Round Lake and Osnaburgh at the turn of the century and a mid-century attempt in the Fort Pelly region. Anglican presence exists today among most Ojibwa communities in Canada, although active missionizing has slowed.

Methodists

The Missionary Society of the Methodist Episcopal Church under the Canadian Conference began the Methodist work on the River Credit, Ontario, in 1823 (Schoolcraft 1853-1857, vol. 6: 738). Four years later, Rev. William Case, the father of Protestant missions in Canada and superintendent of Indian missions and schools, began to proselytize in Canada West,

now southeast Ontario. He and other mobile Methodist minis-
ters preached at Scugog Lake, Mud Lake, Rice Lake, Saugeen,
St. Clair, Walpole Island, Balsam Lake, Osnaburgh, Big Bay,
River Thames, Amherstburg, and other circuit posts in the
area, through the 1830s and 1840s (Copway 1850: 174-181;
Graham 1975; Holdich 1839: 1-59; Jones 1861: 40-49;
McLean 1891: 7-8; Young 1899: 24).

In 1833 the Methodist missions among the Ojibwas trans-
ferred to the Wesleyan Missionary Society, covering both the
United States and Canadian territories (Schoolcraft
1853-1857, vol. 6: 739). In that year, Rev. John Clark became
superintendent of the Lake Superior area stations, a position
he held until 1836. He installed bases at the Sault, as well as at
Keweenaw and other sites on Lake Superior, aided by information on Indian demography gathered by native preachers
George Copway and John Sunday in their 1830 tour of the
lake; these bases led to further moves into Minnesota (Nute
1944: 226; Pitezel 1901: 62-63; Prindle 1842: 56-99).

Along Lake Superior's south shore Rev. Daniel Meeker
Chandler kept the posts from 1834 to 1836, at which time he
replaced Clark (Prindle 1842: 19). Chandler became ill, to be
replaced by Rev. William H. Brockway in 1838 (Pitezel 1901:
106), while Rev. John Pitezel covered the southern shore in the
1840s (Pitezel 1901). At that time the Methodists had twenty-
three Ojibwa mission sites of varying size. Six of these were in
the United States, on Lake Superior and in Minnesota.

The Minnesota movement developed in 1840, when Rev.
Alfred Brunson moved his stormy Dakota mission to Sandy
Lake, where he encountered Ojibwas; he remained there until
1855 (Blegen 1963: 150-151). In 1840 there were two other
Methodist missions in Minnesota, one at Whitefish Lake
under Ottawa minister Enmegabowh (Rev. John Johnson),
the other under Copway and his wife at Fond du Lac. Copway
left the following year (Riggs 1894: 135-141; Winchell 1911:
640) and Enmegabowh replaced him, but in 1849 Enmegabowh's wife had an argument with the resident trader
and the mission post at Fond du Lac ended (Winchell 1911:
644). The Methodists have continued in Minnesota, including
native preachers Frank Pequette and Duane Porter at Nett
Lake and Pine Bend in the 1950s (Lindquist 1952: 19-21).

The last area where the Methodists conducted significant
Ojibwa missions was along Lake Winnipeg, particularly near

Norway House, at the northern end of the lake. In the 1830s, when the Crees and Ojibwas began to drift southward from the trading house toward the Red River settlement, Hudson's Bay Company officials asked the Methodists to supply a mission to the northern post in order to influence the Indians to stay where they were (McLean 1891: 13). In 1840 Rev. James Evans moved to Norway House from Rice Lake, where he had been for twelve years. He remained until difficulties with the Hudson's Bay Company authorities in 1855 forced him to remove himself (Jacobs 1855: 65-67; Young 1899: 34-36, 225-255). The Methodists have continued in the area, including at Berens River from 1893, until the present day.

Presbyterians, Baptists, and the American Board

Although a Presbyterian from the Connecticut Missionary Society was in Mackinac as early as 1802 and undoubtedly had contact with Ojibwas there, it was not until Rev. Jedidiah Morse visited the town on a governmental fact-finding tour in 1822 that the Presbyterians became interested in an Ojibwa mission. The following year the Eastern Missionary Society of the Presbyterian Synod of Pittsburgh sent a preacher who visited among the Sault Ojibwas (Craker 1935: 19-20). In 1824 Rev. Alvan Coe, a Massachusetts Presbyterian, and Rev. William M. Ferry of the United Foreign Missionary Society conducted a school for Indians and others at Mackinac, sponsored by the American Fur Company, which also paid for an Episcopalian mission at the Sault and a Methodist base at Keweenaw. Ferry shuttled between Mackinac and the Sault, conducting his schools which were attended by Ojibwas from as far away as Fond du Lac, until he and Coe quit the field in 1834 (Anderson 1947-1948; Craker 1935: 21-23; Culkin 1926: 79; Elliott 1896: 363; McKenney 1827: 386-387; Neill no date: 3-6). In 1826 the Presbyterian missions were incorporated by the newly formed American Board of Commissioners for Foreign Missions (Schoolcraft 1853-1857, vol. 6: 737).

In 1838 Rev. Peter Dougherty replaced the retired Ferry and chose Grand Traverse as his station (Anderson 1952; Craker 1935: 21-24; Vogel 1967). His mission closed, however, when the Presbyterian Board of Foreign Missions ran out of money after the Civil War. Since then the Presbyterians have sent some missionaries and teachers for brief stays among the

Ojibwas but have conducted no lasting United States establishments (Craker 1935: 45-50). In Canada they had posts at the Red River settlement beginning in 1851 and were near Fort Pelly beginning in 1874.

The Sault was the scene of a small but lasting attempt by the American Baptist Missionary Union. From 1828 to 1855 Rev. Abel Bingham conducted a school there for Indians and other children. The American Board took over the mission of the United Foreign Missionary Society at the Sault in 1826, continuing it for a year (Nute 1944: 225; Schoolcraft 1853-1857, vol. 6: 738). Its better known work took place in Minnesota and Wisconsin, beginning in 1830.

The immediate cause of the American Board's mission was the request of Lyman Warren of the American Fur Company at Chequamegon (on the Warrens' role, see Blegen 1963: 145; Culkin 1926: 7-8, 82; Densmore 1929: 4-5). Warren and the company officials wanted their mixed-blood children to receive an education so that they could succeed in American society, and not grow up as Indians. And so the traders made offers to defray the expenses of a mission. Warren housed the missionaries, providing the funds to build a church and school aimed primarily at the mixed-blood children (Warren Family 1756-1907).

Mr. Frederick Ayer arrived at Chequamegon in 1830, followed the next year by Rev. and Mrs. Sherman Hall. In 1832 Ayer and his new wife went to Sandy Lake to open a school, this time at the request of the American Fur Company trader there. Also in 1832, Rev. William T. Boutwell, who had accompanied Schoolcraft to the source of the Mississippi, joined the Halls at Chequamegon. The following year the Ayers left for Yellow Lake and Rev. Edmund F. Ely took over at Sandy Lake. Ely also traveled to Leech Lake and Fond du Lac. The Yellow Lake base stayed open until 1837. The previous year the Ayers moved to Pokegama, so that in 1837 the American Board was conducting four stations, at Pokegama, Leech Lake, Chequamegon and Fond du Lac (on the movements of these missionaries, see Culkin 1926: 9-21, 44-49, 61-64; Davidson 1892: 434-452; Neill no date: 3-6; Riggs 1894: 117-125; Tuttle 1838: 8, 88; Winchell 1911: 638).

In 1839, however, the Dakota-Ojibwa wars broke up all but Chequamegon (Neill no date: 44; Winchell 1911: 640). Pokegama reopened the next year, leaving two posts. In 1843 the

Ayers moved to Red Lake, feeling that the northern post was ready for conversion. In 1845 Rev. and Mrs. Leonard H. Wheeler, who had arrived at Chequamegon in 1841, went to Bad River, where they stayed until ill health forced Rev. Wheeler to quit in 1867. In the late 1840s whites began to enter the Lake Superior area in search of copper and farmland, and in 1849 the Ayers quit Red Lake. The Elys left Chequamegon in 1853 after the Ojibwas there had been removed to Crow Wing. Hall quit in 1854 and, like the Ayers and Elys, served white congregations elsewhere (on the demise of these missions, see Culkin 1926: 31-32, 122; Foster 1892: 4; Levi 1956: 65-68; Riggs 1894: 143-151).

In 1842 the Ayers had visited Oberlin College in search of missionaries to help with the American Board's work. The next year a small missionary body, the Western Evangelical Missionary Society, began at Oberlin, sending Rev. Sela G. Wright and others to help at Leech and Red Lakes (Foster 1892: 3-21; Schell 1911: 5-118). In 1845 the Pillagers at Leech Lake expelled all the missionaries (Riggs 1894: 156-159) as more recruits arrived in the Lake Superior field. A year later the Oberlin board combined with other organizations to form the American Missionary Society (Beard 1909: 3-32, 65-67) but by 1859 all its workers in the Ojibwa mission were ministering to whites, not Indians, with the exception of Wright. He served the Presbyterians and then the Episcopalians in Minnesota. The Episcopalians removed Wright from Leech Lake in 1882 for "coddling around" and "tampering" with the Ojibwa schoolgirls (Joseph A. Gilfillan to Whipple, 20 September 1882 in Whipple 1833-1934, Box 16) but he stayed in the Presbyterian mission duty until 1894.

Episcopalians in the United States

The Protestant Episcopal Church officially began its mission to the Ojibwas in Minnesota in 1835 when the St. Paul diocese opened. Enmegabowh, the Ottawa minister who helped the Methodists from 1839 until the close of their active Minnesota missions, asked Rev. James Lloyd Breck of St. Paul in 1852 to establish a working post at Crow Wing or Gull Lake. Breck chose the latter and installed a mission with numerous helpers. In 1856 the Pillagers, who had driven off the American Board preachers eleven years earlier, invited Breck to

Leech Lake. He went, leaving others in charge of Gull Lake, but the next year the Pillagers threatened to kill him. As a result, both stations closed, Breck moving to Faribault where he established a school to train Indians for the ministry (Breck 1877; Riggs 1894: 161-164; Whipple 1901: 130). The following year Enmegabowh, who had earlier attended a Methodist seminary in Jacksonville, Illinois, took his first orders of Episcopalian ministry at Faribault and reopened the Gull Lake post (Enmegabowh 1904).

When Henry Benjamin Whipple (Flandreau 1905: 693; Osgood 1958; Riggs 1894: 165-169; Whipple 1833-1934; Whipple 1899; Whipple 1901) became the Episcopalian bishop of Minnesota in 1859, there was only one missionary, Enmegabowh, among the Ojibwas. He opened a Crow Wing station, but all work ended at the time of the 1862 uprising (Enmegabowh 1904: 18-24; Whipple 1901: 132-133). A solid Episcopalian mission began only after the United States created the White Earth Reservation in 1867. Enmegabowh accompanied the Gull Lakers to the reservation in 1869 and became the missionary there (Enmegabowh 1904: 7-9, 25-44; Winchell 1911: 675-682). Rev. Joseph Gilfillan joined him there in 1874 and proceeded to open bases at Red Lake in 1876 and 1878, and at Pembina in 1879 (Aldrich 1927: 41-43; Gilfillan 1873; Gilfillan 1880; Mittelholtz 1957: 72-75; Schell 1911: 116-118).

The Episcopalian missions have continued into the twentieth century, serving currently as schools rather than proselytizing missions (Lindquist 1952: 17-18). Gilfillan quit from old age at the end of the century and Whipple died shortly thereafter, but their establishments continue at Red Lake, Cass Lake, Granite Falls, White Earth and Rice Lake, in Minnesota.

Lutherans

A Lutheran effort continues, too, at Red Lake. Founded in 1954 (Mittelholtz 1957: 78), it is not the first of Lutheran conversion attempts among the Ojibwas. In the 1840s and 1850s Lutherans conducted missions at Frankenmuth, near Ann Arbor in Michigan (Polack 1928: 20-61) and from 1857 to 1868 they operated quarters at Crow Wing (Abbetmeyer-Selke 1930: 20-25).

Other Recent Missions

Other continuing missions include the Christian and Missionary Alliance (Northern Gospel Mission) stations at Leech Lake, Mille Lacs, and White Earth, all dating from 1952, and at Red Lake, which began in 1927 (Lindquist 1952: 19-21; Mittelholtz 1957: 75). In addition, the Northern Canada Evangelical Mission has opened numerous positions in Canada, including one at Round Lake in 1952, and the Mennonites stationed themselves on a dozen Canadian reserves, including Grassy Narrows, since 1953.

Missionary Interrelationships

It is apparent from this survey that the majority of Christian missions have taken place in the United States and in southeast Ontario, the areas where the Ojibwas have encountered whites and white culture most pervasively. In these regions the overall population is greater; there are more railroads and highways, and more interference from white governments. In short, the greater culture contact in these southern areas is matched by the greater missionary contact.

Christian mission efforts did not come to the Ojibwas as one body, however; indeed, there was much interdenominational bickering and rivalry for the Indians' attention. Some Protestant denominations worked together, sharing personnel and resources, and some Catholics and Protestants tolerated each other's presence: Episcopalian Bishop Whipple's claim, "I have made it a rule of my life never to interfere with other Christian work" (Whipple 1901a: 135), did not jibe with all his actions, however. He and Rev. Gilfillan decided to set up mission stations at Gull Lake and Twin Lakes in 1893-1894 with the primary objective to thwart Catholic efforts in those areas, even though the Catholic Indian population outnumbered that of the Episcopalians (Gilfillan to Whipple, 26 January 1894 in Whipple 1833-1934, Box 22).

Anglican O'Meara wrote to a friend in 1847 that while he was away from his post, the Jesuits had tried to "pervert my people," adding that "...with such wily enemies..., I have great need to be both watchful and prayerful lest the enemy gain an advantage over me" (O'Meara, et al. 1847-1848: 12, 13). It is apparent that the missionaries' motives included competition with other Christian denominations as well as the conversion of the Ojibwas. Furthermore, the competition was not limited to Catholic-Protestant animosities. When Anglican Wilson attempted a base at Sarnia, the Methodists petitioned the Canadian Indian Department to prevent the opening; the rivalry was fierce, said Wilson (Wilson 1886: 23).

The competition became even more bitter when denominations vied for government funds and control over Indian populations. Father Tomazin complained that Catholic Ojibwas were subjected by government policy to the rule of Protestant agents and missionaries appointed by the government. He wrote in 1879:

> Most Indians at White Earth were Catholic, yet in spite of this, a satanic Methodist preacher was appointed as the agent. I visited him shortly after his arrival and told him I intended to build a church at the request of the Indians. He replied angerly [sic] that he would not tolerate a Catholic priest on the reservation (Fruth 1958: 13).

Tomazin claimed that Whipple and his "tool," agent Lewis Stowe, used government funds and supplies to bribe the Ojibwas into converting to the Protestant Episcopal Church; when clothes came from Washington, he said, the best always went to the Protestant Indians. Rancor and suspicion were the rules rather than the exception in interdenominational relations.

Missionary Goals, Motivations, and Techniques

Nevertheless, the differences in missionary goals, motivations, and techniques, as well as in attitudes toward the Ojibwas, were not as great between Catholics and Protestants as it would appear from the missionaries' testimony. They were all part of the same missionary tradition of Christianity (on the motives of missions to American Indians, see Vecsey 1971, including bibliography).

They agreed that their mission arose directly from Jesus Christ, the founder, message, and focus of Christianity. Jesus Christ revealed that God and humans are alienated from each other, that God is almighty and humans are worthless without

Him, yet (nay, consequently) humans by their sinful nature will themselves to alienation. The missionaries believed that God willed to be reunited with humans and sent (and continues to send) Jesus Christ, God and human, as the means of reunion or salvation. Only through Jesus Christ, the missionaries agreed, could humans attain reunion with God; without Jesus Christ an individual human could not attain salvation. Such was the revelation of Jesus Christ. The missionaries believed that only those humans who know Jesus Christ will actually attain salvation; therefore, Jesus Christ commissioned his followers to spread his revelation to those who have not yet heard it, and it is the duty of the Christian to spread Jesus Christ's message: Jesus Christ. They were fulfilling their missionary duty by coming to the Ojibwas.

The missionaries shared the belief that humanity constituted a unit, that all humans were descendants of the same Adam, the same Noah. The Ojibwa individual was, thus, a brother to the white, a sharer in the same humanity. Furthermore, the missionaries believed that Christianity was suited to all the members of humanity; there was but one true religion, Christianity, for all the world.

In the missionaries' view, the Ojibwa, as a human, was capable of receiving or refusing the saving grace of God. The Catholics emphasized man's cooperation with God in his own salvation, man's congruity with saving grace; Protestants tended to emphasize God's overpowering role in salvation. But both Catholics and Protestants agreed that the Ojibwas deserved to hear the Christian message. It was the missionaries' duty to help the Ojibwas out of their deficient state by bringing to the Indians the message of Jesus Christ, the knowledge about the true God, and the only means to that God.

Catholics and Protestants concurred that the Ojibwa was capable of receiving the knowledge. The early Jesuits stated that the Ojibwas possessed intelligence, memory, and spiritual maturity (Kennedy 1950: 133-135). Through the centuries the missionaries of all denominations found much to compliment in Ojibwa character. Bishop Whipple praised the Indians' honesty (Whipple 1901a: 129), their composure, gregariousness, heroism, hospitality, amiability and courteousness (Whipple 1899: 41-45). Rev. Gilfillan respected their intelligence, self-control, and reverence for religion (Gilfillan

1901: 89-93). These and other missionaries saw virtues in the natives.

In this regard, especially in the nineteenth century, the preachers differed markedly from their white contemporaries. Newspaper articles in Minnesota in the latter half of the nineteenth century treated the Ojibwas with attitudes ranging from condescension to venom. In joking about starving Indians and condoning the lynching of two mixed-bloods by a white mob, the white writers demonstrated their estimation of Ojibwas as subhuman.

After Hole in the Day's unsuccessful uprising the *St. Paul Pioneer* on 23 September 1863 wrote:

Good News For Indian Hunters. —
The Indian-hunting trade, if the game be at all plenty, is likely to prove a profitable investment, during the present fall and winter to our hunters and scouts in the Big Woods, the Commander-in-Chief, by the General Order No. 60 having increased the bounty for each top-knot of a "bloody heathen," to $200. There is likely to be considerable competition in the trade, and the best shots will carry off the most prizes (Works Progress Administration Writers' Project 1849-1942, Box 170).

The missionaries, for all their ethnocentricisms, did not share in the blatant racism of their white fellows. Obviously they thought the Ojibwas worth the missionizing effort. Some, like Bishop Whipple, championed the Indians' cause against presidents and land-hungry white settlers.

Catholics and Protestants often differed in their missionary approach. Catholics baptized the Indians sooner, as a means to conversion rather than as the last step in the process. They tended to address the entire Indian culture, hoping to incorporate it into the realm of Catholicism; Protestants emphasized individual conversions. Catholics saw their organizational structure, the Church, as a means of knowing Jesus Christ; Protestants viewed the Bible as the principal means of religious knowledge. Catholic missionaries were often more tolerant of Ojibwa culture than were the Protestants; for example, in Michigan Catholics permitted Ojibwas and Ottawas to continue their family feasts and mourning customs, while the Methodists refused to allow such practices and discouraged Indian folklore in all its forms (Kurath, Ettawageshik, and Ettawageshik 1955, vol. 5, Chapter 12: 2).

A strict dichotomy between Catholic and Protestant approaches, however, did not always exist. Catholics and most Protestants tried to learn Ojibwa language, whereas most Methodists insisted that all mission work be conducted in English. One scholar notes that within Catholic ranks, a difference in attitude existed between the field missionaries and the administrative personnel. The former tended to identify with the Indians to whom they preached; the latter tended to identify with the Church, regarding the natives as statistical objects of administrative attention (Baldwin 1957: 100).

A difference also existed between the seventeenth-century Jesuits and the nineteenth-century Catholic missionaries. They both may have agreed that white culture was superior to Ojibwa culture, but the earlier Jesuits approached the Ojibwas and other Indians with a greater degree of cultural relativity. They may not have liked Ojibwa ways, violence, gluttony, but they made a conscious effort not to destroy Ojibwa customs. Despite the Jesuits' ethnocentricism they recognized the arbitrary nature of many societal practices and tried to adapt their message to Ojibwa culture and religious terminology. They studied the Ojibwas closely and tried to create the broadest possible agreement between the Christian message and the Ojibwa traditions. If necessary they simplified their message so the Indians could grasp it. The *Jesuit Relations* described Indian life accurately and incisively because accurate and incisive description was part of the Jesuits' missionary approach.

That is not to say that the early Jesuits did not attempt to change the Ojibwas. They especially tried to alter the Indians' "nomadic" way of life; village life would make the Ojibwas an easier, sitting target for the missions. Contrasted to the attempts by the nineteenth-century Catholics and Protestants, however, the early Jesuits respected Ojibwa culture. The later preachers of all denominations made concerted efforts to end Ojibwa hunting. Rev. Ayer at Yellow Lake and Father Dumoulin at Pembina attempted to gather the Ojibwas into villages where they could be easily reached and where they would cease their hunting. At Keweenaw Father Baraga's energies were spent in organizing a community of Ojibwa farmers. Rev. Breck in Minnesota and Father Pierz in Wisconsin pressured the Ojibwas to farm.

The majority of nineteenth-century missionaries saw their mission as one of civilizing as well as converting the Ojibwas. Civilizing, for Catholics and Protestants alike, meant turning the Ojibwas into as close an approximation of whites as possible. In particular the missionaries wanted the Ojibwas to adopt white sexual divisions of labor, to dress like whites, to live in European-derived homes, to learn white educational skills like reading, geography, history and gardening, and to accumulate private property. The same missionaries who praised Ojibwa generosity and sharing attempted to convert the Indians into proletarians and peasants. For Bishop Whipple, "Honest work for wages is the solution of the Indian question" (Whipple 1899:288). At Keweenaw Father Baraga established family farms for the Ojibwas. He said that for an Indian to become a Christian, the native would have to live in a European-type dwelling, perform European-type work (farming), and amass personal savings (Gregorich 1932: 59). Thus Catholic and Protestant missionaries shared the same attitudes and goals.

Missionary Connections with Government and Business

They also shared a continuing connection with civil authorities and business enterprises. From the seventeenth to the twentieth centuries the missionaries to the Ojibwas in both Canada and the United States have associated themselves with and have been influenced by secular society and its aims.

The early Jesuits labored under a monopoly from the French monarchy from 1632 to 1657 and received government support until the fall of French Canada. They worked closely with the French fur traders, traveling with them, setting up missions at fur-trading posts, and ministering to the voyageurs. In the later years the priests followed the orders of the French military.

The nineteenth-century missions differed little in their connections. The Red River mission of 1818 owed its origin and money to Lord Selkirk and his colonization and trade plans. The Canadian government encouraged and supported the 1830s missions at Manitoulin. The Hudson's Bay Company called for Rev. Evan's station at Norway House; when he displeased the company's leaders, they dismissed him.

In the United States it was not only the fur traders who helped pay for the American Board's missions at Chequamegon and Red Lake, but also the government's Civilization Fund, initiated in 1819, which helped support mission efforts to educate Indians. The government and the missionaries worked most closely in the area of education (Beaver 1966). The government subsidized the Methodist school at Keweenaw, stipulating that the instruction be given in English (Nelson 1965: 58). In 1852, when the Minnesota state authorities decided that the mission schools were not civilizing the Ojibwas fast enough, the governor abolished the literary mission schools and substituted manual labor schools for the natives. This did not mean an end to the government support for the missions; rather, the preachers received pay for their instruction in the new schools. The ministers provided their Christian message after teaching manual skills during school hours (Winchell 1911: 649-651).

In 1869 Grant's "Peace Policy" ushered in an era of greater national support for the missions. Army personnel were replaced by missionary society members as Indian agents. The denominations became the powers on the reservations and controlled the lives of the American Ojibwas with government money.

Even after Grant's policy faded and the Civilization Fund was abolished in 1873, the government in the United States continued to support mission schools through contracts. The government paid the schools for each Indian student enrolled in the institution. It is doubtful that the missions made a profit on these schools, but the missionaries were required to keep their students in the school through the academic year in order to collect the money. As a result, the schools were constructed at a distance from the Ojibwa children's homes, far from parental influence. The Benedictine boarding schools did not allow Ojibwa children to withdraw from classes, once enrolled. A Benedictine explained why the schools were far from the parents' homes: "We do not favor education on the respective Reservations, because parents interfere too much and cause great irregularities" (Order of St. Benedict 1887: 3). This was in keeping with the government desires and rules for the boarding schools, which were designed to acculturate the young as thoroughly as possible by removing them from their native culture.

In the 1890s opposition arose to these contract schools and by 1900 the last appropriations were made for funding mission institutions in the United States. From the 1930s the government gave contracts to secular schools and the mission schools dried up, although missions at Red Lake and White Earth (Elliott 1897: 27) held on to the Ojibwa reservation land which the U.S. authorities had granted them in the nineteenth century.

In Canada as well the missions lost the government's support, forcing the mission teachers to close their schools and become teachers in the secular school system. In both countries the pattern was the same, beginning with government-funded mission schools, changing to manual labor schools with missionary personnel, then to boarding schools with government funding, and finally to secular schools, often staffed by missionaries as teachers.

It is no coincidence that the century of missionary expansion among the Ojibwas occurred simultaneously with the century of government subsidy, just as the earlier French Jesuit labors depended on French support. Missionary expansion was an aspect of territorial, economic, and political expansion in both cases. The missionaries represented their nations as well as their God (Kennedy 1950: 58) and shared many of the general Indian policy goals of the white cultures from which they sprang. Episcopalian Bishop Whipple worked with the United States authorities in establishing and solidifying the reservation system, with its emphases on education and agriculture and its goals of containing Indians within determined boundaries and ridding them of their traditions through persuasion and force. Whipple considered Christianity the best means of making Ojibwas and other Indians civilized American citizens and he saw civilization as the best means of making them Christians (Whipple 1899: 51, 396). Hence he cooperated with government agents and participated in official policies.

Bishop Whipple's participation, however, did not prevent him from taking the role of prophetic critic. In letters to the formulators of Indian policy, through public speeches, newspaper articles, and other writings, he accused whites of illegal and immoral conduct regarding Indians. He castigated the United States government for its lack of concern for the natives' welfare and blamed white land-hunger for Indian militance. He charged that ". . . the Indian Department is the most corrupt in the Government. Citizens, editors, legislators, heads of the departments, and the President alike agree that it has been characterized by inefficiency and fraud. The nation, knowing this, has winked at it" (Whipple 1899: 126), and called for institutional reform. His public defense of the Indians who joined Hole in the Day's uprising enraged many Minnesota whites, some of whom threatened Whipple's life and beat another missionary who protected Christian Indians at Fort Snelling (Osgood 1958: 167-175). The mission movements reflected and depended on movements in secular society but reserved the right to criticize their fellow whites.

Virtually all major Christian denominations have had some contact with the Ojibwas, from the Roman Catholics in the seventeenth century to the Mennonites of today. Despite their theological differences, these missionaries have shared common aspirations, assumptions, and procedures regarding their proselytizing activities, and regarding the Ojibwas themselves. The following chapter examines the Ojibwas' responses to these Christians.

OJIBWA RESPONSES TO CHRISTIAN MISSIONS

O jibwa responses to the Christian missions have ranged from indifference to acceptance. It is the contention of this chapter, however, that conversions to Christianity came in large numbers only after Ojibwas had lost their political autonomy to whites and were subject to diverse pressures from whites to abandon their old religious ways. In addition, this chapter argues that Ojibwa conversions to Christianity have most often been nominal and superficial. The result has been that Ojibwas have turned from aboriginal traditions without profoundly accepting the missionaries' faith.

Resistance to Christianity

The earliest missionaries posed no recognizable threat to the Ojibwas (on this issue see Kennedy 1950: 32). The first Franciscans and Jesuits traveled with little baggage or pretension. Since they did not attempt a radical alteration of Ojibwa culture or subsistence patterns, their message seemed innocuous to the Indians. As a result, the Ojibwas responded to them with mild curiosity, viewing them as harmless associates of the French fur traders who were bringing wealth.

On the other hand, missionaries had nothing of apparent worth for the Ojibwas. The priests were poor, unskilled, unproductive. Father Allouez's account of his travels to Lake Superior left little doubt that the Ottawas and Ojibwas whom he accompanied had no regard for him. They did not want him to join them; they excluded him from their canoes because he could not row his weight. They tried to lose him in the forests. They insulted him and railed against him when he opposed their medicines. He certainly did not make an immediately favorable impression on them (Thwaites 1896-1901, vol. 50: 249-305). Father Louis Hennepin, a Franciscan writing in 1683, noted that the Ojibwas and other Indians were indifferent to the missionaries and their message because the Christians had no leverage over them. Without a miracle, he said, ". . . so long as Christians are not absolutely their masters we shall see little success . . ." (Hennepin 1880: 338).

The situation had not changed by the mid-nineteenth century. Rev. Wright recalled that his fumbling efforts to learn Ojibwa language brought laughter and ridicule from the natives in Minnesota, who perceived the preachers as foolish, ungrammatical fools with nothing useful to offer (Schell 1911: 182).

But already in the nineteenth century, as the numbers of missionaries grew and their power over the Ojibwas increased, the Indian response shifted perceptibly from indifference to opposition. In 1854 when the Lutherans in Michigan encouraged the Ojibwas to relocate, the Indians responded that the Bible was ruinous to Indians, that the preachers were liars, and that Christians wanted to enslave them (Luckhard 1952: 38-39). When Rev. Chandler settled at Keweenaw in 1834, the local Indian leader angrily accosted him, demanding payment for use of Ojibwa land, wood, and materials. The Indian vowed to oppose all attempts at conversion (Prindle 1834: 38-39). Everywhere it was the same. The Ojibwa leadership presented competition and opposition to the missionaries. After sixteen months of proselytizing, Rev. Hall wrote to his sister on 25 December 1832 that the Ojibwas at Chequamegon were not willing to receive instruction; indeed, they "appear a little afraid of the white man's religion" (Culkin 1926: 19). In his year and a half he had interested only one Ojibwa in Christianity.

Elsewhere — for example at Red Lake (Schell 1911: 19-26) — the Ojibwas showed little or no interest in schooling. The parents attempted to keep their children from schools and told the missionaries that attendance at school would have to be matched by payments from the churches to the Indians. They considered attendance a favor to the mission, not anything of worth to themselves or their children. On the contrary, it was a danger.

This reluctance to receive education and religious instruction continued into the twentieth century. Even though Father Borgerding told a *Minneapolis Tribune* reporter in 1916 that in Minnesota "nearly all the old-fashioned Indians are gone now, and the people we have here . . . are a little more than Indians and a little less than white man [sic]" (Fruth 1958: 75), three years later the mission acquired a model-T Ford in order to capture Ojibwa runaways from the school.

Opposition to the missionaries was exacerbated by the Ojibwas' resentment of the intrusions of all whites (Ke-Wa-Ze-Zhig 1861: 5-13). They saw the preachers as part of the white invasion, more as representatives of nations, French, English, American and Canadian, than as members of denominations, Catholic or Protestant.

That Ojibwas smarted under white invasion made the mission work extremely difficult. Christian moral teachings lost their cutting edge when Indians could point to widespread immorality among white Christians like fur traders or government officials. The missionaries were put in the position of having to explain white swearing, sexual abuses, dishonesty, and theft, since these acts were performed by supposed Christians. At Sarnia in the mid-nineteenth century, Rev. Wilson found that the Ojibwas refused to convert because the Christianized Indians they had seen were less moral than the pagans, and they feared that they would degenerate, too, if converted (Wilson 1886: 56). The onus of white sins became all the more difficult to explain when they were committed by the missionaries themselves, for example, Rev. Wright's abuse of Indian schoolgirls, or an Episcopalian Ojibwa deacon's impregnating a Red Lake woman (Gilfillan to Whipple, 13 July 1882, 10 August 1882, 15 September 1882 in Whipple 1833-1934, Box 16; the church bought her a stove and provided her with a weekly stipend in recompense).

The Ojibwas especially resented the parceling of their lands for the use of the missions and the allocation of Indian annuities for mission schools and teachers' salaries. Thus, Chief White Cloud told an inspector at White Earth in 1874 that the clergyman who was agent at White Earth had taken away Indian property without consent or consultation. The chief asked: "Here stands the minister of God, says he comes here to take care of the Indians. Who is his God? Is he a greenback? That is what I am led to believe in my ignorance" (Ruffee 1875: 29). A report on Minnesota Ojibwas in 1920 included the Indian charge that large sums of money, taken from the Ojibwa General Funds, were going to the federal grant for schools run and staffed by missionaries (Scott 1919-1931: 4). Many Ojibwas rejected the Christian mission because of its close connections and identification with the white invasion.

The unsuccessful mission attempted by Rev. Boutwell between 1833 and 1837 at Leech Lake (Hickerson 1965: 1-29) illustrated both the problems encountered by the preacher and the Ojibwa responses to the mission. When Boutwell arrived at Leech Lake, the Pillagers were still beyond the white frontier. They had contacts with fur traders and others but they were still free to make their own decisions. By 1837 they were threatened by land cessions and removal. Boutwell tried to conduct a school for the children and regular Sabbath services. He also attempted to teach farming and animal husbandry, and dispensed medicine, clothes, and food. He interested a few children and a few older men, but everyone else, including all the women, avoided his initiatives, and the young men actively opposed him. He did not attract any sizable or powerful group.

Moreover, he raised displeasure by encouraging individual ownership and cultivation of land when the Pillagers emphasized group activities. Furthermore, his association with the American Fur Company clerk who housed, supplied, and supported him antagonized the Ojibwas who were becoming aware of the fur trader's exploitation of the Indians. When Boutwell and the trader lived comfortably while the Ojibwas went hungry during the winter, the minister won no friends.

In 1834 he bought a plot of land from a woman who had no right to sell it, since it was allocated to her by the Pillager leaders. Boutwell's purchase came while the men were away and aroused their suspicion when they returned. Then in 1836 he administered medicine to a young man who died almost immediately thereafter, making Boutwell suspect of sorcery. By the end of the year the Pillagers were systematically stealing his crops and threatening to kill his cattle. He had to resort to a bribe of flour, tobacco, potatoes and turnips in order to prevent a contingent from killing his farm animals. They warned him that they would force him to leave by the following summer unless he left of his own accord. He moved in the summer of 1837, having made no conversions in his four years of work.

Schoolcraft described the early nineteenth-century Ojibwa opposition to Christianity in the United States, saying that "they have regarded it . . . as a system designed to abridge their natural freedom, and to bring them into a state of society which was not originally meant for them, but which is, on the contrary, . . . suited to destroy them" (Schoolcraft 1853-1857, vol. 5: 151). As recently as the 1920s the Ojibwas at Red Lake actually fled their village to avoid the new missionary attempts made by the Northern Gospel Mission (Mittelholtz 1957: 76-78).

If the Ojibwa opposition to Christianity and Christian missions has appeared so prevailing and intense, how is it that the majority of all contemporary Ojibwas identify themselves as Christians (Ritzenthaler and Ritzenthaler 1970: 97)? Have the better part of Ojibwas living today converted from the religion of their ancestors to the religion of the missionaries?

The seventeenth-century Jesuits baptized hundreds of Ojibwas and related peoples, particularly at Chequamegon and Sault Ste. Marie. The 1669-1670 *Jesuit Relations* wrote that in the previous two years three hundred Indians had been baptized at the Sault (Thwaites 1896-1901, vol. 54: 143). Even though baptism for the Jesuits meant a start toward, not the completion of, conversion, the numbers appeared impressive.

On the other hand, observers around Lake Superior in the early nineteenth century could find no solid trace of Christian beliefs or practices among the Ojibwas (McKenney 1827: 262). If the seventeenth-century Indians had converted, they had not passed down their faith in Jesus Christ to their descendants.

In the nineteenth century the Catholic missionaries again baptized large numbers of Ojibwas. In its five years the Pembina mission baptized 800 Indians, although only 150 had been admitted to Communion (Nute 1942: 415). Father Baraga baptized almost a thousand Indians at Chequamegon (Cadieux and Comte 1954: 23) and from 1835 to 1904 the various missionaries there baptized a total of 3,677 Ojibwas (Levi 1956: 50).

The Protestant missionaries, whose standards for church admission were stricter than those of the Catholics, netted fewer numbers. By 1855 the Sault Baptists had converted twenty-four Ojibwas, the Michigan Presbyterians eighty-six, the Sault and Chequamegon American Board twenty-five, the American Missionary Association twelve, the Minnesota Episcopalians over a hundred. Only the Methodists could match the Catholic numbers, with close to two thousand converts at various stations (Schoolcraft 1853-1857, vol. 6: 735-740). The missionaries claimed to have influenced Ojibwa behavior but by their own standards they had gained few converts and their failures disappointed them, forcing some like the American

Board preachers to cease their efforts. At mid-nineteenth century, the Methodists working among Ojibwas on controlled reserves in Canada were making far better progress than other Protestant missionaries preaching to relatively free Indians.

Christian Control of Reservations and Subsequent Ojibwa Conversions

The 1870s were the turning point for Ojibwa missions in the United States. President Grant's policies emphasized the role of the preachers; indeed, he put the missionaries and their boards in control of the reservations. The preachers now had the leverage that almost two centuries earlier Hennepin had predicted they would need before finding it possible to convert the Indians to Christianity. The Ojibwas were reduced to controlled territory, subject to the autocratic rule of missionaries, especially at White Earth. The Ojibwas there were a defeated, captive audience to the Christian message. By 1875 an observer commented that only at White Earth, where the Ojibwas had to answer to the clergy authorities, was there progress of a social, moral, or industrial nature (Ruffee 1875: 6). By 1881 the *Minneapolis Tribune* was reporting that of the 1,700 Ojibwas at White Earth, 800 were Catholic, 250 were Episcopalian, and only 650 remained heathens (Works Progress Administration Writers' Project 1849-1942, Box 170). Two years later Rev. Gilfillan rejoiced that the Christian services at White Earth attracted an overflow of devout Ojibwas every Sunday, and that the Indians conducted family prayers in their homes (Gilfillan 1873: 2).

In Canada, too, the missionary effort took hold. Anglicans and Methodists claimed (Wilson 1886: 55; Burden 1895: 17-34) that the Ojibwas in southeast Ontario were almost all converts, despite a lingering interest in pagan traditions. At the end of the century only the Rainy Lake and Nipigon areas of Ontario contained relatively large numbers of pagan Ojibwas. Elsewhere in Southern Ontario, almost all the Ojibwas were Anglicans, Presbyterians, Methodists or Catholics, reported Rev. Gilfillan, who claimed that most Minnesota Ojibwas were Christians (Gilfillan c.1911).

In 1921, Christian missions claimed almost all the Ojibwas living in the area just north of Lake Superior (Cadieux 1959: 37) but large pockets of pagans continued where the preachers had not yet penetrated. Along the Berens River, the

Ojibwas in most contact with the missionaries were all converts in 1934 but their relatives down the river, deeper in the forest, remained pagans (Hallowell 1934: 390).

By the middle of the twentieth century, Christianity touched all Ojibwas. In Michigan all the Ojibwas except for those in the small village of Lac Vieux Desert seem to be more than nominal Christians. They participate regularly in Christian rituals; they seem to identify as Christians; their acculturation appears complete, even though they think of themselves as Indians (Kurath, Ettawageshik, and Ettawageshik 1955, vol. 5, Chapter 12: 1, 4). The same seems true in central Ontario (Baldwin 1957: 64-65), and in the Fort Pelly area in 1961 fewer than 5 percent of the Ojibwas identify themselves as traditional religionists (Shimpo and Williamson 1965: 194-200).

Evaluation of Various Ojibwa Conversions

On the other hand, the degree of conversion continues to appear superficial. Among the Fort Pelly Ojibwas the church plays a marginal role in daily life. The Christian ministers remain outsiders; church attendance is low (Shimpo and Williamson 1965: 194-200). Furthermore, vestiges of traditional beliefs persist. In Minnesota the Ojibwas still believe in, and possibly practice, witchcraft; a few old men still seek visions; some perform traditional cures. In Wisconsin, despite the substantial inroads of Christianity, the traditionalists stay active, carrying on their native ways as well as they can recall them. Even in eastern Ontario and Michigan where the Ojibwas are all supposed to be Christians, Indians turn to their traditional beliefs and practices in private and in crises. Little remains of the traditional religion, but the Ojibwas cherish what does remain. In most instances their loyalty to Christianity carries little conviction.

How, then, does one evaluate the conversions that missionaries have claimed of the Ojibwas through the centuries? There exists a range of interpretations which can apply to an Ojibwa "conversion" to Christianity.

Some seeming conversions turned out to be fraudulent. In one instance an Ojibwa woman named Tshusick traveled alone from Detroit to Washington, D.C. in the winter of 1826-1827. She sought the wife of the Indian agent at Mackinac but was directed to the Commissioner of Indian Affairs, Col. Thomas McKenney. She told him that her husband had just died; God had caused the death in order to punish her for failing to accept Christianity. On her husband's death, she vowed to visit the nation's capital to receive baptism into the white religion. McKenney gave her over to an Episcopalian clergyman from Georgetown, who found her well versed in Christianity (and French) and baptized her. Meanwhile, she attended parties in her honor, receiving gifts from the city's social elite. She left town after much publicity and profit. McKenney later discovered that her conversion was a well-rehearsed ruse to acquire wealth at the expense of moneyed whites who were eager to reward Indians for swelling the Christian ranks (McKenney and Hall 1933-1934, vol. 1: 353-367). Such obvious fake conversions were rare.

The baptisms of the seventeenth century carried overt significance as political acts. The French often presented them as rites of alliance to the French king, as types of national adoption like the 1671 rite at the Sault. Any religious change brought about by such baptisms was superficial, if not accidental (Kennedy 1950: 3). They were hardly conversions to Christianity by anyone's criteria.

From the evidence of the Jesuits in their *Relations* it appeared that some of the conversions or baptisms resulted from the Indians' desire to hold on to the alliances they had won and the tangible, monetary rewards to which they were accustomed. Father Allouez effected the baptism of Ottawas and probably Ojibwas at Chequamegon by threatening to leave them; with him would leave the fur traders whose association with the Indians brought wealth (Thwaites 1896-1901, vol. 52: 205-207). Perhaps some of those who agreed to baptism en masse did so out of religious motivation but their number is small.

Others may have become nominal Christians because of the gifts bestowed upon them by the missionaries, or in the hope of future gifts. Others who received baptism in order to marry Frenchmen at Mackinac desired the rite for purposes other than religious conviction.

Still others found the Christian rituals intriguing and attended them out of curiosity. Rev. Hall noted in his Chequamegon journal in 1832 that many Ojibwas had appeared interested in his services, but once their novelty wore off, the

Indians ignored him (Culkin 1926: 38).

Many Ojibwas at the Sault seem to have received baptism and attended services regularly as the result of an epidemic which Father Druillettes claimed to have miraculously cured in the early 1670s (Thwaites 1896-1901, vol. 55: 117-119; 127-131). Extraordinary cures impressed the Ojibwas and led to some conversions. Those who received baptism in these cases may have perceived Christianity to have stronger curing powers than the traditional medicine men. One missionary wrote that a native curer converted to Christianity after failing to cure his daughter of disease (Jones 1861: 270-271).

Paul Radin suggested that the conversions made by the seventeenth-century Jesuits, and particularly those made by Father Ménard at Keweenaw were of the miserable, the maladjusted, the aged, the infantile and the diseased in the Indian populations, and that such baptisms predictably had no lasting effect on the whole of the Indian communities (Radin c. 1926, Envelope 6: 121-123). The evidence supported Radin's contention. On 2 June 1661 Father Ménard described the baptisms he had performed. They consisted of a deserted woman with two children, one of whom died; a poor old man who died shortly thereafter; a man around age thirty who refused to have sex with any Indian women and received constant ridicule from his fellows; a diseased widow; another widow; an eighty-year-old blind man (Thwaites 1896-1901, vol. 46: 127-137). Nevertheless, no evidence exists to suggest that these conversions were insincere or defective. The wretched condition of the converts detracted nothing from the force of their transformations, even though their conversions made no significant impression on the religion of most Ojibwas.

Similarly, throughout the history of Ojibwa conversions there occurred a large number of recorded deathbed baptisms (e.g., Culkin 1926: 41; Morse 1857: 366; Smith 1919; Landes 1971: 162). Perhaps because Christian missionaries emphasized salvation after death in their discussions of the Christian heaven and hell, the Ojibwas felt it necessary to become Christians to help themselves after death. The validity of a conversion, however, did not depend on the time of life when the transformation took place.

Also prominent in the annals of Ojibwa conversion were clear references to material rewards expected upon conversion. For instance, Little Pine, an Ojibwa of Garden River, told of his conversion which came about through a trip to Toronto:

> When I entered the place where the speaking paper (newspaper) is made, and saw the great machines by which it is done, and by which the papers are folded, I thought, "Ah, that is how it is with the English nation, every day they get more wise, every day they find out something new. The Great Spirit blesses them and teaches them all these things because they are Christians, and follow the true religion. Would that my people were enlightened and blessed in the same way!" (Wilson 1886: 82).

For many Ojibwas conversion was a way to share in the power and status of whites, which the Indians associated directly with Christianity. To them the religion was a means of gaining wealth, power, and knowledge, and they wanted to share in those white benefits.

Another factor in Ojibwa conversions was the desire to please the missionaries. The Indians placed a high importance on maintaining surface agreement in societal relationships (Hallowell 1971: 137). The early Jesuits commented on this trait in discussing conversions and were wary of baptizing the Algonkians without some genuine sign of interest. One Jesuit wrote in the 1668-1669 *Relations*, speaking directly of the Ojibwas:

> Dissimulation, which is natural to those Savages, and a certain spirit of acquiescence, in which the children in that country are brought up, make them assent to all that is told them; and prevent them from ever showing any opposition to the sentiments of others, even though they may know that what is said to them is not true (Thwaites 1896-1901, vol. 52: 203).

Consequently, when Father Marquette wrote that there were two thousand Indians at the Sault ready for baptism, the Jesuits held back because of the natives' tendency to say one thing and mean the opposite, to avoid conflict. When Father Hennepin and other missionaries told the Indians the Christian creation myth, the natives agreed that it was a true story. Then they would tell their own creation myths. When the missionaries interrupted them or said that they did not believe the Indian myths, the natives became upset at the preachers' rude behavior (Hennepin 1880: 335). Modern Ojibwas at Lac du Flambeau exhibit the same avoidance of argument in their decision to become Christians, saying that they do not truly think of themselves as Christians, but "the minister was 'good' to them and it would be discourteous to refuse his request" (Gillin and Raimy 1940: 374). Another Ojibwa in Michigan in 1903 explained his conversion as a defensive measure to prevent the missionary from further bothering him (Burton 1909: 111-112).

A further aspect of conversion has been the desire of Ojibwas to develop native leadership when their traditional activities were under attack or being destroyed. Conversion for some provided a means of taking a lead, gaining status in the community, and helping the community itself through leadership. When Ojibwas felt that Christianity could become an Ojibwa institution because Ojibwas were becoming ministers, they gained an interest in conversion. For instance, Peter Jones' presence among the Ojibwas and Ottawas in Michigan in the 1820s triggered the Indians' interest in Christianity, seeing an Ojibwa clergyman as a means of revitalizing their traditions, of reestablishing their communities (Kurath 1954: 315-316).

The records also contained accounts of Ojibwas in both the United States and Canada who, under the influence of missionaries, came to believe in their alienation from the Christian God and the need for reconciliation through Jesus Christ. They affirmed their worthlessness and total dependence on Jesus Christ and hoped to join him in the Christian heaven. They rejected the traditional Ojibwa manitos as false, in favor of an almighty God who provided them with greater meaning than did the manitos. Some of them joined the Christian community and Christian churches, even helping other Indians toward Christianity by becoming missionaries to their people. They were able to transcend peer pressures; their identity shifted from Ojibwa to Christian, as the focus of their lives changed from the manitos to the Christian God. They underwent thorough reorientation (e.g., Copway 1847; *Eliza the Indian Sorceress* 1835; Ferry 1834; Jacobs 1855; Jones 1861: 7-10; *Old Schusco;* Pitezel 1901; Schoolcraft 1848: 207-209; Whipple 1901a: 133-134).

Most of these conversion accounts were recorded by missionaries and it is possible that the preachers colored the Indians' experiences with Christian hues. On the other hand, autobiographical testimonies of Ojibwa conversions leave little doubt regarding the completeness of the transformation. Peter Marksman described his conversion as "the first time I ever felt that I was a sinner in the sight of God" (Pitezel 1901: 47), and he decided to become a Christian missionary to his people. So, too, did George Copway. His conversion in 1830 convinced him of the necessity of educating and Christianizing all other Indians, a task to which he devoted the remainder of his life. For Copway, Christianity was the pinnacle of human achievement and Ojibwa tradition was something to be superseded. He expressed his Christian orientation in saying that "education and Christianity are to the Indian what wings are to the eagle that soars above his home. They elevate him; and . . . enable him to rise above the soil of degradation and hover about the high mounts of wisdom and truth" (Copway 1858: ix). Copway and other native preachers apparently adopted a Christian framework for their lives.

Other Ojibwas, however, interpreted the Christian message through an Ojibwa framework, even as that framework was corroding under missionary pressure. To some, Jesus appeared as another manito, for example, to the Sault native in 1672 who thanked a Jesuit for praying to "JESUS, the God of war" (Thwaites 1896-1901, vol. 57: 209). Others assumed that Jesus would appear to them in visions and help them with their hunting. It seems unlikely that such Ojibwas were rejecting their traditions in favor of the salvific religion of Jesus Christ; rather, they were fitting the Christian deity into their traditional patterns (Rousseau 1952: 185-208).

Moreover, since their traditional religion admitted new revelation without nullifying the old, they were able to accept pieces of Christianity selectively without disposing of corresponding traditional pieces. In short, they were able to hold traditional and Christian beliefs, participate in traditional and Christian ceremonies, interpret the world through traditional and Christian theory, and relate to traditional manitos and the Christian God simultaneously. In such a spirit a contemporary Ojibwa writes: ". . . I understand how the Christian religion came to be. . . . On the other hand I know about my ancestral beliefs, their rights and wrongs, and I respect both teachings as sacred. I understand the loss I would have if I forsook my Indian religion for another and I serve both" (Morriseau 1965: 107).

Other Ojibwas have kept their traditional religious aspects secretly. At Round Lake many "profess to be Christian, but underneath they hold many non-Christian beliefs and are unwilling to discuss these freely" (Rogers 1962: 5). This reticence to divulge traditional persistences has led some outsiders to conclude that Ojibwa religion is thoroughly defunct (e.g., James 1961: 728-731).

Failure of Christianity to Replace Disintegrated Traditional Religion

Certainly most Ojibwa traditions have lost their power and meaning. Under missionary pressure in the last century the majority of Ojibwas have lost trust in the manitos, ceased believing in the myths, and ended the practice of seeking puberty visions. Ojibwa cultic activity, curing practices, and religious leadership have declined or lapsed. The structure of traditional Ojibwa religions has collapsed, leaving fragmented elements which Ojibwas have refashioned through new religious movements. Vestiges of the traditional religion remain but the religion as a whole does not, as this study tries to show.

The Ojibwas have let the bulk of their traditions lapse, but without accepting the validity of Christianity. In Manitoba, for example, Christianity has been successful in undermining Ojibwa religion, throwing doubt on the answers which the traditions used to give to the Indians, but without providing new satisfactory answers to the Ojibwas (Shimpo and Williamson 1965: 109). There are three Christian churches at Pekangekum in Ontario but a minister there asserts that among the local Ojibwas there are "no real Christians" (Burnford 1969: 134). The Ojibwas have given up much of the old without substantially adopting the new.

A useful parallel exists in the history of Ojibwa art. Sister M. Bernard Coleman (1947: 94-111) found that the earliest extant Ojibwa art — dating from 1830 to 1870 — exhibited traditional forms, planned craftmanship, and a meaning-laden symbolism, with many zooic forms connected to hunting. Flowers, many with medicinal values, were presented in the designs with high botanical accuracy. After 1870 Ojibwa art was influenced by European patterns, including the lace patterns taught at Episcopalian missions. The art from the post-1920 period has been incoherent, with different fruits growing on the same branch and inaccurate representation of the natural forms. The artists have lost touch with their traditions, eschewing zooic imagery, in an attempt to copy white styles. Yet they are not able to adopt the European forms gracefully or relate them to traditional themes. The works carry no symbolism and exhibit relatively low standards of artistry in comparison to the earlier work. Ojibwa art stands between a moribund past and an incomprehensible present, with little apparent future in sight.

The same is true for the religion. The traditional religion has been undercut by numerous factors, not the least of which is Christian missionary activity. Christianity has helped destroy the traditional Ojibwa religion but it has not replaced it as the center of Ojibwa life.

THE OJIBWA PERSON, LIVING AND DEAD

The last three chapters have traced the history of Ojibwa-white contacts, including two chapters on Christian missions and Ojibwa responses. The next seven chapters will attempt to describe the salient features of traditional Ojibwa religion as they existed at first contact, and how each feature has changed over the historical period.

Before describing the manitos, the traditional Ojibwa sources of existence and the objects of traditional Ojibwa religion, I shall provide in this chapter the Ojibwa view of themselves as persons, living and dead. I shall recount what constituted the Ojibwa person, the subject of traditional Ojibwa religion.

Ojibwa Ontology and Soul Dualism

This metaphysical topic rarely found ready expression by the Ojibwas. It usually took white observers' questions to bring the subject into discussion. There probably existed a variance in conception among the Ojibwas regarding human identity in its more minute details, and in the historical period acculturation and the formation of a priestly tradition have fostered further variations.

Nevertheless, the Ojibwas' conception of the person derived from their belief in a soul dualism common to native North Americans (Hultkrantz 1953: 51-52). The first observer to realize this dualism was Schoolcraft. He asked an Ojibwa why the Indians left the top of the coffin loose on their graves, rather than nailing it down. The man responded that the purpose was to let the soul escape. Schoolcraft then asked what happened to the soul after death. The man replied that one soul left the body immediately; a second soul left at a later time. When this answer bewildered Schoolcraft, the man explained that during life one soul traveled at great distance during dreams while the body lay sleeping; a second soul was necessary to animate the body since the first soul so often journeyed from it (Schoolcraft 1848: 127; cf. Michelson no date b: 24).

The stationary soul, a body-soul which Åke Hultkrantz calls an ego-soul (Hultkrantz 1953: 77-78, 212-217), animated the body. Located in the heart of each person, but with an ability to move about both within and without the body, the ego-soul provided intelligence, reasoning, memory, consciousness and the ability to act. It could leave the body for short periods of time, but lengthy separations resulted in sickness and permanent separation meant the body's death. This soul, the seat of the will, experienced emotions. Each person possessed one, receiving animation from it.

The traveling soul, sometimes called a free-soul (Hultkrantz 1953: 241-245), resided in the brain and had a separate existence from the body, being able to journey during sleep at will. Its role, however, went beyond that of journeying during dreams. Indeed, it took on many aspects of the ego-soul. It perceived, sensed, acted as the "eyes" of the ego-soul, seeing things at a distance. When a baby seemed dormant, its free-soul could be out gathering information. When a hunter stalked game, his free-soul could move ahead, guiding the man like a scout. In battle the free-soul could warn of danger from its vantage point outside the body (for soul beliefs of Parry Island Ojibwas, see Jenness 1935: 18-20).

Neither of these souls was the entire person, according to the Ojibwas (Hultkrantz 1953: 208). Neither constituted a personality-soul or a unified soul. Each soul had an existence of its own, apart from the body; however, both acted in harmony with the body. The ego-soul traveled to the afterworld immediately at death. The free-soul, or shadow, became a ghost, staying near the grave for a time. Eventually the free-soul departed for the afterworld and rejoined the ego-soul.

Extensions of the Self

The Ojibwas believed that the person consisted of other parts besides the dual souls. The body worked in harmony with the two souls. It was the appearance, the holder of the souls. As souls traveled they could take other appearances, depending on their power. They could appear as plants, animals, and other forms; therefore, metamorphosis was an aspect of Ojibwa metaphysics. The souls and body were not totally bound to each other throughout life.

Within the body the bones and nails, the longest lasting parts, represented integrity; they held the body together.

Ojibwas paid special attention to the bones of the dead, including those of dead animals. As the most permanent parts of the body, they received respect, a fact noted by Alexander Henry in 1763 when he found a cave at Mackinac filled with preserved and unbroken human bones (Henry 1809: 113).

The person also included psychic extensions, such as the blood, hair, afterbirth, spittle and feces. Whether or not they remained in contact with the body, they remained part of the person. For that reason the Ojibwas took care in hiding their psychic extensions, to prevent harm to the person through the extensions. The whole person could suffer when any of its extensions received abuse; thus, all the extensions received protection.

An especially important extension of the Ojibwa person was the name. An Ojibwa might obtain as many as six names during a lifetime: one given at a feast immediately after birth, one received at a puberty vision, a familiar name provided by parents, a nickname, a name representing a totem and a euphonious name (Densmore 1929: 52-53). Only the first two names truly identified the essential person and were usually kept secret, hidden for the same reason that other extensions of the person received protection. The totemic name indicated the person's social identity and was not held secret.

The Ojibwas considered a person's image, including the external shadow, as an integral part of the person, like a name. Drawing another person's picture was a means of influencing that person, just as injuring a person's external shadow might injure the whole person. For the Ojibwas, the person included more than the contents held together by the bones; the body extended beyond the skin.

It is apparent that the Ojibwas respected their bodies, yet they believed in a soul-body dichotomy in which the souls dominated. The souls continued to live after the flesh and bones disintegrated, thereby proving themselves stronger, more permanent, more important. And whereas the souls and body, with all its extensions, harmonized with each other to form the person, the body depended on the souls for life itself. The souls could live without the body; it could not live without them.

First, the body depended on the ego-soul for its animating power. Without the ego-soul's animating power the body could not exist; it would have no consciousness. The ego-soul represented an internal source of existence, just as the manitos represented the external sources of existence.

Second, the body depended on the free-soul's ability to travel in visions. The Ojibwas established and maintained relations with the manitos primarily through visions. Without the free-soul, the Ojibwas' means of relation with the sources of their existence — the manitos — would not exist.

An Animate Universe

The dual souls, then, possessed dual religious functions. They gave the person life and made communication with the manitos possible. The souls were not, however, emanations or reflections of the manitos. The Ojibwas believed that manitos, as well as all animate beings including humans, plants, animals and natural entities, possessed personal souls (Schoolcraft 1839, vol. 1: 42).

The Ojibwa universe consisted of myriad persons, units of body and souls; each body possessed its personal souls. The Ojibwa conception of animate beings included some stones, clouds, and other persons which Westerners would call "things" (Hallowell 1960).

The human person, according to the Ojibwas, participated in the life of the universe in an essential equality with non-human persons (Charlevoix 1761, vol. 2: 155). Humans interacted with the other persons, in harmony and conflict, without the attitude or assumption that humans were innately superior to the other persons (Henry 1809: 130-131). Humans fitted into the universal order; they did not rule over it. For the Ojibwa person, "all objects have life, and life is synonymous with power, which may be directed for the Indian's good or ill. . . . Therefore, the Indian should treat everything he sees or touches with respect befitting a thing that has a soul and shadow not unlike his own" (Jenness 1935: 21).

That is not to say that the Ojibwas never mistreated animals (they often beat their dogs senseless) or that they regarded all the persons of the universe as friends; however, they did respect the persons for the life and power that each one had. The manitos had more power than humans but each herb, each individual animal, held life and power which the human could use and which deserved respect. Ojibwas spoke of bears and other animals as relatives, often calling them "grandfather" or "grandmother" or "brother" (Hallowell 1926: 45-46).

The essential equality between humans and animals made the common metamorphosis between human and animal life sensible. (Metamorphosis between human and plant life or human and mineral life occurred less often.) The souls of humans and animals were the continuity, the essential, lasting parts of the person which could transcend the body.

Furthermore, Schoolcraft cited the Ojibwa belief that "animals in their present state possess their original soul and reasoning faculties, while they are deprived of speech, and that they will have a resurrection or second life as well as men" (Schoolcraft 1853-1857, vol. 3: 520). The equality between humans and other living persons continued beyond the grave.

Death and Afterlife

For the Ojibwa person, death was the permanent separation of the souls from the body. Nevertheless, the person persisted in the afterworld, the souls reuniting and taking on the appearance of the body once again.

The afterworld, located either to the south or west, existed either above or on the same plane as the present earth, not below it. Almost all persons, including animals, went to the same afterworld, ruled by Nanabozho, the Ojibwa Culture-Hero and Trickster, or by his wolf-brother. Existence there had many of the features of the present world, with an abundance of food; thus the dead took their earthly utensils with them from the grave to continue their lives in the beyond.

On the other hand, the dead person's perceptions and participation in reality were thought to be the opposite of that of the living. The dead danced at night and slept during the day. They ate rotten wood rather than meat. Some Ojibwas said that no hunting or warfare continued after death (Kohl 1860: 217). A life without hunting was certainly the opposite of Ojibwa life on earth.

The Ojibwas did not believe in an afterlife punishment for unethical acts on earth. The afterlife did not constitute a moral reward for good deeds performed by the living person. Neither did the afterlife mean a closer communication with the manitos, although theoretically the dead were closer to Nanabozho.

It was, however, a happy place. The dead danced joyfully, creating the northern lights as a reminder to the living of the joy to come after death. Part of the happiness of the afterlife sprang from the fact that practically everyone went there. The Ojibwas did not worry about their destiny after death. They anticipated no punishment in the afterworld for misdeeds committed during life; rather, they enforced their morality through disease sanctions. Sins found their punishment in the present life, not the next.

Nevertheless, the person encountered trials on the way to the next world. The journey took four days, during which the person overcame temptations to remain. The principal obstacle was a rapidly flowing river, spanned by a log-like snake. The person needed to cross over the river on the back of the snake, while the wind blew and the slippery bridge shook. Those who fell into the raging water became toads or fishes, or died forever.

The obstacle seemed related to the skills necessary in the living world for hunting success and survival. If one could not cross a stream in this life, one could not get to the next world. The factor under test was skill, not ethics. For that reason children who died had great difficulty in crossing the stream; they had yet to obtain the skills of life. Some white observers (e.g., Kohl 1860: 217-226) found such an obstacle unfair to children but to the Ojibwas a test based on hunting abilities made excellent sense.

Visits to the Afterworld

Ojibwa knowledge of the afterworld and the road to get there came from the testimonies of living persons who had traveled to the afterworld and returned, or by those who had approached but not entered it. Sometimes the dead conversed with the living and told about the world beyond.

Journeys to the other world were not normal. They took place among the seriously ill, particularly those in comatose states, and those trained to make such a journey. Entering the afterworld usually meant no permanent return to life, although the free-soul might travel between the two realms. The normally healthy person could approach the afterworld in a dream but could not enter it. Once a living person entered and took part in the activities of the afterworld, return would be most difficult (Hultkrantz 1957: 233-234). Those who did come back to life lived abnormally, as one man who played lacrosse with the dead every night after his wife dug him up from his grave (Hallowell 1971: 154).

Some, like that man, did not really die but fell into deep trances indistinguishable from death. Their ego-souls traveled to the afterworld where the dead told them to go back to earth. One youth found his grandmother in the afterworld who took him to a feast where the deceased found his odor disgusting. They danced without heads, legs, and the like; his grandmother told him not to be frightened at what he saw. Reality for the dead differed from that of the living. The dead whistled, whereas living Ojibwas did not; all times and procedures seemed backward. The youth's grandmother sent him back. He came along the road and jumped into a fire which turned out to be his body. He regained consciousness to find his mother mourning him (Jones 1919: 2-23). Similar stories told of persons who returned from the afterworld and advised the living not to feel sorry for the dead; they were enjoying themselves.

Another type of testimony regarding the afterworld was the so-called Orpheus tale, in which a living person attempted to bring back a loved one from a recent death by following and visiting the afterworld (Hultkrantz 1957). These accounts arose from, and in turn informed, the traditional Ojibwa views of the afterworld. Visits by the deceased to the land of the living confirmed those views. Living and dead Ojibwa persons did not lose touch with one another.

Treatment of the Dead

Traditionally the Ojibwas left their dead in crotches or branches of trees, wrapped in a bundle. It was not until the contact period that they began burials. Archaeological evidence has indicated that they buried the bones of their deceased after the flesh was gone (Works Progress Administration 1936-1940; 1942, Envelope 6, No. 3: 7).

At death the body was carried out of the lodge, probably through a special hole made in the wall. The body was then cleaned, dressed in finery, and painted. The burial services took four days or less, with the body oriented toward the direction of the afterworld, south or west. The concern of mourning was for the deceased to reach the afterworld safely. For that reason the family members made speeches to the deceased, giving advice and encouragement for the journey, especially to children, who would have a difficult crossing. They put food with the body so that the soul could consume it on the way. They placed tobacco with the body so that the soul could offer it to the dead and the leaders of the afterworld, Nanabozho and his wolf-brother.

The Ojibwas desired that their loved ones reach the afterworld. They also desired that they leave this world immediately (Kohl 1860: 106-107). They expressed their willingness to let the deceased go and spoke of the unwillingness of the living to join the dead in the afterworld. They loved life too much to depart prematurely. Some Ojibwas might have felt that the dead would attempt to take the living with them, for widows would run through the forest in order to escape from the departed (Jones 1861: 98-100). One mourning speech told the dead person: "You will see your dead relatives. They will inquire about the people who are still living. Tell them we are not ready to come" (Hilger 1951:79).

At dusk following a death, and for the next three nights, the mourners lit fires to guide the ego-soul on its journey. The mourners conducted a feast on the fourth night, burning food for the consumption of the dead person, maintaining communion with the deceased through a shared meal. The burial ceremonies ended with dancing and singing, which matched the ceremonies that the deceased would encounter upon reaching the afterworld.

From the end of the burial ceremonies until the next annual feast for the dead held among the family, the immediate family of the deceased performed mourning duties, particularly the parents and spouse of the dead one (McKenney 1827: 292-294). Mothers carried a cradleboard with a roll of clothing in the shape of their deceased child; sometimes the mourning mother fed the effigy, now an extension of the dead person (Jones 1861: 100-101).

A mourning spouse owed work and mourning duties to the deceased's relatives, particularly a widow to her dead husband's family. She could not remarry; she blackened her face and wore ragged clothing. She eschewed festivities and carried a lock of the dead person's hair in a mourning bundle. She visited her dead husband's grave until the relatives freed her from her obligations.

The mourning period ended with the annual family feast for its dead. At that time the family ate a ritual meal, sharing it with the dead, calling on the dead to help in hunting endeavors. Then the mourners danced and sang in memory of their dead relatives and family members.

Even this ritual did not release the living from communication with and obligations to the dead. Regular offerings ceased but if someone dreamed of the dead, especially if the dead appeared in ragged clothing or in need of food, the living provided aid. Living and dead persons did not lose contact with each other.

The living did not worship the dead. They believed that the dead took an interest in the affairs of the living but the living did not rely on the dead for subsistence. The dead's interest in the living sometimes took the form of revenge for past wrongs; the free-soul made malicious visits in the form of an owl, the traditional Ojibwa bugbear.

As a general rule, however, the Ojibwas did not fear their dead. Some of the deceased visited with the living at their graves, sharing tobacco or food, continuing companionship. On rare occasions the dead could serve as guardians for the living, acting as manitos, but in general the Ojibwas did not consider the dead to possess enormous power over the living (Hallowell 1971: 159-160). The Ojibwa attitude toward their dead was ambivalent. The dead had potential power which might help or harm the living; the living Ojibwa would approach a dead one with some wariness but would accept aid, if offered. But only in rare cases, if at all, did a dead person hold the influence and power of a manito. The living obtained their subsistence, their existence, from the manitos, not from the dead. Deceased humans were still only human for the traditional Ojibwas.

Christian Influences on Ojibwa Ontology

The influence of Christian missions and social disintegration have gradually changed Ojibwa conceptions about the human person. Today most Ojibwas believe in a unitary soul, a personality-soul derived from the Christian conception (Hultkrantz 1953: 33).

Other aspects of the person have lost their meaning, for example, the name. Today most Ojibwas use names received from white officials who could not pronounce the Ojibwa names (Brown 1960). Others have kept traditional names but pass them down as surnames. In both cases the contemporary Ojibwa names fail to identify, fail to exemplify and extend the person as did the traditional names.

Christianity's influence on Ojibwa traditions is especially strong regarding the afterworld. In presenting the Christian message, missionaries emphasized the two Christian afterworlds, heaven and hell, and the need for conversion to Christianity to reach heaven and be united with the Christian God. At Chequamegon Father Allouez hung pictures of the universal judgment and hell, deriving the themes for his sermons and instruction from the pictures (Kellogg 1917: 116). The writings of other missionaries, Catholic and Protestant, indicated their main topic, salvation after death (Lahontan 1703, vol. 2: 518), which they communicated to the Ojibwas.

The otherworldly character of the missionary message contrasted sharply with the Ojibwa concern for this life and the Indians' belief that one's ethical actions would find punishment or reward on this earth, not in the next world. A white Methodist preacher at Rice Lake wrote in his diary in 1830: "Another revolving day has passed, and I am hastening to the tomb. O, may my soul be ripening for a blessed immortality! Oh, may each day advance me towards my eternal rest!" (Holdich 1839: 32). Nothing could have been further from the traditional Ojibwas' view. Their conceptions regarding the afterlife comforted them with the knowledge that life continued after death. Belief in an afterlife denied the finality of death and offered an assurance of reuniting with relatives and loved ones. In these respects the Ojibwas' afterlife served similar functions to that of the Christians' heaven; however, the Ojibwas did not yearn for death as the missionary did. He sought unity with God in heaven; the Ojibwas sought unity with the living world and the manitos in this life.

Not only was the afterlife an emphasis of the Christian mission, but the Ojibwas also perceived it as such. According to a perceptive observer, the Round Lake Ojibwas of today understand Christianity to be "concerned primarily with a person's soul and life after death, while the aboriginal concepts deal with interpersonal relations and the behavior of individuals while here on earth" (Rogers 1962: D2).

Ojibwa beliefs regarding the afterworld have changed under Christian influence, but not without a fight. The struggle has taken place through myths based on traditional visits to the afterworld. The first evidence of such a contest appeared in the seventeenth century (Hennepin 1880: 332) when an Indian woman at the point of death refused baptism from Father Hennepin because she said that Indians who died Christian would be burned in the afterworld by the French. Others told Hennepin that the French baptized Indians to have them as slaves in the afterworld. Still others said that they would not go to the French afterworld because they would surely starve there. Certainly not all Ojibwas believed these charges, but the motif developed and spread through the years.

In the early nineteenth century John Tanner (James 1956: 161-162) heard an anecdote among the Ojibwas and Ottawas in Michigan about a missionary who came around telling Indians to renounce their own religion in favor of Christianity. One man did, but when he died the whites would not allow him into their heaven because he was an Indian. When he went to the Indian heaven, his fellows would not have him because he had renounced their way of life.

This took a more personal touch when an Indian came to Rev. Hall at Chequamegon and told him that a converted Ojibwa had died and was refused admission into the white heaven for his being an Indian. He knew he could not enter the Indian heaven so he returned to his dead body. This story frightened the local Ojibwas and they refused to listen to Hall and the other missionaries (Tuttle 1838:68).

The same tale was current among the Red River Ojibwas and neighboring Crees in the early nineteenth century, as reported by Father Belcourt (Aldrich 1927b: 37). The Manitoulin Ojibwas insisted to Rev. O'Meara in 1840 that they did not wish to enter the Christian heaven because it was different from the Indian one. They feared that they would never be reunited with their dead relatives (O'Meara, et al. 1847-1848: 2).

The same motif was reported at Chequamegon in 1860 (Kohl 1860: 217, 277-278), among the Minnesota Ojibwas in the late nineteenth century (Whipple 1901a: 134), and in the twentieth century among the Berens River Ojibwas. In the last case it was introduced as a true story about an Indian boy who received an education and became a teacher and Christian preacher. Then he became ill and the doctors could not help him; he died. He followed the white man's road and came to a house. He knocked and was told through a crack that he did not belong on that road. He took another road and came to another house where the same message was given to him. He returned to life and did not take up preaching again. The Indians in his area, Lac Seul, gained a renewed interest in their traditional ways because of his testimony (Hallowell 1971: 157). The Ojibwas near Lake of the Woods believe that those Indians who convert to Christianity will have to work for the whites in the white heaven and will not get to see their Indian friends and relatives who live in the Indian heaven (Balikci 1956: 176).

From all Ojibwa areas the pattern has been the same. The Ojibwas have acquired the Christian belief in a heaven and at times used that belief as propaganda against conversion. They have resorted to traditional means of knowledge about the afterworld, specifically visits by the sick and dying to the beyond, in order to bolster their traditions and resist Christianity.

They have been prompted, no doubt, by the Christian practice of introducing a new, alien word to the Ojibwa language to describe the Christian heaven and by the Christian practice of burying the converted Indians in separate grounds, apart from their pagan relatives. An Ojibwa at Chequamegon drew a diagram of the path to the Ojibwa afterworld, including the temptations and trials along the road. He drew on the same picture another path to the Christian afterworld which he said he knew nothing about, since no Indian entered it. J.G. Kohl, the astute German traveler who watched him, was immediately reminded of the separate burial grounds at a nearby mission village. The Ojibwa man colored his ideas about the afterworlds with his knowledge of the separated Christian and pagan cemeteries (Kohl 1860: 210-217).

By the late nineteenth century the Ojibwas in Michigan were devising codes of ethics like the Judeo-Christian Ten Commandments, syncretizing Christian and Ojibwa elements with heaven as the reward for a good life (Blackbird 1887:

104-105). Today many Ojibwas, even among those who have resisted Christian missions, believe in separate afterworlds for good and evil people. The Parry Island Ojibwas think of Christianity as the means by which they have seen a new road to a new afterworld (Jenness 1935: 110). Still others persist in the belief that Indians go to one afterworld, white Christians to another. In general Ojibwas have adopted some Christian eschatological conceptions without accepting the salvific message of Jesus Christ.

Many Indian burial and mourning customs continue, alongside Christian ones, and are often syncretized with them (Kinietz 1947: 146-148; Paredes, Roufs, and Pelto 1973: 160). In Wisconsin the annual feasts for the dead take place on All Souls Eve, a Christian feast day for their dead (Works Progress Administration 1936-1940; 1942, Envelope 6, No. 3: 5). As far back as the seventeenth century the family feasts expanded under Huron influence into village-wide, and even nation-wide events known as Feasts of the Dead, with dancing, games, alliances and revelry. The riches of the fur trade and the increasing interconnections of Indian communities broadened the scope of the rites but the poverty and disjunction of the mid-nineteenth-century Ojibwas put an end to these splendid Feasts, leaving behind the less spectacular feasts *for* the dead (Hickerson 1960).

Through the centuries, the Ojibwas have changed their conceptions regarding the human person, living and dead, particularly under Christian missionary influence. However, fieldworkers in contemporary Manitoba, Wisconsin (Hay 1977: 71-89), and northern Minnesota (Black 1977: 91) describe an Ojibwa personality which is at base the same as the aboriginal one. If these findings are accurate, then the changes in their ontological concepts are doubly damaging to the Ojibwas: first, because of the confusion inherent in the change; and second, because Ojibwas still tend to act the same way, but are much less able to explain to themselves why they act as they do. They are, in effect, alienated from themselves.

THE MANITOS

The Ojibwas believed in numerous manitos of which no one ruled supreme. A matrix of these manitos constituted the ultimate source of Ojibwa existence.

The Sources of Ojibwa Existence

Just as there were many manitos, there were many types of relationships between them and humans. Ojibwas regarded some manitos with awe, some with affection, and others with dread. Ojibwa relations with the manitos covered a wide range of human experience, just as the manitos' influence covered the wide range of Ojibwa existence.

The manitos were the sources of Ojibwa existence; therefore, they reflected Ojibwa life. The primary concern of the Ojibwas was physical survival through hunting. Consequently, their religious concepts and relations expressed their hunting identity and concern for subsistence. Moreover, the Ojibwas conceived of the manitos as the ultimate sources of daily food, of hunting success; it was the duty of the manitos to keep the Ojibwas alive and healthy. In their later conversations with missionaries the Ojibwas contrasted their traditions with those of Christians by saying, for example, to one missionary (James 1855: 3) that Indians prayed for game, whereas Christians prayed for soul salvation.

That is not to say that Ojibwa religion arose from their concern for subsistence, but such a conjecture is not impossible and should not be ruled out. Ojibwa relations with the manitos were as much a means toward the end of providing food as they were ends in themselves. Ojibwa religion reflected Ojibwa life and concerns as much as it reflected the ultimate sources of Ojibwa existence.

The Ojibwas viewed their world as a flat piece of earth, like a muskeg floating in a lake. Below the water was another flat earth; above was the dome of the sky on which a third world was located. The manitos who lived in all corners of this universe were persons, living beings with souls, acting under the same motivations as humans, only with incomparably more power. When an event took place in the universe — a branch put a person's eye out; a storm roiled a lake — the

72

Ojibwas' first response was to ask *who* caused it (Lahontan 1905, vol. 2: 446). They lived in a very personal universe. The most powerful and important of the manitos were the Four Winds, the Underwater Manito, the Thunderbirds, the Owners of animals and other entities, the Windigo and Nana-bozho (Culture-Hero and Trickster). Each of these manitos directly influenced hunting success and determined whether an individual survived or not.

Also concerned with subsistence were numerous minor manitos, a Great Owl who drove game to hunters, little water beings who stole fish from Ojibwas, and the holders of the sun and the moon. Other manitos, such as the Turtle, gave Ojibwas power to see at a distance or conduct shaking tent ceremonies. Still others gave luck and success in war or in overcoming witches. The Ojibwa individual could enter a personal relation with any of the manitos through a puberty vision fast. The Ojibwa community tried to maintain relations with all the manitos through various cultic actions.

Four Winds

The Four Winds resided in the four quarters, the cardinal directions of the universe. Brothers of Nanabozho, they were responsible for the changes in seasons and weather, and the Ojibwas expected them to act in certain ways, depending on the time of the year. Since the Winds were living persons, however, they acted as they willed.

Ojibwa livelihood depended on being able to influence the wills of the Winds. The Indians hoped that a cold North Wind would blow in the late winter to harden the crust of snow so that large game such as deer would be hobbled in their attempts to escape the snowshoe-clad hunters. The animal's legs broke through the hard crust while the snowshoes glided across the top. If the North Wind did not act properly, the Ojibwas could starve. In the summer, too, fishing on the large lakes was made impossible if any of the Winds blew too strongly; therefore, the Ojibwas hoped that the Winds would have pity on them and refrain from heaving the waters too heavily or too often (on the importance of winds over three centuries, see Charlevoix 1761, vol. 2: 43-44; Long 1904: 143; Rogers 1962: A8).

In the Ojibwa Creation Myth Nanabozho gained control over his four brothers in order to secure successful hunting and fishing for the Indians. In some myths, Nanabozho acted as a fifth Wind, for example as the Northwest Wind. The Four Winds always visited in the shaking tent ceremony, rocking the lodge as they entered. As dwellers of the farthest corners of the universe, they represented the universe's totality.

Underwater Manito

The Underwater Manito was not a single manito but rather a composite. It consisted of two main beings, the underwater lion and the horned serpent, whose identity and roles were interchangeable. Perhaps at one time in the distant past they were two distinct beings since they have maintained separate names among some Ojibwa groups, but this is impossible to determine. From the earliest sources (Allouez in Kellogg 1917: 112; Dablon in Thwaites 1896-1901, vol. 54: 153-154) came descriptions of the Underwater Manito, associated with both the lion and the serpent. Like a snake it appeared above ground only in warm seasons.

As a composite, the Underwater Manito influenced the abundance and availability of land and sea animals. With its numerous underwater allies it controlled all game, withholding animals and fish from its enemies. The early Lake Superior Ojibwas offered it sacrifices to obtain good fishing, and in the Creation Myth Nanabozho fought it to secure the right to hunt for future Indians.

The Underwater Manito possessed great and dangerous powers. It could cause rapids and stormy waters; it often sank canoes and drowned Indians, especially children. The Ojibwas associated it with the sudden squall waters of the Great Lakes which prevented fishing, even picturing it in the shape of Lake Superior itself (Kellogg 1917: 104-105). Some Ojibwas thought of the Underwater Manito as a thoroughly malicious creature.

It was not totally evil, however. In some traditions it fed and sheltered those who fell through the winter ice. It offered medicinal powers to those who accepted it as guardian (Radin c. 1926: n.p.). It gave copper to the Indians, who cut the metal from the being's horns as it raised them above the surface of the water (Kellogg 1917: 105). Those who attempted to take the copper without offering proper payment met severe punishment from the Underwater Manito. It was a creature to inspire terror and awe, as well as reverence. Without the aid or benign neglect of this being — part snake, part catfish, part lynx, part mountain lion — the Ojibwas would surely starve or suffer death in raging waters.

Thunderbirds

In order to counteract the influence of the Underwater Manito, Nanabozho created the Thunderbirds, enormous birds of the hawk family seen most often in visions, but who manifested themselves through thunder and lightning (for Thunderbird beliefs see Coleman 1937: 37; Coleman 1947: 68; Grant 1890: 356; Hallowell 1960: 31-37; James 1956: 123-124; Kidder 1918: 127-129; "Thunderbird Legend of the Post" 1930: 128). They threw their lightning balls or bolts to the earth to kill the Underwater Manito or its allies; their powers also punished Indians who broke traditions and moral rules. The Thunderbirds lived in the four quarters and were sometimes thought of as messengers of the Four Winds, but they appeared with other birds in the spring and stayed until the fall. In late fall they migrated to the south after the Underwater Manito's most dangerous season passed. As the Underwater Manito controlled game of the land and waters, the Thunderbirds influenced the game of the air, all birds. The Ojibwas made offerings to the Thunderbirds to obtain success in hunting fowl of all kinds. The Thunderbirds were especially powerful guardians, appearing often in visions, and many Ojibwas received Thunderbird puberty names, including Peter Jones, the nineteenth-century missionary whose traditional name (Kākīwākwōnābī) indicated sacred saving-feathers of the Thunderbirds (Chamberlain 1890: 53).

The appearance of Thunderbirds in lightning and thunder evinced Ojibwa reverence for the frequent and destructive electrical storms. A modern Ojibwa tells that as a child, "we were taught to show respect for the Thunder; we were told to sit down and to be quiet until the storm had passed over. It was just like God going by" (Hilger 1951: 61).

Owners of Nature

Of great importance to the traditional Ojibwas were the Owners of natural entities (Tyrrell 1916: 83), especially the Owners of large animals which the Ojibwas hunted for food. Even though the Underwater Manito controlled land and water animals and the Thunderbirds controlled air animals, each species had an Owner who provided some hunters with game and left others to starve. The two most important Owners were of the bear and the deer, for it was upon the meat of these two animals that the Ojibwas most depended for survival, although each of the animal Owners had decisive influence over the Indians.

The Ojibwas believed that without the aid of the Owners of game animals, individual animals would never be caught; that the hunter depended on the Owner to provide food. If the Owner of a species was insulted or alienated, the hunter would not be permitted to kill, or even find, any member of that species. If the Owner of a species favored a hunter, the Indian would have success. As a result, the Ojibwas treated animals they killed with care and respect, performing rituals for the animals, preserving their bones, offering them tobacco, and thanking the Owner for the kill. Owners of animals were crucial to Ojibwa religion, just as hunting was crucial to Ojibwa existence.

The Ojibwas also recognized Owners of human institutions, especially those concerned with curing and conjuring. The chief patron of the shaking tent ceremony, the Turtle, spoke at every service, accompanied by assistants. Medicine men relied on Owners of curing techniques; Nanabozho's grandmother, Nokomis, acted as the Owner of herbs.

Besides these influential Owners of animals and institutions, there were Owners of certain locations such as waterfalls and springs, and beings who had specific functions which were useful to humans. Each of these numerous Owners of powers possessed specific talent for a certain activity for which they were called in time of need. The Ojibwas chose leaders for specific tasks; one person's leadership never transcended all of the community's needs. The same situation applied to the various Owners; each Owner served a purpose but had no control over activities beyond its scope of powers.

Windigo

Although not central to the host of Ojibwa manitos and possibly not of precontact origin, the Windigo played an influential role in traditional Ojibwa life and thought. The Windigo was a giant cannibal made of ice, symbolizing winter and its starving times. Ojibwas spoke of the Windigo as an individual, yet they believed in the existence of many windigos. Perhaps one was the Owner of the many, but the Ojibwas did not say this directly.

These windigos appeared as skeletons of ice, or as people whose insides were ice, and were naturally most common during the winter, when they searched for human flesh to eat. A human could become a windigo through possession by the Windigo, by the acquisition of the Windigo as a guardian, by witchcraft, or by winter starvation (Tyrrell 1916: 259-261). Both women and men could become windigos, experiencing deep depression and hallucinations in which humans appeared as beavers and other potential food. A windigo developed an insatiable craving for human flesh, sometimes eating family members. The community had the right to kill such dangerous psychotics, since once transformed, they ceased to be human (Henry 1809: 207-209).

Famine was not uncommon among the early Ojibwas, especially in the late winter, and the belief in the Windigo represented a tribal fear of winter starvation. The Windigo's "heart of ice symbolizes an environmental condition, namely, the icy winter of the north, and . . . this note has become associated with the giant-cannibal conception because winter time is the time of famine and of famine-cannibalism" (Cooper 1933: 24).

Other cultures like the Eskimo and Athabascan Indians of the north underwent similar starvation and did not develop such a thoroughgoing belief. The belief in the Windigo represented the central concern of the Ojibwas about physical survival and their fear of winter starvation, particularly in the post-contact period. The Windigo was a creature which turned humans into cannibals by starving them, by weakening and possessing them so that they forfeited their humanity, their identity. The Ojibwa relation with the Windigo was one of absolute terror, yet it was a religious relation because the Ojibwas recognized their dependence on the Windigo for their survival as human persons. They existed at the Windigo's mercy.

Nanabozho

If the Windigo's relation with the Ojibwas was terrifying, their relation with Nanabozho was one of intimate identification. Although he rarely served as an individual's guardian, received few offerings, and seldom appeared in cultic activity, his mythic actions confirmed the Ojibwas as hunters. He secured the right and ability of humans to hunt; he instituted vital cultural elements; he created the present world and formed Ojibwa identity. Without Nanabozho the Ojibwas in their own estimation would not exist.

Totems

Another means to traditional Ojibwa social identity was the totem animal, each person's family mark (Henry 1809: 305). John Long, the late eighteenth century traveler, first used the word "totemism" to describe the Ojibwa relations with these animals (Long 1904: 124 spelled the word as "totamism"), and his misapprehension of the relations helped confuse later theorists who borrowed the Ojibwa term to describe sundry situations worldwide. Long confused totems (patrilinear family marks which promoted exogamy) with .the Owners of animals (potential guardians of humans) in saying that one's totem watched over and protected the individual Ojibwa.

On the contrary, all members of a totemic group considered themselves relatives, and indeed they were in traditional Ojibwa society. When Ojibwas traveled, they left totem signs indicating time and direction so that relatives could share company (James 1956: 165-166). When Ojibwas entered a strange Ojibwa settlement, they sought out relatives and expected hospitality from them. The totemic animals were not persons, living active members of the universe. They did not in any way help the Ojibwas catch game as Owners of animals and other manitos did. They simply were not manitos. The Ojibwas performed no regular rituals or ceremonies in honor of totems, unless one considers family reunions (Bushnell 1905: 69) to be cultic events. The Ojibwas did not regard themselves as descendants of totems, although theoretically the use of animals as family marks helped in joining humans to the animal world, indicating the continuity of nature. Totems deserve mention because of their role in defining Ojibwa social identity but they were not sources of Ojibwa existence in any active sense. Indeed, "the only real function that one can detect for this social grouping is the demarcation of relationship" (Kinietz 1947: 77). The relation between Ojibwas and their totems was not religious since the Ojibwas did not ultimately depend on the totems for continued existence.

Ojibwa Polytheism

The Ojibwas were polytheists. In the nineteenth century Schoolcraft said that they believed in not just one God but in thousands of malignant and benign manitos "who preside over the daily affairs and over the final destinies of men" (Schoolcraft 1839, vol. 1: 41). It is doubtful that the Ojibwas possessed a developed conception of a Supreme Being in pre-contact days, although this is nearly impossible to prove convincingly, especially since most Ojibwas today believe that their ancestors knew and related to such a being.

The earliest Western records presented no conclusive case for a traditional Ojibwa Supreme Being, despite the early Jesuits' enthusiastic use of Indian religious phenomena to prove to European skeptics that religiosity was an innate part of humanity. Father Allouez noted the difference between the Lake Superior Algonkian religion and Christianity, remarking that " . . . whatever seems to them either helpful or hurtful they call a Manitou, and pay it the worship and veneration which we render only to the true God" (Kellogg 1917: 111). He could find no evidence of an Ojibwa monotheism.

Others in the seventeenth and eighteenth centuries claimed to have discovered an Ojibwa Supreme Being. Father Hennepin said that the Indians had an idea of a "Master of Life," but his description noted that each person related to an individual master, for example, a bird (Hennepin 1880: 333). He no doubt referred to personal guardian manitos. Although he was correct in saying that these manitos constituted the master of each person's life, such a description hardly constituted a Supreme Being for the Ojibwas. Father Charlevoix, an eighteenth-century explorer, reported that the Indians had a Supreme Being, but among the Algonkians that being was none other than Nanabozho (Charlevoix 1761, vol. 2: 141-142 called him the Great Hare, "Michabou"). Later in the eighteenth century, Long's portrayal of the Ojibwa Supreme Being turned out to be the Underwater Manito (Long 1904: 80). No early observer clearly described an Ojibwa Supreme Being.

Christian Missions and a Supreme Being Concept

An integral part of the Jesuit missionary message was the belief in a supreme God, the single and total source of human existence, according to Christianity. The priests who preached to the Ojibwas about this God believed at the end of their tenure that they had implanted a God concept in the minds of the Ojibwas (Kennedy 1950: 55). It is possible that such an imprint lasted through the eighteenth century, and that the later observers who claimed that no missionary influence lasted were mistaken.

Even if the traditional Ojibwas did conceive of a Supreme Being, such a conception was later influenced by the missions. Modern researchers who conclude that a Supreme Being concept was aboriginal agree that the present Ojibwa term "Kitche Manito" was the creation of Christians (Cooper 1934: 37). "Kitche" is the Ojibwa word meaning great. The Ojibwa picture of this manito, as contained in a trader's 1804 journal, was of a man who created heaven, water, and the portion of the earth where whites originated. He was the author of life and death, the rewarder of the good and the punisher of the bad (Grant 1890: 354). Such a portrayal indicates more than minimal Western influences.

The term "Master of Life" which Ojibwas and other Algonkians used in the nineteenth century to describe their Supreme Being appears to have come from Christians (Hultkrantz 1953: 414); it is likely that the Supreme Being concept came from Christians, too. That the Ojibwas referred to the French priests as "The Master of Life's Men" strengthens this belief (Long 1904: 39).

None of these clues precludes the possibility of a traditional Ojibwa Supreme Being concept. Neither does the evidence that the Ojibwas used "Kitche" to describe a class of beings rather than a single being. For instance, they referred to large lakes, the Great Lakes, as "Kitche," rather than using the appellation to indicate Lake Superior alone (James 1956: 46).

Likewise, Kohl discovered that "Kitche Manito" referred to an entire class of great manitos. One old Indian told him that there were six Kitche Manitos, one in the heavens, one in the water, and the other four at the cardinal directions (Kohl 1860: 58-60). Although no monotheism existed in such a statement, traditional monotheism was plausible.

Whether or not the Supreme Being was traditional, the Master of Life whom the Ojibwas came to revere was the master of meat, food, and health, as well as master of life and death. If missionaries introduced a Supreme Being concept, the Ojibwas related it to their life concern for obtaining food.

Nevertheless, early Ojibwas did not organize a cult around a Supreme Being. Kitche Manito played no role in traditional Ojibwa myths, did not appear in visions, and did not speak in the shaking tent ceremonies. Even in recognizing the existence of Kitche Manito in the eighteenth and nineteenth centuries, the Ojibwas turned to the manitos in their worship and in their need; they expected no aid from a God so great as surely to be unconcerned about humans (Cameron 1890: 259). Ojibwa converts thought that the Supreme Being heard only the prayers of Christians; no pagan Ojibwas prayed to God (Jacobs 1855: 3).

Contemporary Ojibwas are convinced of the traditional nature of their Supreme Being concept. An old religious leader in Minnesota says that "all the first Indians around here knew there was a God long before the Whites came; only they didn't go to God for things as they do now as Christians. They got their favors from their special helpers then" (Hilger 1951: 60). The Indians' insistence on the pristine quality of the concept has convinced modern researchers that a Supreme Being formed part of traditional Ojibwa religion (e.g., Cooper 1934 and Hallowell 1931).

The testimony of modern Ojibwas, however, cannot be conclusive. Most of them are far removed from their traditional religion, perhaps too far to make accurate statements about it. An Ojibwa at Lake of the Woods told a researcher that the Ojibwas always believed in a Supreme Being, that this God made humans out of clay. Under close examination, however, he admitted that he knew very little about the concept, saying that "some tell us one thing, and some tell us another, and we don't know what to do" (Cooper 1936: 6). His confusion reflected the pull between Ojibwa traditions and Christian teachings about the creation.

The evidence suggests that the Ojibwas have taken up a Christian concept and claimed it for their own. Without being certain of their own traditional concepts they have tentatively adopted new ones. Accepting Kitche Manito, however, has not meant accepting Christianity. On the contrary, the Ojibwas who have spoken most eloquently about the Supreme Being have been the leaders of religious movements which have opposed Christianity while borrowing from it.

Christian influence is even more apparent in modern Ojibwa belief in an evil manito called Matchi Manito. Twentieth-century Protestant as well as seventeenth-century Catholic missionaries have taught the Ojibwas about the Christian Devil (Kellogg 1925: 106-107), sometimes associating it with the Underwater Manito, sometimes with the Windigo. They have even called Nanabozho the Devil or have told Ojibwas that every part of their traditional religion was the Devil's work. Some Ojibwas have believed them and have rejected their native traditions. Others have adopted the belief without converting (Hilger 1951: 61).

Crises of Belief in Manitos

Belief in the manitos continues today, even among Christianized Ojibwas; relations with the manitos have undergone severe crises through the centuries. Christian missionaries threw doubt on the traditional concepts and introduced competing ones, so that Jesus Christ has replaced or supplemented the manitos among some Ojibwas. When hunting failed in the nineteenth century, the Ojibwas' faith in their manitos' power suffered. Some of the Indians blamed themselves for displeasing the manitos by accepting white culture, and they vowed to live henceforth in the traditional manner. Other Ojibwas believed that the Windigo was gaining power, causing starvation despite the efforts of the helpful manitos, and Windigo belief has remained strong. Morton I. Teicher reports that in 1950 over a thousand Ojibwas in northern Ontario spent a summer in Windigo panic, and in the area of Lake Winnipeg the Ojibwas avoid certain areas where the Windigo is thought to reside (Teicher 1960: 4).

Although some have come to doubt the existence of the manitos, most Ojibwas have continued in their beliefs; however, the failure of the manitos to provide subsistence and other powers has shaken the beliefs. As Ojibwa existence has deteriorated, the Indians have suffered through crises of faith. The Ojibwas at Parry Island say that there are manitos everywhere, "or there were until the white man came, for today, the Indians say, most of them have moved away" (Jenness 1935: 29).

The Ojibwas have experienced a crisis of belief in the manitos as well as a crisis of identity. They are unsure about themselves, their existence, and the sources of their existence. Part of their uncertainty derives from their present confusion regarding their origins and the origins of the present world. They are severed from their roots, including their traditional Creation Myth.

NANABOZHO AND THE CREATION MYTH

The Ojibwas have no oral traditions describing the origin of the universe. They say that the beginning of the world was too long ago for them to know of it (Kidder 1981: 14). The Ojibwa Creation Myth, familiar to students of American Indian folklore and religion, presents the major actions of Nanabozho from his birth through his creation of the present world following a flood.

The myth, in the context of the traditional folklore, provides the Ojibwas with a means of knowing what the universe was like, how it came into its present state, what the vital principles of life were, what relationships existed among the world's living beings, what to expect from all forms of life, how to test reality and how societal customs came into being. In short, the myth helped construct the Ojibwas' worldview and explained all important areas of existence.

More specifically, the myth related how the world became ordered so that, through hunting, humans could physically survive. The primary concern, the most important and determining factor in almost every major decision in traditional Ojibwa life was physical survival, nourishment by food made available by hunting. The Ojibwas expressed this concern in and through the Creation Myth.

Ojibwa Oral Traditions

The Ojibwas spent their winters in family units, hunting for food. During this season certain old people in each family unit recounted their oral traditions. One Ojibwa attested to the large number of traditions, saying, "I have known some Indians who would commence to narrate legends and stories in the month of October and not end until quite late in the spring, sometimes not till quite late in the month of May, and on every evening of this long term tell a new story" (Copway 1858: 98). The Ojibwas told the traditions only in the winter, they explained, so that the underwater manitos who hibernated then would not hear them. A summer narration of the stories would bring punishment from these creatures, particularly

84

frogs, toads, and serpents (Coleman, Frogner, and Eich 1962: 5).

The Ojibwas divided their corpus of approximately two hundred narratives into two basic categories: stories connoting news or tidings which related to living human beings; and myths about the manitos and deceased humans (Chamberlain 1906: 346-347; Hallowell 1960: 28; Redsky 1972: 66; cf. Densmore 1929: 97). The bulk of the latter category told of Nanabozho. Of this material, half described him in his role as Culture-Hero, half in his role as Trickster. As hero he created the new world.

Aiding the story-tellers were pictographs (Blessing 1963; Densmore 1929: 174-175; Kinietz 1939: 38-39; Kohl 1860: 387-391), employing symbols derived from natural and invented forms, which recalled to the narrator's mind the essential events in the traditions. These mnemonic devices were so prevalent among the Ojibwas (Charlevoix 1761, vol. 2: 83) that one theorist suggested that the name "Ojibwa" came from their word "ojibweg," meaning those who make pictographs (Hewitt 1926: 116).

The narratives resembled those of other Algonkian Indians in motifs, themes, and underlying concepts; however, there were distinctive Ojibwa traits which were not shared by neighboring peoples, especially in the thorough emphasis on hunting. Apparently the narratives carried certain meanings to the Ojibwas; by discovering those meanings one can discover a great deal about the traditional Ojibwas.

Nanabozho: Culture-Hero and Trickster

It is a difficult task to understand the Ojibwa Creation Myth because even within the Ojibwa cultural context there was a wide variance of opinion about the central character, Nanabozho. The Ojibwas viewed him as a human, manito, hare, wolf, demigod, hero, trickster and buffoon. He was known to take on many forms and many personalities within a single myth. In short, he was a composite, synthetic figure with contradictory and complex characteristics (Fisher 1946: 231).

As Culture-Hero he created the present world and its orderly patterns, its landscape in all its particulars. He called all the persons of the world his relatives and helped join humans to the rest of the living world by inventing totems (Kurath,

Ettawageshik, and Ettawageshik 1955: n.p.), thereby helping in the establishment of Ojibwa social identity. He interceded between humans and manitos, destroyed witches and windigos, called upon the Thunderbirds to defeat underwater manitos and controlled the Four Winds for the benefit of Indians. He served as model and ideal; he originated dances, burial customs, and work. He invented snowshoes (Kidder 1918: 6-7), taught fishing and hunting skills (Charlevoix 1761, vol. 2: 46-47), discovered wild rice and other foodstuffs. He told humans how to protect themselves against disease by making medicines (Brown 1944: n.p.), and he ruled over the afterworld. Nanabozho, "in the mind of the old Indian was the master of life — the source and impersonation of the lives of all sentient things, human, faunal, and floral. He endowed these with life and taught each its peculiar ruse for deceiving its enemies and prolonging its life" (Densmore 1929: 97).

As Trickster he was a witch, a manipulator of his relatives, an example of heinous behavior to avoid. His greed, cruelty, and lies broke the rules of Ojibwa society at every turn. Yet even as originator of death, his misbehavior brought favorable results to the Ojibwas.

Nanabozho's power was not limited to his role in myths. Although no major cults were devoted to him traditionally, Ojibwas offered him tobacco at the sites which he created. He watched over Ojibwas in their pursuits, helped the Indians in their hunting, appeared occasionally in visions and greeted arrivals to the afterworld. His image could protect against disease or influence the winds and waters. In the myths, however, he demonstrated a protean character.

Textual Variations

Even the Creation Myth in its many extant versions (chart 1, pp. 87-88) exhibited wide variances. No two versions were exactly alike. Some devoted much time to Nanabozho's adventures in his travels around the earth; others omitted these aspects completely and told only of the deluge and the re-creation of the earth. Some extensively described his travels with the wolves or his battles with his brothers; others summarized these events in a sentence or two. This variability was due to many factors.

That each Ojibwa family spent much of the year on its own gave it the opportunity to diverge from the mainstream. This pattern was even more accentuated because individual Ojibwas drew inspiration from their visions, affording an even greater chance for divergence.

Furthermore, as oral tradition the myth was subject to the variations due to the aesthetic preferences of the storyteller and the situation in which the myth was told and recorded (Kohl 1860: 88). A receptive audience led storytellers to add details, artistic flourishes, and illustrative addenda. Myths told to ethnologists (Dorson 1952: 19) and other strangers (Wilson 1886: 107-108) most likely differed from those traditionally told to family members sitting around the winter campfire.

Moreover, there were foreign elements which entered the Ojibwa myth, for example from the eastern Dakotas and the Iroquois. The myths which have been collected often show the influence of Christian myths and Western folklore in general (Skinner 1914: 100).

Chart 1: Major Versions of the Ojibwa Creation Myth

Barnouw 1955: 73-85
Blackbird 1887: 72-78
Blackwood 1929: 320-333
Brown 1944: no pagination
Cappel 1931: 30-34
Carson 1917: 491-493
Chamberlain 1891: 196-213
Coleman, Frogner, and Eich 1962: 62-72
Densmore 1928: 381-384
Dixon 1909: 6-7
Dorson 1952: 42-47
Fisher 1946: 231-232
Gabaoosa 1900: 1-7
Gabaoosa 1921: 1-27
Gilfillan 1908-1909: 2-8
Hewitt 1926: 116-117
Hewitt no date a: no pagination
Hewitt no date b: no pagination
Hindley 1885: no pagination
Jones 1861: 32-35
Jones 1917: 2-501

Josselin de Jong 1913: 5-16
Kidder 1918: 1-25
Kinietz 1947: 179-187
Kohl 1860: 387-391
Kurath, Ettawageshik, and Ettawageshik 1955: 25-36
Laidlaw 1914-25, vol. 30: 89-90; vol. 35: 52
Leekley 1965
McKenney 1827: 302-304
Michelson 1911: 249-250
Michelson 1916: 189-194; 220-226
Michelson 1925: no pagination
Michelson no date b: 23-24
Michelson no date d: 1-2
Miscogeon 1900b: 1-25
Miscogeon 1900c: 1-2
Radin 1914c: 1-23
Radin and Reagan 1928: 61-76; 102-103; 106-108
Reagan 1921a: 347-352
Reid 1963
Schoolcraft 1839, vol. 1: 135-171
Skinner 1919: 283-288
Speck 1915: 28-38
Wilson 1886: 107-108
Wright 1894: no pagination
Young 1903: 73-79; 89-94; 171-179; 183-189

The Basic Myth

Despite the variations, the extant versions of the Creation Myth show conclusively that there was a basic, unvarying core to the myth shared by traditional Ojibwa peoples (Kohl 1860: 86-88). Schoolcraft pointed this out when he first collected Ojibwa oral traditions: "Scarcely any two persons agree in all the minor circumstances of the story, and scarcely any omit the leading traits" (Schoolcraft 1839, vol. 1: 135).

For those outside Ojibwa society who wish to understand the traditional Ojibwas, the myth provides stunning insights and valuable verifications. It is surprising, therefore, that only a few modern scholars have attempted analyses of the myth. One saw it as a lunar-matriarchal-agricultural expression (Schmidt 1948). Another used it to describe Ojibwa personality (Barnouw 1955). A third made a cursory look at

Ojibwa motivation through the myth (Parker 1962). A fourth used the myth in evaluating a theory on taboo (Makarius 1973). None was especially profitable for understanding Ojibwa religion or the myth itself. It remains an enigma despite its numerous versions and its importance to the study of the Ojibwas.

The Creation Myth (for sources, see chart A, above) included eight primary episodes: A. the birth of Nanabozho; B. the theft of fire; C. Nanabozho and his brothers; D. Nanabozho and the wolves; E. the death of Nanabozho's hunting companion; F. the shooting of the underwater manitos by Nanabozho involving the stump episode; G. the killing of these manitos involving the toad woman episode; H. the deluge, earth divers, and re-creation of the earth.

A. The Birth of Nanabozho

A virgin or unmarried woman lived with her mother, Nokomis. The mother cautioned her daughter not to sit facing a certain direction but she did and became impregnated by a wind or the sun. She gave birth to several beings, including Nanabozho, and died in childbirth. Nokomis found Nanabozho, a clot of blood, and raised him as a hare.

B. The Theft of Fire

Nanabozho the hare stole fire from neighboring people and gave it to his grandmother. He and his grandmother lived alone; he decided that they should have fire. Against Nokomis' wishes he traveled to another place where people had fire and tricked them into permitting him to steal some of it. They wished to hoard it; because of Nanabozho's action humans came to have fire to use for cooking their food.

C. Nanabozho and His Brothers

While living with Nokomis, Nanabozho wanted to know about his family. He asked if he had a mother; when told of the account of his birth, he decided to seek vengeance against those responsible, sometimes his brother made of flint, other times his father, or his brothers the Four Winds. Nanabozho traveled to a distant place, sometimes an island surrounded by pitch. Through the advice of a bird or other small animal, Nanabozho learned how to kill or defeat his antagonists, usually by shooting at their hair-knot, toe, or shadow, which contained their free-soul, or by shooting at their heart, which contained their ego-soul. In some versions Nanabozho initiated death by killing his brother made of flint. In a speech the hero defended his action by saying that death would leave room in the world for people yet to be born; the scattered flint was used to make arrows for hunting.

D. Nanabozho and the Wolves

Nanabozho wanted to travel with a pack of wolves because of the onset of winter. The wolves said that they were going to find some food they had hidden in the summer and did not want him to join them; however, he persuaded them and they ran together. In the course of their travels Nanabozho and his new relatives had several misunderstandings which eventually led to the wolves' expelling Nanabozho. He asked for a wolf companion to help him hunt for food during the winter and they gave him the youngest of their members to be his brother or nephew.

E. The Death of Nanabozho's Hunting Companion

Nanabozho and his wolf-brother spent the winter hunting. They were an exceptionally successful hunting team, with the wolf providing much of the kill. Because the two were killing so many animals, the underwater manitos plotted to capture and destroy the wolf-brother. Nanabozho dreamed of the danger and warned his companion not to cross any body of water, even if it was covered with ice. Either because he was lured by a deer, or because he wished to hurry home, the wolf-brother disobeyed Nanabozho's instruction, fell through the ice, and drowned.

F. Nanabozho's Shooting of the Underwater Manitos — Stump Episode

After the death of his companion, Nanabozho sought revenge. With the advice of a bird he discovered the underwater manitos' location, disguised himself as a stump, and prepared to shoot the shadow of the leader or leaders. The manitos suspected that the stump, which they had never seen before, was Nanabozho. A serpent coiled around it and a bear clawed it; another bear tried to pull it out of the ground. Nanabozho held firm and they convinced themselves of its authenticity. They fell asleep, thinking themselves safe. Nanabozho forgot the bird's instruction and shot the leaders in the body instead of the shadow. Only wounded, they and all their followers slipped back into the safety of the water to their underground home.

G. Nanabozho's Killing of the Underwater Manitos — Toad Woman Episode

Although some versions contained a preliminary deluge at this point, the great majority proceeded immediately to this episode. After wounding the underwater manitos, Nanabozho met an old woman in the woods. She carried a load of basswood on her back and sang her medicine songs. She was a toad, the grandmother of the underwater manitos, on her way to cure them. Nanabozho learned her songs and curing ritual, killed her, skinned her and put on her skin as a disguise in order to penetrate the camp of the manitos. He then traveled in the water to the manitos' camp where he killed the ones responsible for the death of his wolf companion.

H. The Deluge, Earth Divers, and Re-Creation of the Earth

The underwater manitos caused a great flood in order to drown Nanabozho. He either had a raft at the ready or raced to the top of the highest mountain, climbed the highest tree, and caused the tree to extend itself as the waters rose. Finally the water stopped and Nanabozho was on top of the now-extended tree with water up to his head. He decided to create a new earth, so he told several animals, the beaver, loon, otter and muskrat, who were on the raft or swimming nearby to dive into the water for a piece of the old earth. The muskrat succeeded while the others failed. All died in their attempts but Nanabozho revived them. Then he expanded the piece of dirt brought up by muskrat until it became the present land area, sitting in the waters created by the underwater manitos. He sent an animal out to see if the earth was large enough for all the people and animals. In most cases it was too small and he continued the creation. After completing the earth's surface, he named animals, created laws, placed trees, lakes, mountains and valleys in the proper locations; then he went off to hunt.

Ojibwa Mythic Worldview

In its entirety the Creation Myth described the universe to the traditional Ojibwas. It consisted of a flat island earth with another beneath, water separating the two. There were the Four Winds, the sun, and the underwater manitos, as well as animals and other forms of life, all associated in some way with Nanabozho.

The myth also described the animating features of each living person, particularly when Nanabozho had to locate the heart, or hairlock, or toe of his adversary as the location of one of the souls (Radin and Reagan 1928: 70-71). Not only humans had these animating forces; so, too, did all aspects of "Nature." In the myth, entities like the sun, flint, and animals acted with intelligence and will; they were living persons. The myth derived this point of view from Ojibwa religious conceptions and in turn formed those conceptions. The individual Ojibwa, thus informed, interpreted the universe in a like manner.

The worldview of the Creation Myth was one which did not make a sharp dichotomy between the orders of living beings. There was a hierarchy and interdependence within the universe, based on the amount and type of power possessed by individual persons. A structural analysis (Fisher and Vecsey 1975) shows a fundamental difference in the understanding of reality between animals and humans, particularly between wolves and Nanabozho, but he needed the assistance of animals, birds and trees in defeating his adversaries. The wolves had the ability to work magic in their hunting; Nanabozho depended on such power to survive the winter. In all of his battles Nanabozho needed birds' knowledge; in general his success depended on the cooperation of the other living beings of the universe.

The myth presented two complementary views of the universe's structure. There was a conflict between persons in which some proved themselves more powerful than others, for example, Nanabozho over his brothers. Success, however, was based not on individual prowess but on aid given by friendly persons, guardians, and helpers (Radin and Reagan 1928: 63). This accurately portrayed traditional Ojibwa worldview and life, in which individuals sought guardians through vision quests in order to gain powers.

Nanabozho's powers were illustrated by his ability to transform himself and appear in various disguises, particularly by his transformation into a stump. The myth informed the Ojibwas that beings could take the form of other entities; metamorphosis was a fact of life. Indeed, one of the characteristics of life and power was the ability to change appearance. That ability to change emphasized the fluidity between animal and human forms.

The myth provided means by which to judge reality. These means were observation and dreams. When the mysterious stump appeared, the underwater manitos were suspicious, knowing as they did the ability of Nanabozho to transform himself. They decided to test the stump empirically, by feeling it, watching it, pulling it. Only after empirical testing were their suspicions allayed.

In the myth dreams were used as means of receiving warnings and information. Nanabozho's grandmother dreamed that her daughter would be impregnated by the wind or sun, and Nanabozho dreamed that his wolf-brother would drown if he tried to cross the body of water. Dreams were valid bases on which to act.

The myth provided the means by which its own information could be validated. The Ojibwas were keen observers of the world around them; they had to be in order to survive. If the myth was not consistent with their empirical knowledge, they would have been hard pressed to believe it as they did, but since they interpreted events around them employing the means provided by the myth itself, the myth received constant reinforcement. As A. Irving Hallowell stated,

Experience and belief must be harmonized if beliefs are to be believed. The Indian is no fool. He employs the same common sense reasoning processes as ourselves, so that if he firmly holds to certain beliefs, we may be sure that they are supported in some degree by an empirical foundation. Thus experience is obviously the crux of religious rationalization. But dogma furnishes the leverage which makes the reconciliation of experience with belief possible (Hallowell 1934: 393).

It is clear that the myth influenced personality, society, and action, just as they influenced myth. Dozens of examples could be given of Ojibwas acting like characters in their myths; let one suffice. An old Ojibwa couple whom Benjamin Armstrong knew lived by a lake. One day a moose entered the lake to escape from wolves. As it crossed the water, it was forced to swim. In such a position, up to its head in water, it was helpless to prevent attack by human hunters. The old couple got in their boat and gave chase. As they approached it, the man said, "Bo-zhoo! moose, you are always afraid of an Indian. Don't hurry, we want to get acquainted with you" (Armstrong 1892: 171). All the while the woman was telling her husband to slit its throat and hamstring before it could escape to shallow water. In his hunting technique the man acted precisely as Nanabozho did when he hunted moose and ducks, addressing his victims as friends and relatives, lulling them into acquiescence before the kill. The old man acted like the mythical model.

The Ojibwas followed Nanabozho's lead when they performed societal customs originated by Nanabozho in the myths. The Creation Myth told of his mourning customs, sweat bath ritual, puberty fast for a vision and other cultic actions which became normalized for the Indians through his use. He supplied revenge as a means of maintaining social equilibrium when he fought the killers of his mother and his wolf-brother. In traditional Ojibwa society, with no written laws or regulations, revenge was often the only means of enforcing intracommunity and intercommunity order. Through the myth Nanabozho established societal balance.

The Creation Myth's Central Concern: Hunting

The central meaning of the Creation Myth, however, was the alleviation of hunger through successful hunting. A twentieth-century Wisconsin Ojibwa referred to the Nanabozho narratives as " . . . stories of the olden days, of how the Indians eked out their existence, and of how they tried to keep in good health" (Works Progress Administration 1936-1940; 1942, Envelope 12, No. 9: 1). In the myths Nanabozho always searched for food to alleviate his hunger and interspersed throughout the Creation Myth were tales relating how he hunted game and created food. He caught ducks, moose, and other animals through his ruses, serving as an example of hunting technique to the Indians. In one narrative he created tripe-de-roche, a lichen resembling human flesh, by scraping his burning buttocks along the ground (Young 1903: 214-220). Boiled in a porridge, this bitter but nutritious substance kept many Indians and whites from starving during hard winters (Charlevoix 1761, vol. 2: 124; Henry 1809: 221; Long 1904: 156).

In narratives outside the Nanabozho cycle hunting was the major theme and hunting success was often the reward for proper actions. The folklore, like religion, reflected the need for food and the means of obtaining it. The Creation Myth reflected the hunting life; for example, John Tanner told that while hunting animals in the winter he had often fallen through snow-covered ice and almost drowned, just like the wolf-brother (James 1956: 44). The myth, however, did more than reflect hunting life; it sanctioned hunting as the means of sustaining life.

When Nanabozho contended with his brothers, it was for the expressed purpose of providing good hunting and fishing for the Indians, who were hampered by strong winds (Speck 1915: 30), as well as avenging his mother's death. The Ojibwas evoked Nanabozho's image when they needed the strong winter Wind to crust the snow. They formed a hare in the snow which caused the Wind to blow (Flannery 1946: 266). In cult as well as myth Nanabozho controlled the Winds to make hunting and fishing possible.

In the Creation Myth, Nanabozho's success against his enemies was due to his ability to locate their vital spot (Radin and Reagan 1928: 64-71), a hunting necessity. Ojibwa hunters employed a technique called muzzi-ne-neen, which consisted of drawing outlines of animals, indicating the position of the heart. This "x-ray" style of art was particularly prevalent among the Ojibwas, and Nanabozho was the creator of the practice. Through the myth he taught the essentials of hunting.

As good a hunter as he was, Nanabozho was no match for the wolves with whom he ran. They were not only fast, but they also worked magic, thus they were extraordinary hunters. When Nanabozho separated from them, he took with him a wolf to be his brother. They formed a hunting pair, a theme which was distinct to the Ojibwa Culture-Hero cycle. They were so successful in killing game that the underwater manitos sought revenge, for the animals of the world complained of their depleted numbers. Thus the motivation for the underwater manitos' killing of the wolf-brother was explicit: he was too good a hunter; he was killing too many animals (Blackwood 1929: 196; Kinietz 1947: 181-183; Michelson no date). The battle between Nanabozho and the manitos was clearly over the issue of hunting: where and how much could Nanabozho and his "relative" hunt for food? Nanabozho's subsequent revenge and victory over the underwater manitos was his assertion of the right to hunt successfully. His earlier distribution of flint made hunting easier and his theft of fire made the cooking of food possible. Each episode in the myth was directed toward hunting from one angle or another. After creating the new world, Nanabozho released animals to roam the world, after which he went hunting and successfully captured a flock of ducks or other game.

Structural Analysis of the Myth

A structural analysis (Fisher and Vecsey 1975) of the myth shows that the idea of death permeated every aspect of it. A death of some kind appeared in each episode, except for the theft of fire. Each death led to a benefit of some kind. The mother's death resulted in the birth of the Culture-Hero. The death of the flint brother produced the small pieces of stone with which to make arrowheads. The disagreement which led to Nanabozho's expulsion and obtaining a companion was his killing of one of the wolves. The deaths of the wolf-brother, toad woman, and underwater manitos ended in Nanabozho's right to hunt.

Seen from the point of view of the myth, existence seemed to be a struggle between factional "families," represented most specifically by Nanabozho and his "relatives" in opposition to the underwater manitos. In this struggle death seemed necessary for the continuation of life, as in intertribal revenge raids.

That death was necessary for life was most evident in the earth diver episode, in which the animals who dove for the earth usually died in the attempt. Even the muskrat, who succeeded in getting a piece of the earth, died before he could return to the raft. Their deaths were essential preconditions for their success.

Taken as a structural whole, the myth taught the Ojibwas how to survive in their frequently hostile environment. The two main structural lessons of the myth concerned death and animal-human relationships. It taught the Ojibwas the beneficial importance of death, a vital lesson in a hunting culture in which the death of animals was necessary for the continuance of human life. To the Ojibwa "the animal has the same right to life that man has. It is necessary to use the animal for the subsistence of man, but the animal is sacrificed regretfully for this purpose" (Burton 1909: 243-245). The myth expresses exactly this sentiment.

Nanabozho's two main acts of revenge in the myth were against the Winds and the underwater manitos. The former was to make conditions conducive to hunting and fishing; the latter was to assert the rights of hunting. Thus, in the course of the myth Nanabozho overcame two sets of adversaries, the Winds and the underwater manitos, both for the purpose of providing for and maintaining successful hunting to alleviate hunger, and to continue human life.

What is especially intriguing about this interpretation is that it reveals an implicit duality of the universe: the world above the present earth and the world below its surface. In the course of the myth Nanabozho controlled the masters of the sky and the masters of the waters which surrounded the earth he created.

The Ojibwas had no moieties; neither did their closest neighbors, the Ottawas and Potawatomis, although other Algonkians did and their categories were invariably Earth and Sky (Ritzenthaler and Ritzenthaler 1970: 51). The Ojibwas were familiar, however, with the duality of earth and sky, as demonstrated in the myth.

To the Ojibwas the sky beings — the Thunderbirds, Four Winds, birds, sun — were generally helpful to humans, although not always predictable. Sky imagery meant power in visions, whereas Ojibwas tried to avoid water beings in their dreams. Nanabozho's kinship was with the Winds; he was sometimes thought of as the Northwest Wind or the East Wind. Throughout the myth Nanabozho received help from birds; they usually gave him information which led to the death of his adversaries. In one sequence, Thunderbirds distracted the underwater manitos while he shot their chief. In traditional Ojibwa life birds were both signs of spring and the first food of spring after the starving times of winter. They were literally a godsend for the starving Ojibwas in late winter.

The underwater beings were not evil. They were dangerous guardians of the earth's food supplies. Serpents and other water reptiles were intimately associated with all meat, all land animal food. Ojibwas remarked that "in ceremonial pow-wows, the serving of any kind of food to the participants is forbidden. An imitation of the thunder birds must first be given before serving the meat, as meat of any kind is regarded as reptilian in nature" (Works Progress Administration 1936-1940; 1942, "Types of Dances Practised by the Chippewas of Lake Superior": 20). In the myth Nanabozho controlled the underwater manitos, with their influence over game, to insure the continuation of bountiful hunting.

The duality of the universe was not an explicit or major theme of the myth. Nanabozho did not create the duality; he was born into it. The antagonism between the two sides of the present world, sky and underworld, was not even emphasized in the myth. Rather, Nanabozho dealt with the world as the Ojibwas perceived it. First he battled with his "relatives," the Winds; then he battled his "enemies," the underwater manitos. Instead of presenting a disjointed duality, the myth demonstrated that both aspects of the world had to be controlled for the sake of successful hunting.

Historical Changes in the Myth

Since the corpus of Ojibwa myths, and the Creation Myth in particular, laid the foundation of Ojibwa reality, the Ojibwas turned to them to help in explaining the rapid changes of the historical period. Myths were always a flexible medium; they expanded and diverged to meet the new situations brought on by contact with Europeans, migrations, and new social conditions.

As Ojibwas moved onto the prairies and plains they borrowed new folkloric materials from their neighbors (Skinner 1919), as they borrowed from Europeans (Hallowell 1939b and Skinner 1916a). Nanabozho took on new roles, for instance, as a blacksmith, copying the smiths provided each agency by the United States government ("Winneboujou" 1930: 130). He worked his tricks on whites and mastered modern inventions like the automobile.

Ojibwas turned to the Creation Myth to explain phenomena they did not understand. When Alexander Henry showed some Mackinac Ojibwas a cave filled with human bones, they said that during the great flood the inhabitants had fled to the cave for shelter and had drowned (Henry 1809: 113). But the Indians needed new twists of myth to explain the appearance of whites, the disappearance of animals, the loss of sovereignty. By the twentieth century they were using extramythic material to explain their myths. One Indian, in explaining why Nanabozho had seven wives, said he may have been a Mormon (Kurath, Ettawageshik, and Ettawageshik 1955: 57). The Ojibwas were becoming defensive when narrating their myths to whites. The Indians had to rationalize their mythic realities in terms acceptable to their white listeners.

Perhaps the most important application of the Creation Myth in the historical period was its development into the myth of the origin of Midewiwin. The Mide priests emphasized Nanabozho's actions after the flood and his creation of humans, the latter borrowed from the Christian tradition. They reinterpreted his conflict with the underwater manitos in order to depict the primeval need for Midewiwin and its sacred inception. In modern times many Ojibwas know of Nanabozho as the giver of Midewiwin.

Midewiwin helped syncretize Christian and traditional Ojibwa oral traditions but the syncretism did not end there. Ojibwas identified Nanabozho with Noah and sometimes mentioned Kitche Manito in their texts, giving the Supreme Being a transcendent role in the mythic doings. Nanabozho became the creator of humans, fashioning them out of clay.

In other cases the Ojibwas tried to maintain the primacy of their Culture-Hero over the Christian characters, for example, by placing Nanabozho further back in time than Jesus Christ and the Christian Devil (Dorson 1950: 47). Sometimes the Ojibwas used their myths creatively in combating Christianity, defending traditional beliefs and practices. In one narrative told by an Ojibwa to the traveler Kohl (1860: 201), the Devil offered a heavy book to the newly created first human couple. They rejected it, saying it was too heavy to carry around while hunting. Then the Supreme Being offered them birchbark scrolls, the mnemonic devices used in telling myths and Midewiwin texts. These they could carry around while hunting. Furthermore, the birchbark scrolls contained sacred knowledge, in contradistinction to the evil heavy book, the Bible. The traditional Ojibwas had no apparent concepts of Supreme Being or Devil, yet they were willing to use the Christian concepts against Christianity and its missionaries by showing in the myth that the Bible was a gift from the Devil and the birchbark scrolls were a gift from the Supreme Being. In addition, the myth determined the relative worth of the two gifts by contrasting their effects on the hunting life.

Crises of Belief in the Myth

Into the twentieth century the Ojibwas persisted in their telling of the Creation Myth in all its essential details. They held tenaciously to it. By mid-century, however, their hold began to loosen. Under missionary influence, they lowered their estimation of Nanabozho, regarding him more as Trickster than as Culture-Hero, embarrassed about the often ribald aspects of his escapades. Christian Ojibwas referred to him derisively; some accepted the Christian opinion of him as the Devil himself.

The older, conservative Ojibwas bemoaned a situation in which their children and grandchildren, taught in Christian schools, no longer wanted to listen to the old stories, as the young ones turned away from their traditions.

In many contemporary Ojibwa communities, there are no storytellers who know the complete Creation Myth. Collectors of Ojibwa oral traditions find the old stories more and more fragmentary in recent tellings. Many of those who tell the myths do so hesitatingly and with embarrassment. They say that they do not believe the myths; they are simply repeating what they were once told. A white observer describes the present situation: "At present, the older Ojibwa seem to feel that they are the last link with a distinctly Indian past. They recognize the fact that those who can relate the native traditions with sureness and relative completeness are rapidly becoming few in number" (Coleman, Frogner, and Eich 1962: 4).

The Ojibwa myths have retreated in the face of white dominance. The narratives which formerly provided the Indians with bases of reality, which explained and validated the traditional hunting existence and its customs, have atrophied. It is significant that a recent myth about Nanabozho ends with his retreat from active life. As he withdraws, he says "He is finished, is going to a rock formation because the white man is coming" (Dorson 1952: 51). The Ojibwas' structure of beliefs, their identity, their trust in the manitos and relations with them — all based in the Creation Myth — fall to pieces as Nanabozho departs.

OJIBWA RELATIONS WITH THE MANITOS

The manitos were the objects of traditional Ojibwa religion. The Ojibwa communities passed down their knowledge of the manitos through myths, told around the family camp-fires in winter. Individual Ojibwas, by themselves and in community circles, validated their beliefs and communicated with the manitos through ceremonies.

Ojibwa ceremonialism lacked the ornate, formalized pomp found among agricultural Indians of North America. Ojibwa rituals were concerned primarily with hunting and other food-gathering pursuits. Individuals and individual families undertook ceremonies according to their own schedules, not in a standardized tribal calendar. Nevertheless, group as well as individual rituals existed for the purpose of maintaining Ojibwa relations with the manitos.

Individual Ojibwa Knowledge of the Manitos

Ojibwas gained personal knowledge of the manitos through visions, direct experience and interpretation of natural and cultural phenomena, and the shaking tent ceremonies and other forms of divination (Hallowell 1934: 393-394). These means of religious knowledge were described in myths and served to reinforce their authority.

For the Ojibwas the puberty vision established a personal, lifelong relation between an individual and a manito. It was the most crucial religious experience and formed the basis for all other visions. Through the visions the Ojibwa person communicated directly with manitos and established criteria for judging all other phenomena.

Visions and other ceremonies were sufficient to uphold the religious beliefs of the Ojibwas, but everyday events found interpretation through the beliefs and further reinforced them. Natural and unnatural occurrences helped to validate the beliefs, because the Ojibwas saw the manitos acting through those events. If a manito promised an Ojibwa a successful hunt and that Ojibwa caught a deer, belief in the manito as a powerful and trustworthy being increased. By the same token, the existence of cannibalism validated the Ojibwa belief in windigos.

Provided with a mythic worldview, the Ojibwas interpreted their world accordingly. That myths reflected the empirically observable environment and cultural structure adds credibility to the observation that the Ojibwa religious outlook was a "relatively coherent and self-contained system of beliefs" (Hallowell 1934: 389), supported by the evidence of visions, common and uncommon occurrences, and ceremonies.

If visions were the means for individual Ojibwas to validate their beliefs and gain new knowledge and aid from the manitos, the shaking tent ceremony was the means for the Ojibwa community to gain access to the objects of Ojibwa religion. The ceremony provided the two-way communication between humans and manitos which characterized Ojibwa religion, and formed the crux of the community ceremonial system.

Traditionally most Ojibwas practiced some forms of divination in order to obtain information about future events, situations beyond their sight, and phenomena beyond their understanding. These included scrying, scapulimancy, body trembling and stone rolling, none of which directly pointed to the manitos or increased knowledge about them, but which used the manitos' powers.

Scrying was a practice in which the diviner gazed into a smooth surface or clear water in order to find lost objects, discover game, and learn the whereabouts of enemies and windigos (Cooper 1928: 205-210). More concerned with hunting was scapulimancy, a practice laden with taboos against participation by children. In this form of divination, Ojibwas attempted to locate animals by observing the shapes, colors, and other characteristics in the bones of animals, particularly shoulder blades, which were often placed near a fire to cause meaningful cracks and burns (Cooper 1969: 29). Less common were prognostication by watching the trembling of parts of one's body (each part signaling a future event), and divination to determine the course of war parties by rolling stones across smooth ground (James 1956: 110-111). Each form manifested the powers, but not necessarily the will, of the manitos.

The Shaking Tent

The shaking tent ceremony, to the contrary, conjured the manitos in order to make manifest their will and knowledge (Cameron 1890: 264-265). The ceremony required a specialist, an expert whose abilities stemmed from the puberty vision. Almost all of these experts were male, although women could practice the ceremony after menopause or if they were especially ambitious and powerful, blessed by important manitos connected with the rite.

The earliest description of a shaking tent ceremony was in 1609 by Samuel de Champlain among the Algonquins (Biggar 1925, vol. 2: 86). Father LeJeune saw it among other Algonkians in 1634 (Thwaites 1896-1901, vol. 6: 163; vol. 12: 17). Common to woodland Algonkians, prairie Algonkians, and plains Athabascans across the northern belt of America (see Hultkrantz 1967), the shaking tent ceremony was for the Ojibwas "an institutionalized means for obtaining the help of different classes of spiritual entities by invoking their presence and communicating human desires to them" (Hallowell 1942: 9; besides Hallowell, others who have studied Ojibwa shaking tents include Cooper 1944; Densmore 1932; Flannery 1946: 266; and Verwyst no date c). The expert who conducted the ceremony was called a djessakid; his specialty was invoking and conjuring the manitos.

His abilities came from his vision; he could not sell them or transfer them to others. A djessakid learned his skills from his manito, not from a teacher; neither did he inherit them from his relatives. When a youth had a vision which granted him the power to conjure, he did not immediately practice the ceremony. Its performance needed maturity, strength, and tested skills. Some youths waited until receiving the same vision four times before conducting the rite (Hallowell 1942: 21-25). In any event, taboos prohibited youths from its performance. Young children were not permitted to play at being djessakids; the ceremony was too powerful and would cause them harm. Invoking the manitos was not child's play. Even powerful djessakids refrained from overusing the rite because it drained one's power and could endanger the health of relatives, especially spouses and children. The shaking tent ceremony was a very serious matter, despite the humor associated with its performance.

Djessakids performed the ceremony for specific reasons, not simply to communicate with the manitos. They sought to gain information about people who were not present; find the causes and cures for diseases of those present; obtain knowledge of enemy movements during a war; foretell events; locate game for hunters; find and return lost objects, and protect the community against imminent windigos (Hallowell 1942: 53-69). In short, the ceremony acquired information hidden by time, space, and faulty human understanding by calling on the powerful manitos.

Occasionally the conjurer summoned the dead from the afterworld to testify about their past conduct on earth which might have caused disease among their descendants. At other times the djessakid called the free-soul of a witch to the shaking tent in order to force the witch to cease evil activities which were creating illness or shortages of game. The chief sources of the rite's revelations, however, were the manitos themselves.

When the community asked the djessakid to perform, he took a sweat bath in order to purify and strengthen himself. He sang to the accompaniment of his drum while the vapor caused by cold water on hot stones filled the sweat lodge where he sat. Then he beat on his drum as his assistants constructed the tent.

No two tents were the same; in general they consisted of five to ten poles, freshly cut, around ten feet in length. One end of each pole was buried two to three feet in the ground. These posts formed a circle about four feet in diameter. They were bent outward at their middles and inward at their tops, and bound laterally so that they joined in an elongated concave. The posts were then covered with bark or skin, and medicine rattles were hung at the top which was left open.

At sunset the conjurer approached the tent, around which the community gathered. He addressed the manitos, reminding them of their obligations to him and of the powers they granted him. He told them that the gathered Indians desired the manitos' presence. Then he summoned the manitos to the tent for the ceremony, singing that they should enter as he himself went in.

Inside the tent the djessakid knelt or lay on boughs, while the audience sat around outside, throwing tobacco offerings

into a small fire. The smoke blew the Indians' devotion upward to the manitos.

After a while the manitos arrived, each making distinctive
sounds. The Turtle, his assistants, the Four Winds and others
flew in the top of the tent, causing it to shake violently. These
were persons, not abstract powers. They possessed life, vitality,
and personalities which distinguished them from one another.

The people addressed the manitos, asking questions and
seeking advice. The voices of the manitos responded, offering
remedies, prescribing actions, and telling secrets. If the Indians needed information about a distant place, or if the souls of
the dead or witches were required, the Turtle or his assistants
made the errands while the djessakid sang about the manitos.

In 1764 Alexander Henry witnessed such a ceremony at
Sault Ste. Marie. The main question in the minds of the
Indians then was the intention of the British toward the
Ojibwas and other natives who were warring on the whites.
The Turtle traveled to Fort Niagara and Montreal to ascertain
the number of British troops. He found boatloads of soldiers
on their way to attack the Indians and suggested that the
Ojibwas sue for peace immediately, promising safety and
prosperity if such advice were followed. The natives sent a
large delegation, heeding the Turtle's instructions (Henry
1809: 166-173).

Throughout a typical ceremony an audience bantered with
the manitos, particularly with the Turtle. The people sitting
around the tent called out for him to speak and engaged in a
witty, often ribald, repartee with him. At one ceremony witnessed by Hallowell (1942: 44-50), the Ojibwa audience joked
with the Turtle about his slowness afoot. When he returned
from his errands, he told the Indians that he had not really
gone anywhere, but had hidden himself behind the poles
inside the tent. At the end of the rite he refused to leave the
tent until forced out by the conjuring master. The Turtle had a
distinctive voice (something like Donald Duck's) and appeared
at every ceremony, so that the people felt comfortable and
familiar with him. They passed tobacco into the tent for him to
smoke; he joked about the quality of the offerings while
sucking on his pipe with long whistling inhalations.

This stream of levity misled some white observers to consider the rite unimportant, because the Indians were not
always reverent (e.g., Joseph N. Nicollet in Bray and Fertey

1970: 216-218). However, the participants could also be sol-
emn — for example, at Fond du Lac in 1826 (McKenney 1827:
328-330)—when asking vital questions. The Turtle performed
crucial errands as well as conducting the humorous entertainment.

Sometimes the conjurer performed special tricks of his own
to show the power and presence of the manitos. He escaped
from a knot of ropes or made the tent shake by simply placing
an article of clothing inside it while he stood outside. These
tricks tended to increase the reputation and prestige of the
individual djessakid, but their primary role was to support the
belief of the community in the manitos.

The means by which the Ojibwas communicated with the
manitos in the shaking tent ceremony, as well as in visions, did
not involve possession by the manitos. The Ojibwa individual
related to the manitos as to other persons; the manitos spoke
with the Ojibwas but did not possess them, except in the case of
the Windigo (Teicher 1960: 111). In all other cases, revelation
came from manitos to humans without any loss of personal
integrity on the part of the humans.

Apart from the immediate reason for holding a shaking tent
ceremony, the rite affected the community considerably, as A.
Irving Hallowell has shown. Individual problems found solution; cures were accomplished, lost items found. But more
important, the ceremony provided a tangible validation of the
beliefs about the manitos. The Ojibwas heard the manitos'
voices, thus proving their existence and continuing interest in
the community's welfare. When the manitos diagnosed a
disease, saying it was caused by sin and calling for cure by a
public confession, they not only explained the existence of
disease but also enforced morals for the good of the community (Hallowell 1942: 85-86). The shaking tent ceremony
gave the Ojibwas an opportunity to speak directly with the
manitos, and provided clear evidence of the manitos' many
powers and concern for humans.

Ritual Acts and Paraphernalia

Many of the ritual components of the shaking tent ceremony—the sweat bath, prayers, songs, offerings, paraphernalia and taboos—appeared in other Ojibwa ceremonies.
In addition, each component—including sacrifices, body-

painting, pictographs, dances and feasts—stood on its own as a traditional rite.

The Ojibwas used the sweat bath, the low lodge in which a person bathed in steam created by pouring cold water over hot stones, in all important ceremonies and undertakings. The bath purified and strengthened a human before entering into contact with the manitos, before consulting a curer, before an important decision, or simply by itself as a curing rite.

The most common prayers — verbal communications to the manitos—were petitionary, thanksgiving, and invocatory. Ojibwas presented prayers to the manitos in times of need, particularly to obtain food and restore health, most often combining the prayers with songs, offerings, and other ritual components. There were no set formulas for prayers, and they usually consisted of but a few words. Ojibwas prayed to the Underwater Manito while crossing lakes in stormy weather, and to Nanabozho while hunting for food.

Like prayers, Ojibwa songs communicated human wishes to the manitos, hoping to influence them. Ojibwas acquired their songs primarily through visions. Manitos gave songs to visionaries as reminders of the powers bestowed on them; hence, songs were the property of the visionaries. As one missionary in Minnesota discovered (Gilfillan 1901: 66-67), Ojibwa individuals spent their leisure hours singing, playing on a drum, communicating with their manitos.

Songs consisted of a few cryptic phrases; all were designed for a purpose, usually to obtain food through hunting. A song describing a deer was not meant as mere description, but rather as an incantation which permitted the singer to catch a deer (Kohl 1860: 394-395). Some Ojibwas knew at least one song for each species of game, to be sung to the Owners of the species before going out on the hunt (Burton 1909: 114-115).

Other songs recalled myths and other oral traditions, thereby invoking the powers gained through the myths. For example, from Ontario near Lake Huron the lament of the toad woman, "Nanabush is killing our chief, alas, alas, alas" (Davidson 1945: 304), reminded the Ojibwas of Nanabozho's victory over the Underwater Manito and the achievement of human hunting power. By singing the song, the Ojibwas reenacted that triumph, praised Nanabozho, and reminded the Underwater Manito of the rights of humans.

Songs accompanied the administration of medicine and other ceremonial acts to give the rituals potency (Cameron 1890: 261). It was the lyric of the song which provided strength. New lyrics applied to an old melody constituted a new song.

Songs and prayers often accompanied offerings, which served as invocation, petition, and other forms of prayer in their own right. The Ojibwas frequently made offerings of tobacco to the manitos as a means of tying the giver to the receiver of the gift. Nanabozho created tobacco so that humans would have something to give the manitos, who craved it and depended on humans to provide it for them. Ojibwas offered tobacco to angry seas, to killed animals, and to the earth when gathering herbs. They either smoked it in their pipes, threw it into a fire, or left it unsmoked in a place associated with a certain manito. It has been suggested that they burned the tobacco or other offering in order to move a manito into action, and left the tobacco unsmoked in order to maintain good relations with a manito (Barrett 1911: 360-366). More likely, they burned tobacco to appeal to the manitos of the upper world, including Thunderbirds, Four Winds, and Owners of animals, and left tobacco on the waters or the ground to appease the underwater beings (Charlevoix 1761, vol. 2: 147-148).

A more drastic form of offerings used by the traditional Ojibwas was the sacrifice of their dogs in order to influence a manito. Like the simpler tobacco offering, the dog sacrifice was performed on its own or in conjunction with other ritual components to form a substantive ceremony. The Ojibwas said that the dog was created especially for the purpose of sacrifice (Kohl 1860: 38-39). Alexander Henry mentioned that his Ojibwa companions performed three dog sacrifices in 1763-1764, all made to the waters (Henry 1809: 108; 127-128; 178).

In all their ceremonies the Ojibwas used paraphernalia which aided in human-manito communication. The djessakid's drum and rattles acted as prayers in invoking the manitos. When smoked in hunting rituals, wild oats, beck, water parsnip and other herbs had the power to charm and attract game (Yarnell 1964: 177-179). The fragrance of these plants influenced individual animals as tobacco influenced the Owners of animals. Other Ojibwa charms such as seashells were used to attract wealth, assure safety, entice lovers, work evil and counteract such evil. Most charms did not appeal directly to the manitos but used their powers to achieve goals. Guardian manitos gave the Indians these charms to symbolize vision blessings. The majority of charms were intended to assure hunting prowess and success (Cooper 1946: 288).

Hunting was also a major concern in Ojibwa taboos. In the treatment of game, the preparation of foods, and the procedure for hunting, the Ojibwas were restricted by rules which warned of famine and starvation as results of misconduct. Expectant mothers and fathers were prohibited from eating certain foods. Menstruating women avoided contact with hunting men. There were proper times for fishing, improper approaches to hunting, and regulations against mixing two species of fish in the same cooking pot (Hilger 1951: 7-9; Jenness 1935: 80-81). In ceremonies these taboos were accentuated, preventing women from becoming djessakids before menopause, preventing youths from performing powerful religious rituals. The common theme of traditional Ojibwa ritual taboo was the inability of the unprotected and the weak to come into direct contact with the manitos and their embodiments. If the purpose of ceremonialism was to place humans in contact with the objects of their religion, taboos represented a negative cult which kept manitos and unqualified humans apart.

Ojibwa ceremonialism was sparse. It used no masks or intricate choreography. Nevertheless, the Ojibwas used body painting (Henry 1809: 198) in order to mimic the manitos and thereby enter into a closer relation with them. By looking like the manitos the Ojibwas stressed the continuity in their rituals between the objects and subjects of religion.

Ojibwa artistry contributed to ceremonies in the use of pictographs. Not only did these drawings serve to remind the Ojibwas of their songs and other texts, but they also influenced the manitos by portraying them. The image of a manito, like the image of an animal or human, was an extension of the person. Ojibwas could cause illness in humans by drawing their picture in "x-ray" style and violating it. They could catch animals by drawing their pictograph and placing an arrow through it. In like manner, although to a much smaller degree, the Indians could influence the manitos by re-creating their form. Drawing such pictographs formed an important part of Ojibwa ceremonialism.

Although dancing often accompanied ceremonial songs, it was most common in the more elaborate rituals. Dances imitated the movements of the manitos, thereby bringing humans closer to the objects of their religion; dances also provided an opportunity for the community to gather together as a unit.

Feasts were common elements in the major Ojibwa ceremonies in which large numbers of people participated. Like dances, feasts gave humans the opportunity to share activity with one another. This companionship also applied to the manitos, who received their portions through burnt offerings of food at the feasts. Feasts were an important way for the community to sit down as a community in common with the manitos; their shared food formed a bond between humans and manitos.

Ceremonial Cycles through Seasons and Lives, to Promote Ojibwa Existence

The Ojibwas directed their ritual activities to the manitos in conjunction with seasonal food-gaining pursuits, liminal stages of growth in a person's life, and immediate crises, especially those concerning hunting and health. Not all Ojibwa ceremonialism was religious in its primary intent but all ceremonies made at least a passing mention of the manitos.

Through the course of a year an Ojibwa community celebrated the following rituals (Kurath, Ettawageshik, and Ettawageshik 1955: n.p.). At the time of the first maple sap run in the spring, at the appearance of the first berries of each species through the summer, during the wild rice harvest in the fall, when the first animals were killed in the late fall, the Ojibwas conducted thanksgiving feasts for the manitos, providing them with burnt food offerings, prayers, dances and songs. Throughout the winter each family told and retold the tribal myths, thereby recalling and invoking the manitos for the good of the group. At midwinter the family held a feast to the bear Owner and to the bears themselves. At midsummer the extended family made petitionary prayers and offerings to the manitos at a painted pole ceremony. In addition, each person presented a feast and offering to guardian manitos at some time during the year.

The Ojibwa community also conducted ceremonies for its members at appropriate stages of their development. When a child was born, its family gave it a feast at which it received a name (Bray and Fertey 1970: 185; Cameron 1890: 252-254; Keating 1824, vol. 1: 155-156). An old person, man or woman, was asked by the child's parents to bestow a name on the child during the feast, given approximately a month after birth; the old person received gifts for this service.

It was important that the old person be healthy and of high repute in the community, having been either a successful hunter, talented artisan, or powerful curer, because success, talent, and power were considered to be results of blessings from the manitos. As Frances Densmore has shown, the Ojibwas thought that by bestowing a name on the child, the old person was bestowing on it the blessings of the manitos. These blessings had been given to the old person through a lifetime of visions, especially those obtained during the puberty fast, and they were passed on to the child to be of use until the child could make its own fast for manitos' blessings (Densmore 1929: 53).

At the feast the old person held the child and told of the lessons learned during the puberty fast vision, telling the guests, the parents, and the infant the name to be given. In general, girls received names signifying protection; boys were given names signifying powers. A feast ensued at which guests consumed great quantities of food so that the child, who could not yet eat, would have such feasts in its maturity (Jones 1919: 331-335). The feasters tried thereby to assure the child would have an abundance of food throughout its life. They said prayers for the long life of the child and for its health.

This ceremonial pattern continued through a person's growth, at the time of killing the first animal of each species, at puberty, at war initiations, adoptions, clan gatherings, preparation for death, mourning and feasts for the dead. The major themes of these rites of passage were the hopes for abundant food, successful hunting, good health and long life, the Ojibwa ideals.

At the time when a boy killed his first animal, his parents gave a feast for him and his relatives at which they asked the blessings of the Owner of that species. These feasts mirrored the first fruits celebrations held during the seasonal cycle, only the former benefited the boy who crossed the threshhold from childhood to the status of young hunter.

The most important of the life cycle ceremonies was the puberty vision quest, performed by girls and boys alike, although girls had additional rites of seclusion and cleansing at the time of their first menstruation. The vision quest consisted of an extended fast, climaxing in a vision of the manitos, one of whom would serve as lifelong guardian for the faster. The vision established a personal relation between the human and the objects of Ojibwa religion. The vision was followed by a celebration feast.

The girls' menstruation rite was not strictly a religious act. The manitos were mentioned only briefly during the period of seclusion. Each girl stayed in an isolated hut, blackened her face, and avoided all males. Her powers during menstruation were said to interfere with hunting success. Prohibited from touching her body with her hands, she carried a scratching stick. Her eating and drinking utensils could not be used by any other person.

A similar ceremony existed for young men about to enter battle for the first time. They, too, blackened their faces and followed taboos similar to those practiced by menstruating girls. In addition, they kept ritual observances through their first war party. These heightened the youths' transition to manhood but did not ostensibly invoke the manitos.

Other community rites included feasts by which families adopted new members, and yearly meetings of clans. These involved ritual components such as sweat baths, dancing, and feasts, but they made no mention of the manitos. They were means of changing one's status and solidifying the community's bonds but were not apparently religious.

The Ojibwas invoked the manitos at ceremonies associated with death. Occasionally, when an old Ojibwa was no longer self-supporting, he or she was either left on an island to die or killed by the family. In either case, the family gave sweat baths, dog sacrifices, prayers, songs and dances to the manitos for the blessing of the parent (Long 1904: 110-111). At the death of any family member the Ojibwas conducted mourning ceremonies which asked the manitos' aid for the living community. Periodically the community remembered its dead with feasts, held either within a small family circle or among the larger extended family (Henry 1809: 134-135). In the early historical period these feasts for the dead expanded into opportunities for political alliances, ostentation, and entertainment (Thwaites 1896-1901, vol. 23: 209-223). Their primary function continued, maintaining relations between the living and the dead.

The relations between living and dead animals created the need for Ojibwa animal ceremonialism, performed when hunters killed bears, deer, beavers, moose, and large fish such as sturgeon (Casagrande 1952: 113-115; Hennepin 1683: 333-334; Kellogg 1917: 112). It was necessary for the Ojibwas to treat their game properly so that when the dead animal met with the Owner of its species, it would suggest that further game be permitted to its killers (Hallowell 1926: 144-145).

Ritual activity surrounded the hunt. Before seeking game, the hunters divined to learn its whereabouts and offered tobacco and prayers to Nanabozho, the guardian manitos, and the Owners of animals (Bray and Fertey 1970: 211-216; Radin 1928: 661). Attempts were also made to gain the help of the Four Winds in arranging weather conditions conducive to successful hunting. Hunters often took sweat baths to purify and strengthen themselves before setting out on their hunt.

Upon killing an animal, especially a bear (Charlevoix 1761, vol. 1: 184; Hallowell 1926; Henry 1809: 143-145), the hunters conducted a conciliatory mourning ceremony. They apologized to the animal, explaining their need for its flesh and fur for their survival. They asked it to speak well of them when it reached its Owner. They laid the animal out on a blanket, kissing and stroking its head, calling it friend, grandfather, or grandmother, and placing trinkets, tobacco, and other gifts around it. Some blew smoke into its nostrils so it could inhale the offered tobacco.

The hunters cut up the animal, offering some parts of its body to the Owner of the species. They held a feast at which only men could eat select pieces of the animal. The hunters gathered the animal's bones and placed them in a tree, in order to prevent dogs from chewing on them. The bones, lasting extensions of the animal's person, were not to suffer mistreatment. Such offenses would prevent the hunters from obtaining further game and would result in starvation.

At certain times the hunters especially wished to thank the manitos for hunting success. The Indians held feasts at which they ate enormous quantities of meat and other food. It was the duty of all the invited guests to eat every morsel of food placed before them, often as much as twenty pounds of meat for each participant. The feasting thanked the manitos and showed the hunters' confidence in future hunting success (Henry 1809: 201-202; Kellogg 1917: 111).

The Ojibwas held other ceremonies in times of medical crises. They appealed to the manitos with prayers, offerings, and sacrifices when accidents befell them, or when epidemics threatened their villages. Often they hung pelts, tobacco, and other offerings on a central pole in order to prevent the spread of disease. Individual cures were rituals in themselves, incorporating many of the ceremonial components for the patient's recovery. The Indians held their medical rites as they needed them, not according to a fixed schedule. Ceremonial structure was also flexible enough to incorporate new elements as new situations arose.

Historical Changes in Ojibwa Ceremonialism

In the historical period Ojibwas altered their ceremonies under the influences of missionaries, traders, government officials, other Indians and the new needs of Ojibwa life. Contemporary Ojibwa rituals differ markedly from those of the seventeenth century.

Ojibwas quickly adopted ritual paraphernalia of the Jesuits. When the missionaries gave the natives crucifixes, icons, and rosary beads, the Indians wore them as charms and decorations and hung them on offering poles in times of crisis (Hennepin 1683: 337). In their ritual acts the Ojibwas adopted French customs, for example, kissing each other on both cheeks (Nelson 1965: 165).

The priests attempted to implant the Catholic ceremonial calendar and taught Christian hymns to replace the traditional Ojibwa songs. They composed French airs based on folk melodies and plainchant and introduced antipagan lyrics. In the nineteenth century the Catholic clerics brought Austrian folksongs to the Indians as part of a new ceremonialism (Kurath 1957: 32-41). The Protestants, too, taught Christian hymns which the Ojibwas accepted and mixed with old forms to create what one Ojibwa man called "half breed music" (Burton 1909: 137). Some Ojibwa melodies took on Christian lyrics; more often the Indians learned translations of Christian songs.

Missionaries were struck by the Indians' eagerness to learn new songs. Many twentieth-century Ojibwa songs show the influence of both Catholic and Protestant melodies. The Ojibwas' desire to learn the mission hymnody sprang from their traditional ideas about the power of songs. Humans received songs from manitos during visions; each song contained effective power (Densmore 1938: 175). When the Christians sought to share their religious songs with the Ojibwas, the Indians were willing to receive the new sources of power, devoted to the influential Christian God.

The early Catholic missionaries devised feasts and other ritual components to correspond to and supplant the traditional rites. Fathers Allouez and Marquette and other Jesuits tried to redirect Ojibwa sacrifices and offerings, permitting the Indians to continue these acts, but for the honor and worship of the Christian God (Kellogg 1917: 112; Thwaites 1896-1901, vol. 54: 181). The priests forbade only a few aboriginal dances, preferring to syncretize traditional ritual activity with the new religious focus.

The later Catholics and the Protestant missionaries frowned on the continuation of traditional Ojibwa rituals, viewing them as obstacles to conversion. The clerics attempted to turn religious rites into social events and create a new corpus of ceremonialism as Christian cult. When Ojibwas wished to continue their dancing and feasting as part of Christian ritualism, the missionaries objected. In Michigan Joseph Greensky and his fellow Ojibwas formed their own Methodist congregation in the 1830s when the Christian missionaries refused them the right to celebrate Christian rituals in the noisily jubilant traditional style (Walker 1964: 41-43). Peter Jones and other native preachers impressed upon their fellow Ojibwas the similarities between traditional and Christian cults (Jones 1861: 96, 172), but the Indian and white missionaries insisted on replacing the old rituals with Christian forms, such as replacing tobacco offerings with Bible readings.

White officials and traders also discouraged the continuation of traditional religious ceremonies. Some refused to smoke with the Ojibwas at their rituals; others ridiculed the shaking tent ceremony and other religious rites. That whites failed to observe traditional rituals and received no supernatural punishment weakened the Ojibwa belief in their traditions.

Development of New Ojibwa Rituals

In some cases Ojibwas were successful in joining traditional and Christian rituals. Joseph Abita Gekek, a Pembina Ojibwa, helped to convert Red Lake Ojibwas to Catholicism in 1882 by instituting a Prayer Dance, using a drum blessed by one of the Benedictines. The dance followed traditional form but was directed to the Christian God. Later in the year, however, Father Tomazin saw the Indians dancing with rosary beads around their necks. Infuriated, he slashed their drum and thereby turned the Ojibwas against the mission (Fruth 1958: 15-16). In 1890 a Wisconsin Ojibwa initiated a Spirit Dance, in which he placed an empty glass on a stool and covered it with a white cloth. Then he sang sacred songs, during which time the glass mysteriously filled with water. This he called spiritual water and anointed people with it, giving it to them to take internally, saying that their souls and bodies would be thus purified (Works Progress Administration 1936-1940; 1942, "Types of Dances Practised by the Chippewas of Lake Superior": 3). His ritual, followed by a dance, joined features of the Catholic mass with the works of wonder traditionally associated with the shaking tent ceremony.

Missionaries themselves helped in the formation of new, syncretistic rituals. Their emphasis on the Matchi Manito resulted in a yearly ritual at Manitoulin and in Michigan at which Ojibwas gathered to shoot the supremely evil spirit in order to prevent disease (Hamilton 1903: 232; Kurath 1959: 213). This ritual joined the Christian belief in an evil being with the traditional practice of transferring sickness to an effigy and destroying it to restore health in the community.

Still other Ojibwa rituals developed by the traditional means of inspiration through visions. Under the direction of the manitos any Ojibwa might institute a dance, feast, or other rite. The Lac Court Oreilles Eagle Dance came from a boy's vision of eagles flying in droves across the sky. Other dances accrued during the historical period in similar fashion. The Old Age Dance, performed by very old men and small boys, originated in the 1870s when a very old, feeble man at Lac Court Oreilles surprised the community by showing up at a ceremonial dance. He sat in the drum circle and gave a long speech, telling the youths to lead good lives and be faithful to their creator, God. He composed a song, which Ojibwas still sing at the dance: "God, I praise Thee for the long life you have given me on this earth" (Works Progress Administration 1936-1940; 1942, "Types of Dances Practised by the Chippewas of Lake Superior": 5-8).

In the twentieth century the Ojibwas around Lake Superior's south shore perform approximately forty dances and feasts. Many of these are purely for secular enjoyment, or they commemorate events like the participation of Indians in the First World War. But others are based on myths or visions and seek to communicate the will of the community either to the manitos or the Christian God. Some of the dances derive from other Indians, for example the Dakotas and Winnebagos. Steady diffusion of songs exists among all the Great Lakes Indians and their neighbors, so that it is often difficult to determine the tribal origins of many songs and dances (Blessing 1958a: 16).

The Plains Ojibwas (Skinner 1914: 318) have adopted an especially large number of new ceremonies, including the plains Sun Dance, probably obtained from the Crees. Ojibwas allowed individual participation in the Sun Dance only after a male had a vision. Only those men who dreamed of Thunderbirds were permitted to participate, and the chief purpose of the ceremony was to communicate with the Thunderbirds to bring rain (Hallowell 1931; Skinner 1921: 313-315). As with other new ceremonies, the Ojibwas adapted them to fit their immediate needs.

Ojibwa ceremonial activity increased rapidly from the late seventeenth to the late nineteenth centuries. In the proliferation of dances and feasts, the most important became religious movements in their own right. Midewiwin, the Dream (Drum) Dance, the Ghost Dance and the peyote religion were foremost among the new religious movements which brought new ceremonies to the Ojibwas. All of these movements showed the influence of whites and other Indians; the foreign ceremonial elements were clear. Nevertheless, the Ojibwas persisted in many of their traditional ritual practices, changing them to fit new circumstances.

Ceremonial Crises, and the Diminishment of the Shaking Tent

Yet even as the number of ceremonies increased, the Ojibwas began to lose faith in the efficacy of their rituals. Divination, shaking tent ceremonies, and animal ceremonialism failed to secure the game necessary for survival. Medical rites failed to cure new diseases brought by whites. Even in the early nineteenth century, artist Paul Kane "found few remains of the ancient rites in the Great Lakes region; already acculturation had suppressed many of the old ways and replaced them with a kind of apathy" (Harper 1971: 15). Schoolcraft found that Ojibwas near Sault Ste. Marie ceased their offerings and other rituals where whites had desecrated the land (Schoolcraft 1848: 78). When the ceremonies failed to provide food and health, Ojibwas performed them less often, with less conviction, and with an eye toward the Christian God rather than the traditional manitos.

In Michigan especially the Ojibwas accepted Christian ceremonies as the core of their ritual life. Today the Michigan Ojibwas' major religious activities are Methodist camp meetings and Catholic feasts which include some aboriginal elements. Ojibwas also participate in the Dakota-inspired Dream Dance but that has degenerated into a tourist attraction with little religious import. In many areas the Ojibwas continue their mourning rites and family feasts, including the naming ceremony for newborn children, but in Michigan Christian ceremonialism has replaced traditional forms (Kurath 1954: 311-316). In all Ojibwa areas the rituals which surrounded the hunting and gathering pursuits of traditional Ojibwas have nearly vanished. Rituals concerning menstruation, war initiation, and adoption are rarely performed, even in areas where the Indians ignore Christian ceremonies.

Through all the changes in their religious ceremonialism, Ojibwas have managed to maintain use of and belief in their shaking tent ceremonies, even as the frequency of those ceremonies has decreased. Even djessakids who converted to Christianity continued to believe that the manitos communicated with the Indians in the conjuring rites. In 1834 an Ojibwa convert told Rev. Chandler that his former performances of the ceremony were controlled by an "unseen influence" which he knew to be the manitos. As a Christian he decided that those manitos represented the Devil; nevertheless, he still believed in their presence in the ritual (Prindle 1842: 29). Similarly, Old Schusco, a former djessakid, told Schoolcraft that the manitos directed the shaking tent ceremony and related to humans through it, although since converting he considered those manitos to be evil (Schoolcraft 1848: 210). Kohl heard of another djessakid who reaffirmed on his deathbed that he practiced no deception in the shaking tent. He did not speak the voices of the manitos; they themselves moved the tent and spoke to him from the top of the tent. The old man truly believed in his past work as the means by which humans and manitos maintained relations (Kohl 1860: 279-280). When, in 1900, Father Verwyst accused a former djessakid of trickery in the ceremony, the old Ojibwa was insulted and professed his continuing belief in the manitos' presence in the rite (Levi 1956: 210).

Despite the skepticism of missionaries, traders, government officials and other whites, the Ojibwas have persisted in their belief in the efficacy of the shaking tent ceremony. Though Ojibwas admit that some of the djessakids are fakes, their faith in the institution of conjuring remains intact. Even though fewer and fewer Ojibwas are able to perform the rite, especially in the United States, they retain their primary traditional means of communication between the manitos and the community.

Hallowell wrote in 1942 that even Christian Ojibwa communities continued their shaking tent ceremonies. He concluded:

> To my mind, the occurrence of conjuring in such cases is an index of the vitality of native beliefs, attitudes and values despite a veneer of acculturation. When conjuring entirely disappears we can be certain that the behavioral world of these Indians, as constituted in terms of their aboriginal belief system, already will have collapsed (Hallowell 1942: 88).

In subsequent years conjuring has further decreased. It has not disappeared but in many Ojibwa communities there are no effective djessakids.

Ojibwa faith in the shaking tent ceremony cannot last indefinitely in the absence of the ceremony itself. Neither can traditional Ojibwa religion be considered a living organism with a viable future when its two most important ceremonial aspects are moribund. Ojibwas rarely practice the shaking tent ceremony, which formerly joined communities to the manitos. The puberty vision, which in early times joined individuals to the manitos, exists in a similar, decayed state.

PUBERTY FASTING AND VISIONS

The past four chapters have described important aspects of traditional Ojibwa religion, including ontology, theology, myth and ritual. All of these aspects helped inform and shape the central event of an aboriginal Ojibwa's life: the puberty vision quest.

Quest for Personal Identity through a Guardian Manito

At the traditional naming ceremony the old Ojibwa lent to the child a part of identity, associated with ability and power, which he received from the manitos. The purpose of the ceremony was to pass on to the child the benefit of the old person's puberty vision. Even though the child would never know what that vision had been, nor ever fully understand the blessing received, the child was receiving an identity which it could use until it obtained its own.

It was up to the child to maintain those borrowed blessings and to gain more through life, because "a child was given power by its namer, but it rested somewhat with the child whether this power was developed. Throughout the Indian's belief in spirit power we note the necessity of cooperation on the part of the individual in order that he might have the full benefit of that power" (Densmore 1929: 54). All persons in traditional Ojibwa life had to obtain their own personal identity and power in life; nobody, except for the old person at the naming ceremony, was going to share.

A human did not begin life with power and full identity; those came partially as a result of naming and, more particularly, from the vision acquired through the puberty fast when an Ojibwa gained the aid of a manito (Thwaites 1896-1901, vol. 54: 138-143; Charlevoix 1761, vol. 2: 145). Only by obtaining such aid did an Ojibwa become a complete person and gain an identity. To the traditional Ojibwa,

All those talents and traits of character which we think of as functions of a total personality are regarded by the Ojibwa as isolated, objective items which may be acquired in the course of life by individuals who are fortunate enough to coerce them from the supernaturals. In Ojibwa thought, there is no original and

121

absolute "self"; a person freshly born is "empty" of characteristics and of identity. Consequently tremendous pressure is exerted upon a young person to pursue the supernaturals and move them to fill up his "emptiness" (Landes 1971: 124).

Thus, it was the duty of the Ojibwa child to gain an identity beyond its borrowed one, and thereby become a functioning member of society. This was accomplished chiefly through fasts for visions. As among other Indian peoples the vision was "socially recognized and made the very cornerstone of their cultural life" (Benedict 1923: 24). Furthermore, the vision was the cornerstone of the individual's religious life, the establishing of a personal relation with a manito. The relation formed the person's character. Among the Ojibwas the chief trait of character sought in the vision quest was the ability to hunt successfully, although health, long life, and the ability to doctor, gamble, fish, divine, fight and trap were also sought.

The puberty vision had cultural and religious dimensions. Its goals were to enhance social prestige as well as form a relation with a manito. For the Ojibwas, social prestige was based on the ability to hunt, an ability granted by the manitos. One Ojibwa's claim that his great puberty vision had made him a hunter highly attractive to women was not a vain boast since, as a hunter, he had community prestige and wealth, and therefore made a good "catch" as a husband (Jones 1919: 305). Moreover, the Ojibwas considered hunting to be a sacred activity, not only requiring the aid of the manitos, but also indicating that aid through frequent success.

An individual Ojibwa acquired only one manito guardian and received its blessings, but any number of manitos might appear in a vision. These personal beings could be appealed to, influenced, cajoled, insulted and alienated, just like human beings. The vision was the effective means of communication between individual Ojibwas and manitos. The human sought initial contact through fasting and the manitos responded through the visions.

The vision which resulted from the puberty fast was not the only occasion in which the manitos would appear to the Ojibwas. There would be visions in which the guardian manito appeared to tell the whereabouts of game or help in divination, war, and other pursuits. The Ojibwas distinguished between dreams (which were further classified as common dreams, meaningful dreams, and children's dreams) and visions (Schoolcraft 1853-1857, vol. 6: 664; Radin c. 1926, Envelope 4). The former were journeys of the free-soul; the latter were visits from the manitos. The puberty fast vision was the most important of all life's visions, for it established the faster's identity, and initiated a lifelong relation with the objects of Ojibwa religion, the foundations of Ojibwa existence. The puberty vision gained the help of the manitos and set the pattern for future visions which no longer required the preparatory routine of the puberty fast.

Rules regarding Fasts and Visions

There were rules regarding the proper attitude toward the manitos sought in the vision fast. The first was to refrain from asking too much or too often. There were myths which illustrated this theme, specifically about a boy who overfasted at the insistence of his father, even though the boy had already obtained as much power from the manitos as he would need in his lifetime. As punishment he turned into a robin. The Ojibwas believed that a person who sought too much power endangered health and life; the results could threaten family and descendants. Thus, fasters were discouraged from fasting for excessive periods of time. As one Ojibwa explained, "from experience the older Indians had learned that one who fasted too long became mentally unbalanced" (Works Progress Administration 1936-1940; 1942, "Significance of Charcoal"). Oral traditions recounted how youths became so preoccupied with obtaining power that they lost their sense of obligation to humans and ended up as murderers and social outcasts, or as robins (Jones 1919: 302-311).

The successful faster was not to describe the vision unless absolutely necessary for an important cause. Immediately after receiving the vision, the youth sometimes told a parent; doctors sometimes told their patients about their doctoring visions before beginning a cure. Ojibwas kept their visions secret because telling a vision brought the manitos to the teller and that should be done only when the manitos were actually needed for aid. Also, the instruction provided to the faster by the manitos was secret; it was not everybody's business. The vision was a personal matter between manito and individual. Telling a vision could destroy its efficacy. Because of the prohibition regarding the recounting of visions, researchers have collected accounts of only a few visions.

An Ojibwa was never to claim nonexistent patronage from a manito. Legends told of boastful hunters who falsely claimed vision power from manitos. Outraged, the manitos tortured or killed the boasters (Landes 1971: 210). The lesson of these stories was not that the Ojibwa should mask pride in gained accomplishments and power; indeed, pride was a virtue to the Ojibwas. But one should never make false claims on a manito; neither should one forget that game was caught only through the permission of the manitos.

In general, the attitude toward the manitos as expressed both in Ojibwa myths and life was twofold: a) a human should not make inordinate demands on the manitos; b) a human should not abuse power or it would hurt the abuser (cf. Fisher 1946: 233-235). Both of these rules resulted from an Ojibwa respect for the manitos and other persons of the universe.

It should not be concluded that an Ojibwa owed the benefactor manitos a constant adoration. Many Ojibwas never mentioned or regarded their manitos except when needed, although curers did pay lavish attention to their special manito helpers (Kinietz 1947: 160) and many Ojibwas had yearly feasts to their individual manitos by pouring tobacco on the water or into a fire. In any event, from early life the Ojibwa child learned to respect the manitos for their powers and to hope to obtain some of those powers through fasting for visions.

Preparing the Ojibwa Child for a Vision

After naming a child, Ojibwas addressed it as though it were an adult, because it had an identity, albeit a borrowed one. They encouraged the child to be independent and urged it toward its puberty fast. From around the age of four or five, the child's parents or grandparents directed it toward the goal of a successful vision. Just as Nanabozho fasted for and received a vision as a child, so should the youth. This was a rule of life for all Ojibwas. Girls as well as boys needed the help of manitos. Although they were not exhorted as much as were boys to make a long vision fast, girls often conducted the long fast and received powerful visions (Landes 1971: 8-9). There were Ojibwa women who became respected curers and able artisans because of their visions. Some females even took up hunting and other roles usually practiced only by males, for example, a La Pointe woman whom Richard E. Morse met in 1855 (1857: 353-354) and an occasional woman became a warrior or djessakid through successful vision quests (James 1956: 288).

Not everyone who sought a vision was successful. There were some whose lives were ruined by their failure to obtain the aid of manitos in visions, although it was rare for an Ojibwa to be totally unsuccessful. One Wisconsin Ojibwa man, whose mother had kept him from completing his fast, was forced to rely on a manito he had dreamed about before his birth. This made a poor substitute for a manito acquired through a fast for visions, but it was better than no guardian at all (Barnouw 1954: 83-84, 88). Some Ojibwas made several attempts before acquiring a manito; at other times the visions that did occur were considered dangerous, evil, or useless. In these cases, the youths rejected the visions. It was the duty of the child's parent or grandparent to state in advance what visions were considered powerful or helpful, and which were considered weak or harmful. Sometimes — for example, at Parry Island — the child's tongue was scraped to remove the effects of an unwanted vision (Jenness 1935: 50).

Normally an Ojibwa could reject an unwanted vision; blessings were not irresistible. Sometimes, however, the manitos compelled the visionary to receive them. One man dreamed (in Kohl 1860: 422-425) on ten consecutive nights of the Underwater Manito; each time he rejected the creature. Finally he could resist the call no longer and went to the water. Following the instructions given him in the vision, he called for the manito to appear. The serpent arose from the water and gave him powers which made him a rich and powerful sorcerer, but which resulted in the deaths of his wife and children.

Timing was very important in seeking and receiving a vision. If a child received a vision too soon in life, it might cause illness because of the youth's immature incapacity to understand or accept the vision. On the other hand, waiting too long for a vision might lead to listlessness and indirection, especially among boys, because of a lack of guidance from the manitos (Jenness 1935: 48-49). The Ojibwas felt that the vision fast should occur before the child engaged in any sexual activity. Parents had to know the right time for their children to make the vision quest.

Consequently, human guardians prodded their children toward the vision fast, but without pressing them beyond their capacity. Parents repeatedly tested the individual youth, for example by offering it a choice between charcoal (worn on the face while fasting) and food. Through rewards and punishments the child learned to choose the charcoal, that is, to make a fast. The youth was nagged to eat sparingly, even to make short fasts, to build up an increasing ability to live without an abundance of food. One nineteenth-century observer noted that "it is very natural that the Indians should make a great faster into a brave, for they are so often obliged to fast involuntarily, that the energetic defeat of hunger and thirst must become a national virtue among them. They make a virtue of a necessity" (Kohl 1860: 374). By the time of puberty, although frequently before, the youth was prepared to attempt an extended fast in order to obtain a vision of manitos who would give the youth a personal and powerful identity and full membership in the human community and in the universe at large.

It was important to attempt this fast during either the late fall or early spring. The Ojibwas considered the summer an inappropriate time, possibly because of the presence of the underwater beings, possibly because many of the aspects of nature present in the summer — leaves and other greenery — would be dead before long. Since one of the goals of the vision was long life, this omen was considered unlucky. The Ojibwas sought aid especially from the Thunderbirds, Owners of animals, and other manitos of the upper world. The Indians avoided visitations from the underwater manitos.

The Visionary Event

After a number of years of preparation, the youth at age ten, eleven, or later, made the fast for a vision. For a few days the parents or grandparents provided only a little supper; then they constructed a small lodge or chose a place away from the main camp in a secluded spot. They marked the child's face with charcoal to warn other Ojibwas that the youth was fasting and not to offer food. The charcoal also served to make the youth look "pitiful," a desired condition.

They gave the youth no food for five days, then a little, then none. Between the sixth and tenth days the youth was expected to have the vision. The longer the youth waited, the stronger the vision. It was thought proper to refuse the first few visions offered, to seek the strongest vision possible. The youth was not encouraged to fast beyond the tenth day; if the faster insisted, some food would be provided on the tenth day and on every fifth day thereafter, until the vision came.

Sometimes the human guardians told the youth to concentrate on something in order to facilitate the fast (Blessing 1961b: 10). In special cases the youth was wrapped in a robe, making it impossible to see light. Small pieces of lead were put in the mouth to draw the saliva. Through such sensory deprivation a youth could obtain certain types of visions, often of fog or rain manitos (Radin c. 1926, Envelope 5a).

Very few Ojibwa puberty visions have been recorded. The following thirteen examples, reported in ten different sources, date from the mid-nineteenth to the mid-twentieth centuries. These detailed summaries are not direct quotations.

1. On the eighth night of my fast, I heard rustling in the branches; I was frightened. A man approached me and told me not to fear. He asked me why I was fasting in the tree; I answered: to gain strength and knowledge. The man was pleased with the answer and told me that a council had been held that night and a favorable decision had been made regarding me; I should go hear it. We floated together upward, as if up a mountain, and at the top was a lodge in which there was a large white stone. At next look, there were four men sitting around it. I started to sit, but the stone started sinking; they had forgotten the proper foundation on which to lay it: a tanned deer-skin. They put it down. The lodge was filled with persons, a great council. I saw the earth beneath me, spread out, with its four corners. The sky was quite near me. They asked me whether I chose down or up; I chose up. The four men were pleased, and they told me to ascend. The stone became a ladder, and I ascended higher and higher to where four white-haired old men were sitting around a pillar, with a dazzling dome arched above. They told me I could rise no further, but that health, strength, long life and all the creatures of nature were mine. They told me that they would be the intercessors in prayer between me and the Master of Life. They especially told me not to forget that all the beasts were mine. All around were countless birds and game; I would be a great hunter. I came back down to

the white stone, and the four men and the council told me it was good, and to pray to my guardian spirits. I returned to my bed (Kohl 1860: 233-242).

2. I heard a voice and perceived a black form hovering over me. The form asked me why I was weeping; I said it was because of my mother's recent death. I was taken by the hand and led out on the limb of the tree where I was sleeping. The black form was a female. She told me not to be afraid, that the limb would hold us. We took three steps, i.e., three days journey. We came to a tall mountain, which we climbed. She waved her hand and the mountain opened. We went down a ravine and into a room with a supernatural light. I was frightened. A person at the back of the room told me I had been called because I mourned for my mother. The voice told me to look around, to see how the speaker lived. There was a lamp hanging in the middle of the room: the lamp of the sun. Behind it was the sun itself. Sun told me to look down, and I saw the earth, trees, forests, mountains, the big sea, the round of the world. I saw the vault of heaven so close I could grasp the stars. I looked forward and saw myself and was frightened. The sun said to be happy because my image was always before him. He said that the Four watch over me and are a gift of the sun. He said I would live long and have silver white hair like himself. He gave me a bird which soars high and a white bear with a brass collar. Then the woman led me back; we climbed down all night. A black dog ran past, so I promised to sacrifice a black dog to the woman in the spring (Kohl 1860: 204-209).

3. On the fifth night, I dreamed of a large, beautiful bird. I had decided to reject the first vision, so I did. As it left, I saw it was a chickadee. The next morning, my grandmother said chickadees often fool people. On the eighth night another great bird took me to the north where there was only ice. There were very old birds there who promised me long life and health. I accepted, and was brought back to my lodge. As he left, I saw he was a white loon (Radin 1914b: 2-3).

4. On the fifth night, I was alongside a lake and had had nothing to eat for a long time. I came upon a large bird as I looked for food. I said I was lost, and that people were looking to shoot me. The bird brought me a fish from the lake. He told me I would have good hunting and fishing luck and would live to be old. I would never be shot since this bird was very rarely shot at (Radin 1914b: 3-4).

5. I saw those who looked like people. They called me their grandchild, and told me they had come to pity me. I was taken roundabout, and I was shown what the earth was like, and what the deep sea was like. I saw how big the sky was, where the stars were, the many beings who lived among the stars. The manito who exists above appeared to me. It filled the sky, and pleasing words were spoken to me. I saw the roads where the sun goes, where the moon and the stars go (Jones 1919: 303-305).

6. A middle-aged man invited me to a dance. We went to a large lodge where I drummed and sang. I attended several times, and at the last one I saw a great herd of deer, with war bonnets. These bonnets were really horns. A medium-sized female albino deer came to me and told me that she was the king of all animals, that she was not ferocious, that she was harmless. She said I had gained great power, and would henceforth command all the beasts of the forest (Works Progress Administration 1936-40; 1942, "Types of Dances Practised by the Chippewas of Lake Superior": 19-20).

7. When I was a boy I went out to an island to fast. My father paddled me there. For several nights I dreamed of a chief who finally said to me, "Grandson, I think you are now ready to go with me." He danced around me as I sat there on a rock. I glanced down at my body and noticed I had grown feathers. I felt just like a golden eagle. The chief had turned into an eagle too and he flew off to the south. I spread my wings and followed after him. After a while we arrived at a place with many tents and people, the summer birds. After returning north I was left at my starting point. The chief promised to help me whenever I wanted it (Hallowell 1955: 178).

8. I was standing by the shore. A very large turbot offered to take me into deep water. I was reluctant to swim underwater but the turbot reassured me. We reached deep water after a long trip and I could see a great distance. The turbot showed me all the different animals. After a long time we came back (Rogers 1962: D7).

9. I was far away, in a sacred country. In the evening I saw many kinds of people going to one place. I knew who they were. Half-man spoke with me; I understood what he said but I couldn't remember it. I went to another country and in a big house I found Great Horned Owl. I stayed only a few minutes, during which time Owl told me many things. Before Owl's big family came home after traveling all day, I left (Rogers 1962: D8).

10. On the fifth night of my fast I was led to a conjurer's hut by a flock of wild geese. Inside the swaying hut, which I had entered through a hole at the top, were a spikebuck and six spirits. Later they were joined by a beautifully-dressed lady whose approach was heralded by singing and laughter. Her home was behind the sun. These taught me how to cure people and told me the songs to sing in summoning their help (Casagrande 1960: 478).

11. When I was twelve I blackened my face and fasted. On the third night a man came and told me he was coming for me, that I would be blessed if I believed him. I refused to go with him having been warned by my father against taking the first visitor. Then another man came, telling me that they had seen my pitiable condition, that I would never be killed if I went with him. I would live to be an old man, blind before dead, and my body would be as solid as his back. I would have many children and they would be strong as his back. He was the leader of a number of men. I was to return home, and he told me to turn around toward him as I left. I turned and saw he was Turtle. Turtle had blessed me (Radin 1936: 253).

12. At the age of twelve or thirteen, when I had my first menstruation, my mother sent me to the forest and encouraged me to fast for a vision, asking pity of the Master of Life, to help my poor family. It was the middle of winter. On the sixth night I heard a voice saying, "Poor child! I pity your condition." I followed the voice as it summoned me, on a shining path going upward. After a short distance I saw on the right a new moon with a bright flame coming from it, giving great light. On the left was the setting sun. The Everlasting Woman told me her name. She gave me her name and said I could give it to another. She gave me long life on earth and skill in saving life in others. I went on and saw a man with a large, circular body and rays from his head like horns. He said not to fear; he was the Little Man Spirit. This name was for my first son. He told me to continue. The path led to an opening in the sky. There was a man with a halo, whose breast was covered with squares. His name was The Bright Blue Sky, the veil that covers the opening to the sky. He said not to be afraid. He gave me the gifts of life and the power to endure and withstand. I saw myself encircled with bright points which rested against me like needles; there was no pain; they fell at my feet. This happened several times. Each time he reassured me. Then awls and nails stuck into my flesh but still no pain. He said it was good and told me to continue; I would live long. I got to the beginning of the opening to the sky. I had arrived; I could go no further, he said. He told me to return to my lodge on a kind of fish swimming in the air. He told

me to eat when I got back. I rode the fish back, with my hair floating behind me. After this, animal food disgusted me (Schoolcraft 1848: 169-171).

13. In my dream I saw a person coming from the east, walking on the air. He looked down on me, telling me to watch a great high pine tree. I saw that its branches reached toward the heavens and its roots reached deep into the earth. I gazed at the tree while he sang and pointed at the tree. It waved its top and heaved the earth and waters around its roots. He stopped singing and all became still. He taught me the song:
> It is I who travel in the winds,
> It is I who whisper in the breeze;
> I shake the trees,
> I shake the earth,
> I trouble the waters on every hand.

While I sang, the winds whistled, the tree waved its top, the earth heaved, the waters roared; they were all agitated. Then he said he was from the rising sun and would visit me again, saying, "You will not see me often; but you will hear me speak." Having spoken, he returned toward the road from whence he came (Müller 1969: 172-173; from Copway 1850: 39-40).

These thirteen accounts provide a composite picture of the traditional Ojibwa puberty vision. The similarity among the accounts indicates a unified Ojibwa tradition which continued into the twentieth century. The detailed imagery of the summaries suggests that the Ojibwas endeavored to remember their visions, the central events of their personal religious lives.

Effects of the Experience

The visionary returned from the experience with a vivid memory of the event, a new name, a token of remembrance, a promise of future help and a song. The latter was obscure to all but the visionary, but like the name, it gave other Ojibwas a clue to the guardian manito's identity. The youth never asked anyone for an interpretation of the vision, and people could only guess at the manito guardian's identity through the visionary's new name, songs, and other visible hints. As Charlevoix saw in the eighteenth century (Charlevoix 1761, vol. 2: 147) some Ojibwas painted pictures of their manitos on rocks; others tattooed their manitos' image on their bodies, indelible reminders of the lifelong bond between visionary and manito.

Paul Radin theorized that the youth was encouraged to experience a religious thrill in the vision. He suggested that the vision's content was developed as the person grew older and learned the proper format, including the folkloric elements (Radin 1914b: 7-10). This does not seem probable considering the preparation given the youth by parents and grandparents, the knowledge of myths which were recounted every winter, and the ever-present divination and medicine ceremonies of which the youth had knowledge at the time of the vision quest. Although the thirteen vision accounts came from mature informants who may have altered some details of their remembered visions through the years, the summaries most likely reflected the actual puberty visions accurately. The Ojibwas fasted for visions of manitos, not simply for religious thrills as Radin posited. Furthermore, all the accoutrements of the vision — the tokens, songs, tattoos and pictures — indicated the content of the visions, the manitos themselves, and the visionary displayed these accoutrements immediately following the successful puberty quest.

Visionary Patterns

What is significant about the correlation between mythic material and individual visions is that in a society in which visions played as important a role as they did in traditional Ojibwa life, there was always the chance, in fact the probability, that visionary revelations of one faster would contradict that of another. Individual visions could lead to divergent ideas about the manitos and the nature of the universe, unless the visions were carefully prepared for and rehearsed.

The Ojibwas were not doctrinaire; they held no explicit codes or dogmas, no articles of faith, which everyone had to believe in order to remain an Ojibwa. The Indians were willing to admit the possibility of mutually contradictory beliefs. They held that each vision was partial revelation; nobody had total knowledge of all the manitos. In turn, no manito had total knowledge or power. Nevertheless, there was general agreement among the Ojibwas concerning the structure of reality and what to expect from living persons. There existed an Ojibwa consensus of religious assumptions. Informed by myths and reinforced by parental teachings, shaking tent ceremonies, and empirical evidence, these agreed-upon (but uncanonized) beliefs and perceptions were very difficult for an individual to challenge.

The young Ojibwa making a puberty fast was told what to expect from the vision; nobody fasted for something hazy or undefined. He or she sought something specific, and in most cases the visions matched the expectations. Generations of visionaries met the same manitos in the same patterns. It seems likely that in cases in which visions did not match the familiar pattern of myth and instruction, the fasters rejected the visions as useless or meaningless. They resisted bad visions if they could, and they ignored unexpected visions except in extraordinary cases. In almost all cases the visionary found the expected, the usual. Indeed, "stereotypes of character, phrase, and incident appear in every dream. These are identical with the stereotypes of the traditional tales, myths, and religious ritual" (Landes 1971: 9).

The Ojibwas did not tell each other their visions, thus avoiding differences of belief. Since most manitos appeared only in visions, and since visionaries did not compare their experiences, opinions about the manitos varied. Nevertheless, the thirteen summarized accounts displayed a remarkably standard form and content.

Two major patterns were especially prominent. The first involved the type of relationship which the visionary established with the manitos, a relationship grounded in the manitos' pity for the one fasting. The second concerned the results, the promised rewards, of the quest and successful vision. These rewards included hunting achievements, good health, long life and personal prestige. The encounter with the manitos translated a pitiful fasting youth into a powerful visionary.

Pitying Relation between Manito and Faster

The first pattern appears especially in visions 1, 2, 4, 5, 11 and 12. Among the Ojibwas, as among other Algonkian (and Siouian) peoples, the theme of supernatural pity for fasting Indians was common in myths, fasts, and historical dealings. In myth, Nanabozho left his grandmother to fast. While walking he heard a voice say, "I pity you. I sympathize with you. You don't know where you are going. You have nothing to eat or protect yourself. If you will make good use of the power which I give you, you will be able to feed yourself & protect yourself"(Michelson 1925).

Through the fasting process the Ojibwas attempted to evoke the manitos' pity, and in the vision the manitos recognized the Ojibwas' pitiful state. The Ojibwas were using "the fast in a personal relation with the supernatural. They believed that by fasting the supplicant underwent such suffering, made himself so weak, that the spirits were overcome with pity, and so granted him whatever he desired" (Blumensohn 1933: 451).

The Ojibwas entered into their relations with the manitos just as they would with human persons, using, for example, the term "grandfather" to describe both the manito and the biological grandparent. There existed no linguistic dichotomy between humans and other persons (Hallowell 1960: 21-23). Although the manitos controlled Ojibwa destinies, holding the greatest share of power in the universe, the Ojibwas expected no qualitative difference between the behavior and motivation of humans and manitos. Indeed, "in Ojibwa idiom, to 'pity' another is to adopt him and care for him as a parent or grandparent cares for a child. Consequently the pitying supernatural is bound to the protegé by the firmest loyalties that exist in Ojibwa" (Landes 1971: 6).

A relationship based on pity was common to the Ojibwas, common enough to warrant a pitying conjugation of verbs, indicating an action which was performed in a certain way which was deserving of pity. Ojibwa was perhaps the only American Indian language, perhaps the only language in the world, with such a form (Verwyst no date b: 1). Rev. Gilfillan wrote that the expression, "he is poor" was one of the most common in Ojibwa language (in Hale 1893-1894: 317). The pitying relationship was firmly grounded in Ojibwa life.

The fast dramatized the Ojibwa dread of starvation and defined the state of hunger as one deserving of pity. In myths and common speech the Ojibwas characterized themselves as always hungry and the fast simply accentuated and highlighted that condition. Quite possibly they pitied themselves and expected the manitos to do likewise. Thus, they appealed to a code of conduct which they themselves followed, that is, providing food to the hungry, even to strangers. Missionaries, travelers, ethnographers and other white observers through the centuries have commented on the thoroughgoing Ojibwa generosity, in times of hardship and plenty alike. The Indians expected the manitos to extend the same courtesy.

Ojibwas sought the pity of the manitos not out of any feeling of innate guilt, but rather out of feelings of incompetence, emptiness, and inadequacy. As one missionary observer of Minnesota Ojibwas stated, "They say much in regard to their poverty . . . , but *never* speak of their sins or evil ways, never ask for forgiveness, or for anything which has reference to character" (Wright 1894: 186; emphasis his). The Ojibwas certainly did feel remorse for their improper actions against manitos, animals, humans and other persons; they received punishment for these wrongs. However, they never thought of themselves as born sinners, evil by nature. They could commit sins, individual acts, but they did not consider themselves sinners. Rev. Hall found this attitude a serious obstacle to his attempt at implanting Christianity among the Ojibwas. At Chequamegon they would not accept the Christian premise that all humans were sinful from birth. Rev. Hall hoped he could instill the Christian anthropology but he had his doubts: "They do not feel that they are sinners, and of course will not apply to the physician" (Culkin 1926: 60).

The Ojibwa youths in vision fasts felt pitiful because they were powerless, talentless, helpless and devoid of permanent identity, as indicated by their state of hunger. Their ontological emptiness was symbolized by the emptiness of their stomach; they were begging the manitos to fill both voids. They correlated a full belly with self-esteem and sought both food and identity in the same vision quest.

The Ojibwas did not act out of a magical technique; rather, they appealed in a very personal way to very personal manitos, expecting the same generosity as would be expected of humans. There was no guarantee that the manitos would respond, any more than there was a guarantee that every human would provide food during times of starvation, but if both the faster and the manitos followed the accepted rules of behavior, there was every probability that the fast would result in blessings through a vision.

It is interesting that the Ojibwas approached Westerners in a manner similar to the approach to manitos, begging and attempting to evoke pity. One trader complained that the

Ojibwas were "the greatest and most shameless beggars on earth; give them ever so much, they will still continue to ask for more until they receive a decided refusal" (Cameron 1890: 249). The arrival of traders among the Ojibwas was an impressive event, with the whites' wealth, guns, and potential for sharing those blessings with the Ojibwas. As a result, many Ojibwas treated whites as manitos or as extremely powerful and mysterious beings endowed with the manitos' powers (Barnouw 1950: 42-48). One Ojibwa boy, on seeing his first white man, an American soldier near Leech Lake, was frightened by the strange being. "We thought him a spirit," he recalled, "and as he talked we were convinced that he was a Great Medicine Man of some great tribe of whom we had scarcely heard" (Smith 1919:n.p.). The Indians tried to share in the whites' power through the standard technique of begging for pity, used so often in obtaining a vision of the manitos. An Ojibwa chief at Mackinac in 1766 spoke of himself and his people as "poor," "hungry," and "sincere," in asking an Englishman for supplies. The Indian begged for the man's charity and pity just as he would a manito (Clements 1919: 238).

The relation between visionary and the manitos was one in which the manitos offered support, consolation, assurance and protection. These attitudes appear prominently in visions 1, 2, 5, 8, 11 and 12 above, in which the manitos told the faster to trust them, not to be afraid, to rely on their aid. The manitos presented themselves as friendly benefactors, intercessors between the faster and the universe.

The relation strongly emphasized the personal nature of the manitos; here was no distant force to be tapped by rote. The visionary could depend on the manitos because of their personal interest and care, not because they were coerced to help through a formula. Furthermore, the visionary was not possessed by the manitos. Simply, the manitos revealed themselves and promised future aid. Though the visionary and guardian manito entered a relationship, there was no mystical absorption or loss of self. The identity gained through the vision and its consequent relationship remained separate from the manitos' identities. Ojibwas could not transform themselves into their guardian manito, not even the most powerful visionaries or curers.

Goals of the Vision: Hunting Success, Good Health, Long Life

The second common pattern of the visions indicated what the Ojibwas wished to gain from the manitos as a result of the visions. The thirteen summarized visions consistently promised the faster hunting success, good health, and old age, especially visions 1, 2, 3, 4, 6, 11 and 12. The visions also used a common theme in which the faster in the vision was given the ability to see the universe as it was thought to be: the sky, earth, sun, four quarters, inhabited by animals, trees, and other persons. Particularly in visions 1, 2, 3, 5, 7, 8, 12 and 13 the manitos seemed to reveal the structure of the universe. Later in life the Ojibwa visionary would be able to use this knowledge in divination, curing, locating game and healthful herbs, and interpreting natural phenomena. In a very literal sense this was a revelatory vision because in it and through it one was able to see the universe clearly. This ability would be invaluable throughout life.

The vision revealed to the visionaries their individual importance. Like their myths, Ojibwa visions emphasized the achievement of power and control. This was evident in visions 1, 2, 4, 5, 6, 7, 10, 11, 12 and 13. The one fasting heard from the most powerful beings in the universe that they had a personal interest in his or her welfare and that they would help whenever needed or called upon. What a feeling of pride and self-importance the Ojibwa youth must have felt as a result of such a revelation! Furthermore, the manitos promised success, talent, power and respect throughout life as a result of the vision, as in 1, 2, 3, 4, 6, 10 and 12. An Ojibwa told of his vision: "And yonder on the mountain-top was where I saw many goods, and all the various kinds of food there were, likewise silver. 'That is yours,' I was told. . . . That I should thus have dreamed was on this account, by a manitou [sic] was it willed in my behalf that the people should desire me to be a chief" (Jones 1919: 301-303). Visions similar to this were not rare and were instrumental in forming the Ojibwa personality with its emphasis on self-esteem and pride in individual accomplishment. Certainly accomplishments resulted from the manitos' aid, but that aid came because the individual was chosen personally for success by the manitos. That in itself made the individual important in his or her own eyes as well as in the eyes of the community.

The vision transformed the Indian. No longer was he or she a pitiful creature: hungry, tired, empty. The manitos told one Ojibwa boy during a vision of a noble war council: "Thou art still young, and thou art at the same time poor, wretched, and persecuted. But hereafter thou wilt be as grand as those thou seest there in the field, and will become, thyself, a mighty hero" (Kohl 1860: 376). The visions did not cause a change in religious belief but the person's orientation changed in the direction of the guardian manito. In addition, the visionary underwent a transformation, from nobody to somebody.

The vision reaffirmed the individual's relative isolation from other human beings and oriented the visionary toward the helping manitos, particularly the guardian. A transition took place; "formerly the boy had been dependent upon older *human* beings, who, in addition to teaching him necessary skills, had trained him to rely upon himself to the extent of his capacity. Henceforth he was to rely primarily upon *superhuman* beings . . ." (Hallowell 1971: 361; emphases his). The change in the visionary could be as radical as an alteration in gender orientation. Occasionally Ojibwa men adopted the clothes, mannerisms, and roles of women as a result of their puberty visions (Grant 1890: 357).

Other humans might not notice the visionary's new powers but those powers would become evident through hunting and other successes. It was a common theme of Ojibwa myths that the least likely person received vision power which would be greatly useful in a crisis (Jones 1861: 89-90). Since the Ojibwas were not supposed to abuse the benefits of the manitos, it was common for an individual to save the promised power until it was needed in an emergency. Nevertheless, the individual knew the power was available, remembered the vision distinctly, and maintained the identity and self-esteem gained in the vision.

Historical Failure of Visions to Achieve Goals

Of course, hunting and other successes might not come, even after an apparently powerful vision. In such a case the visionary might wonder what he or she had done to alienate the guardian manito; or suspect witchcraft and seek an even stronger guardian to counteract the evil; or doubt the efficacy and even existence of the manitos. The Ojibwa worldview provided explanations for such failures, unless they took place consistently. The nineteenth and twentieth centuries witnessed such failures repeatedly, resulting in Ojibwa bewilderment and a communitywide crisis of faith in visions for guardian manitos.

Only rarely now do Ojibwas fast at puberty to obtain visions of the manitos. Although in the seventeenth century the Jesuits found the vision quest a major obstacle to Christian conversions (Thwaites 1896-1901, vol. 54: 139-143) and in the early twentieth century the Ojibwas at Rainy Lake still used their dreams and visions as weapons against Christian teachings (Cooper 1936: 22-23), today the practice has fallen into almost total disuse. From Wisconsin (Kinietz 1947: 124), to eastern Ontario (Jenness 1935: 52), in Manitoba (Shimpo and Williamson 1965: 62-63), Minnesota (Blessing 1961b: 9-10), and north-central Ontario (Rogers 1962: D5; Sieber 1950: 151-152), only an occasional adolescent Ojibwa secures a guardian manito through a vision. Where the practice persists, it remains out of sight of the community and does not cohere to the whole of modern Ojibwa life.

The depletion of game, the severe changes in Ojibwa environmental and societal conditions, the influence of Christian missionaries, and the religious persecution by United States and Canadian governments have worked together toward eradicating the vision quests. For the most part the quests have been eclipsed. One Lac du Flambeau Ojibwa told what had happened when he was young in the late nineteenth century: "My grandfather was teaching me . . . ; he was showing me how to do in the woods; but before I had my dreams, the agent made me go away to boarding school" (Gillin 1942: 552). Rubber hoses and razor straps served to prevent the boy from continuing the old Ojibwa ways.

Even in the nineteenth century the Ojibwas became aware of the changes in their lives. An old Indian woman on the southern shore of Lake Superior lamented:

Then the Indians were much better than at this hour. They were healthier and stronger . . . , stronger in their faith, more pious and religious. . . . They lived long and became very old. . . . They could all fast much longer. . . . They ate nothing at all for ten days and longer. Hence they had better dreams. . . . Now their dreams are weak. They often make a mistake and even if they have dreamed well, they do not know how to find the animals at the right place (Kohl 1860: 368-369).

The old Ojibwa's comment pointed out the first major shock to the Ojibwa vision practice: game was depleted, first by the heavy fur trade, then by white settlements. The Ojibwas were baffled; they could find no game. Starvation became an all-year experience, instead of confining itself to the winter. The results were devastating, for example, in Manitoba

> When, for reasons not fully understood by the band members, the game quickly disappeared . . . , the band members were able to understand this phenomenon only in their own frame of reference. Lack of success in hunting in spite of their dedication and skill, most possibly meant some serious diminution of the blessing and protection of their deities. Mental and emotional security was disturbed, and tension developed (Shimpo and Williamson 1965: 206).

Ojibwa subsistence, self-confidence, assurance in the manitos' blessings and vision questing declined in sequence.

For the Ojibwas worldly success, symbolized by hunting achievements, good health, and long life, came as a gift from the manitos. The manitos were the source of Ojibwa existence because they provided the Indians with animals for nourishment and medicinal powers for health, thereby making long lives possible. Continued existence was impossible without the blessings of the manitos. When an Ojibwa boy encountered manitos in his puberty vision, one thing they promised him was the ability to catch game. More specifically, when he later went out to hunt, the manitos brought the animals to him and permitted him to kill them. The hunter could take pride in his hunting achievements, but only as symbols of his relations with the manitos. He knew that he was powerless to find and kill animals unless the manitos granted him success. They allowed him to live; his existence depended on them. His continuation as a person relied on his continued relations with the manitos.

In the nineteenth century when game was scarce and many Ojibwas starved, belief in the manitos did not waver, but their own self-confidence did. They could no longer count on catching enough game to eat. Poor and pitiful, with the manitos not providing aid, the Indians were becoming increasingly dependent upon white traders and government agents. Traditionally they had relied on their relations with the manitos for their identity; now these assumed relations were failing them. Nevertheless they trusted in the manitos, continuing the vision quests of traditional times, at least as Paul Radin found in Michigan and Ontario, where conservative adults prodded the youths (Radin 1936: 233-234).

The Ojibwas then applied their visions to religious movements — like the Wabeno cult — which promised hunting success, or to other religious movements which promised a closer relation between humans and the manitos. A vision formed the base for the Dream (Drum) Dance of the late nineteenth century. The vision came to a Dakota girl; the Ojibwas adopted the movement partially because her vision coincided with their beliefs about manitos and the means of individual revelation. Once the Ojibwas accepted the Dream Dance, they changed it locally, as at Whitefish, Wisconsin, as further information was revealed through visions to an adolescent member (Barrett 1911: 327-332). Visions and dreams played roles in the Ojibwa adoption of the Ghost Dance and the peyote religion, and in the formation of a small religious movement in the early twentieth century on the Berens River. Dreams also formed the bases for new dances, feasts, and other forms of cultic activity. The Ojibwas found new applications for their traditional practices involving vision revelation; however, they were not fasting for these visions. The visions related less and less to traditional myths, and concerned themselves decreasingly with the fulfillment of individual Ojibwa identity. Most of the Ojibwas continued, however, to believe in the manitos' power.

Diminished Visionary Activity

By the early twentieth century, much of the continuity between traditional and current visions was lost. Under the influence of missionaries who belittled the manitos and whose God seemed to provide whites with wealth and success, the Ojibwas began to doubt not only their own but also their manitos' powers. They started to accept some of the claims of Christianity and speak of their traditional beliefs in the past tense: "Just as Christians approach God for favours through his ministers or churches, so the Indian approached the servants of the Great Spirit, the manidos [sic], and sought their aid" (Jenness 1935: 47). They no longer understood their past traditions, which barely connected to their present situation.

Their visions which had formerly fought Christianity, now assisted in conversions as Ojibwas accepted some Christian beliefs and denigrated their own abilities. The visions of a native religious leader at Round Lake, Ontario, led to the facile acceptance of Christianity by the Indians in the area.

> This man told the people that his "power" was going. Each night he dreamed of a white light or a bright area which drew closer all the time and moved across his field of vision to the north. He was powerless to stop this. Later the people learned that a bishop was traveling through the area at the time. Accordingly it was thought that Christian power must be greater than that of the shamans (Rogers 1962: A28).

Through his vision the Ojibwa man symbolized the losing struggle of traditional Ojibwa beliefs against the inroads of Christian teachings. He and his fellow Indians accepted the verdict of the missionaries among them, that the old Indian ways were dying, to be replaced by Christianity.

The Ojibwas have not abandoned their idea of a correct relation with power figures. White officials on a mundane level and Jesus on a grander scale have become potential sources of blessings, often through the medium of dreams and visions. Dream revelations are not foreign to Christianity; indeed, missionaries to the Ojibwas have turned often to dreams for divine guidance. Father Pierz, when he despaired of ever learning Ojibwa language received encouragement in a dream in which appeared a great banquet, a priest, an Easter egg, ripe fruits, and other Western folkloric baggage. He wrote that

> I was confirmed in my view of the higher inspiration of this dream by a sequence of dreams which followed from time to time. They let me realize how fatherly was the good God or my guardian angel, who, whenever necessary, instructed, warned, exhorted or corrected me for my faults (Furlan 1952: 77).

For some Ojibwas Jesus has replaced the traditional mani-tos, becoming a source of strength and blessing. For example, he reportedly cured an Ojibwa on Parry Island through a dream:

One night I dreamed that Jesus approached me, clothed in a loin cloth and with bleeding wounds as He appears in pictures. I threw myself at His feet and asked for a blessing. Then I awoke, and told my friends that Jesus had blessed me and was restoring me to health. I recovered my health, and am now as strong as ever (Jenness 1935: 48).

Ojibwas do not make quests for visions of Jesus, but he appears in dreams, offering the kind of consolation and aid formerly given by manitos. An Ojibwa woman has told of her puberty vision in which a porcupine manito promised aid, but that was in the past: "Yes, the porcupine formerly granted me favors; they were like the favors I now get from God. Whenever I wanted a favor, or was in need, not knowing where to look for help, I just thought of him and wished that he'd help me. I thought of him the same as I now think of God" (Hilger 1951: 48).

This process appears in hymns and other popular manifestations of Ojibwa attitudes toward the Christian God. One song from Michigan, significantly entitled the "Grandfather Song," describes the poor, weak, and helpless Ojibwa who asked for Jesus' aid. The lyrics speak of the poverty of the supplicant, asking for charity (Kurath 1954: 313-314). This theme, not foreign to Christian hymnody, derives mainly from the Ojibwa view of visionary-manito relation.

The problem for the Ojibwas is that Jesus does not consistently provide them with the worldly success that the manitos once did. Some Ojibwas look to Jesus as a replacement for the discredited manitos. They hope that he will give them the type of prosperous and healthy existence that they think he has given to the white race. But when they compare themselves with whites, they see that the Christian God does not bless Indians. They cannot believe in their old manitos and they cannot trust Jesus. Their poverty persists as their traditions fade. Christianity aids them in reaching heaven, they say, but its usefulness on earth is slight. They are set adrift without their visions and Christianity will not rescue them.

DISEASE, HEALTH, AND MEDICINE

Medical Concern of Traditional Ojibwa Religion

Typical of the northern hunters of native America, aboriginal Ojibwa religion was intimately concerned with health and the curing of disease (Ritzenthaler 1953: 241-244). That is not to say that Ojibwa religion arose from medical concerns, but one of the most important applications of the religion was health. Whereas the Indians' religion — relations with and beliefs about the manitos — was an end in itself, the reigion had daily concerns: primarily hunting, and secondarily the maintenance of health and the curing of disease.

One way of describing such a concern is through a definition of symbols. Religious symbols point to and participate in the subjects of religion as well as the objects of religion. In so doing, they tell observers something, although not everything, about both. Thus, the hunting and medicinal concerns of Ojibwa religion were symbols of Ojibwa daily concerns. It was natural for the activities and interests which concerned the Ojibwas to reveal themselves in their religion, just as the manitos revealed themselves.

Traditional Ojibwa concern for health showed itself through other aspects of the religion. The manitos promised health and long life in puberty visions and often provided the visionary with specific knowledge of herbs and other medicines. Religious leadership meant medicinal leadership in Ojibwa society. Writing of the twentieth-century Indians' values, Frances Densmore said, "Health and long life represented the highest good to the mind of the Chippewa, and he who had knowledge conducive to that end was most highly esteemed among them" (Densmore 1928: 322). Ojibwa cultic life addressed health concerns; myths described the origin and treatment of disease. In short the concern for health touched every corner of traditional Ojibwa religion, as it pervaded Ojibwa life. Whites often observed that Ojibwas were exceptionally healthy people; one rarely saw a crippled, diseased, or mentally retarded Ojibwa (Gilfillan 1901: 59). Nevertheless, disease, health, and medicine were constant topics of Ojibwa conversation (Kohl 1860: 110).

The Ojibwa concern for health directed itself to the individual, although the community's health was also important. In traditional times it was the duty of the family leader to maintain the health of the members of his small community; in later times this situation changed somewhat, both broadening in larger communities and narrowing to individualistic concern.

Health and cleanliness were related values to the Ojibwas. They burned refuse, aired bedding, bathed frequently, washed their hair, used sweat lodges, washed their cooking and eating implements, and sweetened their homes with fragrant medicinal herbs and roots (Ritzenthaler 1953: 179-181). Early travelers may have found the Indians' habits disgusting, but such views were more a matter of cultural variances than an indication of unhealthful native practices.

The connections between Ojibwa religion and health surfaced through the causes and cures of illness. The Ojibwas distinguished between the immediate causes, or agents, of disease and their ultimate causes or meanings. They chose cures to fit the ultimate causes as well as the agents (Hallowell 1939a: 191; Hiller 1937: 1; Ritzenthaler 1953: 190-192; Rogers 1962: D22-23).

Causes of Disease

The Ojibwas attributed the origin of disease to the misbalanced hunting relationship between humans and animals. One myth recounts (Reid 1963: 85-88) that early in the history of the world when no disease existed, humans and animals coexisted as friends; however, the humans wanted to eat animals. When they did, the animals began to prey on one another. Then the killing became too widespread and humans killed more animals than they needed. The animals held a council and commissioned the mosquito and fly to spread disease among humans. When Nokomis saw the humans' condition, she felt pity for them. She called Nanabozho, who discovered from chipmunk the herbal cures of all diseases. These the Culture-Hero distributed among the humans.

As a result, even though the Ojibwas considered many ailments and accidents to be natural, they considered none normal. Disease was a condition introduced, not original, to the world.

Minor accidents and ailments could all fall under suspicion from the other causes of disease, including the manitos, witches, and the dead. Thus, one could suffer a fall or a cut, and still suspect the work of a witch.

The second immediate cause of disease was the intrusion of a foreign object into the body. This could be a feather, shell, stone, worm, insect, or other small object. The intrusion might be the work of a witch, the dead, or the manitos, and thus the Ojibwas had to look beyond the immediate cause to the ultimate cause.

Likewise, the Ojibwas attributed some diseases to soul-loss. This could occur through a soul's wandering in a dream, or through malicious actions of the dead, manitos, or a witch. Soul-loss might also result from foreign intrusions which jarred the free-soul from the body, or from mental anguish which made the body an unpleasant place for the free-soul. Conceivably all diseases were related to soul-loss to some degree (Hultkrantz 1953: 448-463), although the Ojibwas did not state this explicitly. The ultimate causes of soul-loss could be natural or supernatural.

Disease also came about from improper contact with sources of power, not through a breach of ethics but an unintentional contact with powers beyond the person's control, for example, menstrual blood which could cause illness in men and obstruct hunting. Although menstrual blood was not evil — it possessed curing properties — it contained powers which should not come into contact with men too weak to associate with them.

A further application of this concept concerned the religious leaders themselves. Although human, they possessed great power which they controlled to a greater or lesser degree. This power could cause harm as well as good, depending on the circumstances, and some medicine men — sorcerers — might have caused illness to Ojibwas because of a lack of control over their power. They did not mean to cause disease, but their power escaped their control, or a person came into contact with their power without proper precaution or preparation.

The same was not true of witches. Father Allouez noted that seventeenth-century Indians of Lake Superior attributed diseases to the malicious work of witches (Kellogg 1917: 113-114). By the early nineteenth century belief in them was even further entrenched. Cameron told of boasts by medicine men that they could kill or harm others, besides being able to chase away game or bring destructive natural phenomena. He wrote that " . . . an Indian seldom imputes any unfortunate event to natural causes but invariably believes that another Indian whom he thinks has a spite against him, has been employing his art in conjuring to make him unhappy or unsuccessful . . . " (Cameron 1890: 262). Tanner saw at close range how one Ojibwa who harmed another became ill shortly thereafter. The ill man begged his enemy to cease revenge, and although the accused man denied any part in the disease, his accuser attempted to kill him. The afflicted man's actions showed how strong the belief in witchcraft was (James 1956: 154-157).

Ojibwa witches used numerous means to cause disease in their enemies. They also influenced game and natural phenomena and thereby could harm others by withholding sources of food. By thwarting attempts to secure game, they caused starvation or facilitated Windigo possession. Their chief means of attack, however, was by causing disease.

Their methods of inducing disease included sketching their victim's image on the ground and placing poison on the spot to be harmed, or tying a carved wooden image of their victim to a tree with a thread, and when the thread broke, the victim would die (Henry 1809: 121). Witches also scratched their victims with poisons or poisoned their food. They could also mix poisons with extensions of their victim's body, for example, nail parings. They shot objects into their enemy's body and stole their victim's soul. Through their control over animals, they could cause a beast to molest their victim (Jenness 1935: 85-86). Artist Paul Kane fell suspect as a witch at St. Clair, Ontario, when his realistic paintings of Ojibwas stirred Indian fears that he would gain control over them by painting their likenesses (Harper 1971: 52). Some religious specialists caused illness through soul-loss by the shaking tent ceremony. While in the tent they summoned their victim's soul and imprisoned it, thereby causing illness and eventual death (Michelson 1925: n.p.).

Many of the devices used in witchcraft mirrored hunting techniques, for example, the muzzi-ne-neen, or "x-ray" style of art used in gaining power over animals to be hunted. The principle remained the same: the image (an extension of the person) influenced the life and actions of the person, even when removed from the body. The same powers that enabled specialists to cure disease played a prominent role in causing disease.

Particularly fearsome to the Ojibwas were witches who posed as bears, either by wearing the skins of bears or by metamorphizing into bears. These bear-walkers owed their powers to their personal manito, the bear, and traveled in disguise at night, causing disease among their victims (on bear-walkers, see Dorson 1952: 26-34; Radin c.1926, vol. 1: 85-90).

Closely associated with bear-walkers were fireballs, glowing objects which traveled at night. Some Ojibwas said that these were bear-walkers themselves; others said they were a different type of witch. In either case, they caused disease at night. If caught, the fireballs or bear-walkers returned to their human form, usually that of an old person, and tried to buy off their captors (on fireballs, see Works Progress Administration 1936-1940; 1942, Envelope 15, "The Firewalker"; Hilger 1951: 71; Levi 1956: 193-201).

The Ojibwas particularly suspected witchcraft of Indians from other clans, outside the family circle. Indians visited foreign communities only if they had relatives in them. Removal from a home base increased the fear of witchcraft. Behavior regarding strangers was circumspect, though polite, dictated out of fear of offending people and thus bringing on the opportunity for vengeful witchcraft.

Traditional Concept of Sin

Another major cause of disease was sin (for this entire issue, cf. Hallowell 1939a). The traditional Ojibwas had little civil or political coercion to enforce community ethics. Their chief means of social control was anxiety about diseases caused by sin.

The Ojibwas held beliefs about the proper relationship between humans and the rest of the universe, particularly the manitos but also including other humans, animals, plants and natural phenomena, which were thought of as persons. Misconduct in relations with any of these entities, but particularly the manitos, could be thought of as a sin. Ojibwas did not view themselves, however, as naturally sinful or evil. They held no such opinion of sinful human nature. Rather, sins were specific actions which broke the rules of the universe, offended the living entities of the universe, and were avenged by the manitos.

Failure to share with others, improper treatment of the dead, cruelty to animals or humans, incest, sexual perversions, homicides: these were all sins, punishable by disease. The Ojibwas did not expect nemesis after death; their concern was for disease and hunting failure in this life. On the other hand, punishment did not necessarily come at once. It could wait for years, even transferring itself to the descendants of the sinner. As a result, one could never be sure which sin caused a disease.

Sins against manitos included ritual misconduct or neglect, either intentional or unintentional. Sins also included pride in the human-manito relation, that is, claiming too much power as a human, not giving credit to the sources of one's success, or claiming the help of manitos who were not in fact guardians.

One offended the manitos, too, through one's actions toward other humans, but in actuality the Ojibwas emphasized their sins against animals whom they hunted. Killing animals without purpose was avenged by the Owner of that species. Improper disposal of the killed animal's bones, or torture of the animal before killing, or bestiality, also resulted in disease brought by the manitos. It would be incorrect to view these sins as taboos. They were not the improper mixing of powers; rather, they were unethical acts against persons, and thus they offended the manitos, the ultimate upholders of morality. In this regard, the Ojibwas held a broadly directed ethical system which cared about nonhuman persons. The Indians were vitally and morally concerned about their treatment of animals and even plants used for medicine. Punishment for sins against these persons was either the withdrawal of game or disease. Punishments were delivered by the manitos and indicated the two most prominent concerns of the Ojibwas, hunting and health.

In order to protect themselves from disease, then, the Ojibwas were obliged to lead proper, ethical lives. That did not insure them health, since the forest was filled with enemies and accidents, but ethics and health were closely entwined. The gaining of a powerful manito was another key to health and long life, since the guardian manitos provided such rewards to their favorites. Individuals protected themselves against disease by wearing charms, especially those which were prescribed in visions and dreams. These could be herbs, or a composite of herbs and other powerful material representing the blessings of the manitos. Worn always, these charms even protected the wearer from the weapons of enemies in war. In historical times, some Ojibwas wore Christian sacred objects such as rosary beads or medallions as talismans. Protection from disease was also effected through propitiatory offerings to the manitos and the observance of taboos, as well as the avoidance of those suspected as witches.

Diagnosis and Cure of Disease

When an Ojibwa became ill, the first thought was of diagnosis. Individuals used their visions, their communication with their personal manitos, to attempt to find the cause as well as the agent of the ailment. In the vision, patients found out for themselves the cure as well as the cause, especially in cases when herbs were the sole cure. One might also envision the cure for another person's sickness; any Ojibwa with a guardian manito would have some ability in this regard, and family members shared their cures.

In order to combat a witch, however, Ojibwas called on their most powerful curers. In particular, the diagnostic specialist of the Ojibwas, the djessakid, performed a shaking tent ceremony in order to discover the cause of the disease, be it witch, manito, or ghost. The djessakid's powers were primarily concerned with diagnosis, not necessarily with healing.

Once diagnosis was made, the Ojibwas decided the proper cures or combination of cures. Indeed, the various cures were rarely used by themselves, but more often in series. John Long observed one rite in the late eighteenth century which consisted of sweating, prayers, and the use of herbal medicines (Long 1904: 137).

If the disease was caused naturally, the Ojibwas turned to surgical or herbal cures. The Indians used massages for sprains, localized burning for rheumatic pain, enemas for constipation, surgery for torn flesh and broken bones, trephination for headaches, scarification with herbs for muscular pains, and sweat baths for colds and respiratory ailments.

Although they used sweat baths in conjunction with other rituals, the Ojibwas took sweat baths as disease prevention, as cures for natural illnesses, and in curing diseases caused by improper contact with power. The sweating removed impurities and uncontrolled powers from the body. Father Charlevoix found that the Ojibwas used sweat baths as panaceas (Charlevoix 1761, vol. 2: 175), and Lahontan said that they never went a week without enjoying one (Lahontan 1703, vol. 2: 469). The baths served as purifying preludes to ceremonies, and as curatives in their own right.

The Ojibwas used herbs in cures for both natural and supernatural diseases. Densmore listed sixty-nine plants used by the Ojibwas which whites believed possessed medicinal value (Densmore 1928: 299). This number represented approximately 17 percent of the 400 plant species used by Great Lakes Indians in food, technology, and medicine, or about 3 percent of the 2,000 plants of the area (Yarnell 1964: 143). Huron Smith claimed that 65 percent of the plants used by the Ojibwas had medicinal worth, although he did not specify how many the Ojibwas used for the purposes whites claimed they should be used for (Smith 1932: 348). The natives used numerous herbs and, Hoffman's claim notwithstanding (Hoffman 1891: 159), they did not learn their uses from the Catholic priests.

Ojibwas used medicines for stomach pains, fits, fainting, blood diseases and general ills. They took many as teas made of a number of plants boiled together, others as emulsions, ointments, lotions and aromatics in sweat baths. The various herbs functioned most commonly as emetics or cathartics, but also as expectorants, diuretics, and narcotics. Some modern Ojibwas attest that their people had herbal concoctions to prevent conceptions or to abort fetuses (Balikci 1956: 189), but no evidence exists to support this claim.

Many whites, including Alexander Henry, spoke of the efficacy of Ojibwa herbal cures. The medicine he described consisted of the blood of a garter snake's head, mixed with water and given by the tablespoon to help in the delivery of a child. Henry noted, however, that despite the knowledge of some Ojibwa herbalists, many Indians were so credulous about medicines that Hudson's Bay Company agents were able to trick them into buying sugar, coffee, pepper, allspice, cloves, tea, nutmegs, ginger, and other spices as purportedly powerful drugs (Henry 1809: 116-117; 326-327).

Herbs had their greatest power as part of a ceremony. The Ojibwas used ritual in combating disease, with or without herbs. Just as witches could cause disease by making effigies of their victims and then harming these, curers could transfer the illness from the victim to an effigy which could then be shot or destroyed; the disease would perish with the effigy. This procedure was used either as a protective device in the case of a village besieged by disease, or as a cure of an individual (on effigies, see Hilger 1936: 40; Kohl 1860: 281-282; Ritzenthaler 1953: 209-216). The principles of sympathetic and contagious magic used by witches were counteracted by the reverse process. Other means of thwarting witches included granting the victim a new name and thus a new extension of identity, in order to confuse the witches' magical powers and maleficent intent.

Disease could be prevented not only by rituals, but also by propitiatory offerings and sacrifices when individuals or the group who offended a manito were subsequently punished. The Ojibwas sacrificed dogs to prevent disease. Their most common curing ritual for the community, however, was the tree offering. The Ojibwas hung cloth, beads, herbs and other offerings on trees, later replaced by Christian crosses which the early Jesuits planted in Indian villages (on offerings and sacrifices, see Balikci 1956: 179; Kellogg 1917: 112; Killy 1948: 61; Winchell 1911: 610). Ojibwas usually conducted these offerings for their community in times of epidemic.

The widely used sucking rite, noted by Father Allouez in the seventeenth century (Kellogg 1917: 114), existed for individuals. When a disease intrusion was diagnosed, a sucking doctor specialist among the extended family performed the cure, usually accompanied by sweating, herbal cures, prayers and other ceremonial components. The doctor often employed a medicine stick (see example in Winchell 1911: 610, and Plate IX) about nine inches long with a hoop at the end, filled with clay and connected to leather thongs. With this he hit the patient's body to chase away the disease. The curer's prayers, songs, and directives also had power in prying loose the disease-causing object, whether it was placed there by manitos, witches, or the dead. While playing a drum, the doctor called upon the guardian manitos and sucked on the patient through a small bone tube, spitting the removed objects into a receptacle. Only when the objects were all removed was the patient cured.

When an Ojibwa's disease resulted from sin and consequent punishment from the manitos, the prerequisite for cure was confession (Hallowell 1939a: 191). By themselves, herbs or the sucking rite, even propitiation, were powerless in these cases; the piacular rite was needed first.

Such confessions took place during the shaking tent ceremony. The djessakid and the attendant manitos called upon the patient to testify, just as they might call upon the parents of the patient and elicit confessions of wrongdoings. Even deceased parents could be called back to provide witness, if they had committed sins which now devolved upon their offspring. By so doing, as Hallowell demonstrates (1939a: 196-197), the djessakid reinforced community ethics by demonstrating the forbidden behavior which caused disease. The community was there to hear the confession and to learn what was unethical. The entertainment of the ceremony also provided moral instruction.

Occasionally, but apparently not very often, Ojibwas performed ecstatic shamanistic journeys in order to bring back the captured souls of their patients. Usually the djessakid was able to summon the witch who captured the soul and demand its return; however, in exceptional cases, the curer entered a trance, metamorphized, and traveled great distances, even to the afterworld, in search of the patient's soul. These flights did not necessarily coincide with the shaking tent ceremonies. One shaman in northern Michigan (Smith 1896: 283) turned into a hawk and caught the raven-witch who had stolen the patient's soul, and returned it before the victim died, blowing it into the man's mouth.

To traditional Ojibwas, disease had its reason, its meaning as well as its cure. Everything was explained; everything made sense. Medicine and religion were thus closely allied, the manitos causing and curing many illnesses. Disease could be terrifying in its inexplicable destruction; Ojibwa medical beliefs and practices made sense of it. Their conceptions of the causes and respective cures of diseases which could prevent a hunter from subsistence constituted a significant part of religious thought, just as their preventive and curing rituals made up a large part of their religious ceremonial life.

Historical Crises in Medico-Religious Balance

The coming of whites upset the medico-religious equilibrium. In the historical period the Ojibwas formulated another concept of disease, that caused by whites, created by germ intrusion and resistant to Indian cures.

Father Hennepin in the seventeenth century presented the picture succinctly and ominously. "They know roots and herbs with which they cure all kinds of diseases," he remarked; "they have sure remedies against the poison of toads, snakes and other animals, but have none against the small pox [sic]" (Hennepin 1880: 284). A century later David Thompson the trader and explorer reported (Tyrrell 1916: 321-325) the havoc created by a smallpox epidemic in 1781-1782 among the Ojibwas in Minnesota and southwest Ontario who contracted the pox by wearing the clothes of whites whom they had killed. It spread like a forest fire, killing anywhere from one-half to three-fifths of the Indians in the villages where it hit. Because Ojibwas were living in larger villages, communicable diseases could spread faster and cause greater harm than in traditional times when the family bands remained at a distance from one another. The survivors sacrificed all they had to the manitos in desperation, leaving themselves destitute. The dogs and wolves who ate the corpses of the smallpox victims caught the disease and died. Wild game left the area to avoid the contagion and many other Ojibwas died of starvation. The natives looked to the manitos and the traditional understandings of disease but found no answer, no relief, no meaning. They were devastated.

Smallpox was not the only disease which periodically decimated the Ojibwa population. There were serious epidemics of measles and tuberculosis in the early nineteenth century. Other white diseases such as scarlet fever and cholera struck the Indians, who had no immunization to them. Smallpox did the worst damage. Recorded epidemics occurred in 1781-1782, along Lake Superior in 1846 (McDonald 1929: 115), and in Minnesota and Wisconsin 1882-1883 (Fred Smith to Whipple, 20 September 1882, S.I.R. McMillan to Whipple, 1 February 1883 in Whipple 1833-1934, Box 16), the last still recalled vividly in Wisconsin in the 1930s (Works Progress Administration 1936-1940; 1942, Envelope 9, No. 6, "Totem Pole Ceremony").

In most cases the Ojibwas blamed themselves for mistreating the manitos (or in later years, under Christian influence, the Kitche Manito), but even their improved behavior, sacrifices, and prayers brought no cures, not even under the inspiration of the Shawnee Prophet in 1808. The medicine leaders were powerless against these new, white diseases; the results were terror and a series of crises of religious faith.

The Ojibwas, whom early observers described as healthy, became increasingly disease-ridden. Tuberculosis, pneumonia, high infant mortality, influenza, venereal disease, smallpox, and other diseases reduced Ojibwa life expectancy to 30.8 years in 1953 (Ritzenthaler 1953: 219). Village life, change in clothing, housing, and foods all contributed to deteriorating health.

What effect did the drastic deterioration in health and life expectancy have on Ojibwa religion? It shook the faith in the religious specialists as well as in the manitos and turned them in at least three different directions.

Increase of Witchcraft Accusations

First was the apparent increase in witchcraft accusations. When families became incorporated into large communities where unrelated Indians lived, the anxiety regarding witchcraft increased. Anyone in the area could be a witch. Particularly suspect were the religious leaders themselves, often nonrelatives with no kin loyalties. Jealous of their threatened powers and prestige, the specialists competed with one another and accused each other of evil. Because in traditional times they were thought of as the causers as well as the curers of disease, the increase in sickness brought with it an increase in accusations against the leaders.

Into the twentieth century the Ojibwas still fear strangers, and fear of their own leaders is total. In 1923 a Bad River man was camping with other Ojibwas on a hunt. With them was a Lac du Flambeau medicine man. On the last day the Bad River man killed nine deer by a stroke of luck. A few days later the Lac du Flambeau man accused him of insult and threatened him. Months afterward the Bad River man heard a shaking tent ceremony in the woods at night and knew he was being witched. He went home and the next night started talking to himself. He became seriously ill from the Lac du Flambeau medicine man's witchery (Works Progress Administration 1936-1940; 1942, No Envelope, "The Wrath of a Juggler"). Whether or not the Lac du Flambeau man was guilty of witchcraft, the inbred suspicion of strangers and medicine men combined to find cause for sickness, or perhaps actually to cause the sickness.

The fear of witchcraft has spread in the modern period. At Parry Island, "probably there is not a single adult on the island who has not been accused of sorcery at some time or other, and who has not himself suffered some misfortune which he attributes to the same cause" (Jenness 1935: 97). At Berens River those who are most friendly are most often accused of witchcraft, creating suspicion in all social relations (Hallowell 1960: 40). Ruth Landes' description of the Ojibwas in south-western Ontario bears out the pervasiveness of witchcraft fears in modern Ojibwa society. No activity is safe because all companions can be witches; no relationship is safe, even within families. Whereas her description is extreme in terms of the evidence from all other quarters, it indicates the growth of witchcraft fears in modern times (Landes 1968: 11-13). Aboriginal Ojibwa beliefs about disease, health, and medicine carried the seeds of uncontrolled witchcraft paranoia; those seeds germinated under fertilizing conditions of epidemic crises and have grown into widespread recriminations in contemporary Ojibwa personal relations.

New Religious Movements to Restore Ojibwa Health

The second response was a series of native religious movements whose partial cause was the desire of Ojibwas to right their disastrously unbalanced relations with the manitos and with each other. In particular Midewiwin, which arose in the eighteenth century, taught its members herbal knowledge for a price, honored the manitos and Kitche Manito in order to restore health, and emphasized ethical behavior as a means to maintain health and enforce the faltering societal morality. When Midewiwin declined in the twentieth century, having failed to restore Ojibwa health, its medicinal aspects declined too, and it was overshadowed by other movements, both native and white.

On the plains and prairies, the Sun Dance took hold around 1900; its primary purpose in the twentieth century has been the curing of disease by appealing to the manitos and Kitche Manito in a new way. The Dream Dance — imported from the Dakotas in the late 1870s — did not at first emphasize curing, but in many areas where Midewiwin weakened, the Dream Dance took on curative importance. The Chief Dance, originally a war dance and used as such in World War I, has undergone a distinct change in its purpose so that by the mid-twentieth century its goal is to prevent disease in communities. Finally, the peyote religion has reached some Ojibwas and presents itself as a medicinal panacea.

Medical Crises and Conversions to Christianity

The third response to the medical crisis of Ojibwa faith involved the Christian missionaries and white medicine. Many Ojibwas became impressed by white health or white curing, including that performed by missionaries, and turned toward Christianity as the answer to their medical dilemma.

The early Jesuits, including Father Allouez, carried around chests filled with medicines which they used for curing. One which Allouez favored especially was theriac, a popular remedy of medieval Europe consisting of opium and spices like nutmeg, cinnamon, or mace. When he lost his chest and an Indian doctor found it, the doctor returned it, saying that the medicines were too dangerous for natives like him to handle (Kellogg 1917: 106-107).

Father Druillettes's arrival in Sault Ste. Marie in 1669 was followed closely by an epidemic. The disease helped rather than hurt the mission, however, because of the miraculous cures which the priest claimed to have performed. The Jesuits reported that the cures led directly to conversions (Thwaites 1896-1901, vol. 55: 117-131; vol. 57: 219-237).

Priests and other missionaries, conscious of the role played by cures, prayed to their God to alleviate illness in order to bring about conversions. Nineteenth-century Protestants, too, such as Rev. Barnard and others, attempted to impress their Ojibwa charges by performing homeopathic cures (Schell 1911: 82-92). Father Baraga gave a Catholic relic to an Ojibwa woman, telling her to use it in healing the sick (Hilger 1936a: 292-296).

The traders, too, used medicines in order to influence the Ojibwas. John Long placed a tincture of opium (laudanum) in the rum which he so freely distributed among the Indians to sedate them when they drank (Long 1904: 149). In the face of failure of traditional means to cure new diseases, many Ojibwas turned to white medicine, if not white religion. In 1886 Rev. Wilson wrote that "they make medicines themselves from roots and herbs, but prefer generally to get the White man's physic" (Wilson 1886: 90).

In many cases the Ojibwas recognized that the whites were the cause of disease. A curer opposed Rev. Ayer at Yellow Lake by stating that the sickness prevailing among the Indian dogs the previous summer derived from the missionaries (Tuttle 1838: 81-82). A girl who fell very ill in the 1930s near Emo, Ontario, was told that her disease stemmed from her attendance at a Catholic school and her subsequent conversion (Landes 1968: 52). Native religious leaders attempted to use uncontrolled diseases as weapons against the missions, Christianity, and whites.

Nevertheless, even when Ojibwas concluded that the missionaries were causing disease, their very power to do so impressed the Indians, perhaps leading to conversions. In traditional Ojibwa thought the causes and cures of disease were often one and the same. The mission literature was filled with accounts of conversions brought about by deaths of Ojibwas in contact with the missionaries, even immediately after baptisms (e.g., at Leech Lake, Schell 1911: 80; at LaCroix, Pierz 1947-1948: 281-282).

The governments took a part in the competition with native medical practices and thereby weakened the traditional religion. Although the Ojibwas continued to distrust the white doctors who were placed on United States reservations as part of treaty agreements and reservation policies, the Indian Service discouraged traditional medicine and actively competed with the curers. The Bureau of Indian Affairs handled health services in the United States until 1955, when the Department of Health, Education, and Welfare took over, creating an Indian Health Service within the Public Health Service. This free health care (which still exists) has made serious inroads, as have similar programs in Canada. As white doctors gain prestige, they do so at the direct expense of the native leaders. White medical practices directly undermine the traditional concepts so that, for instance, at Round Lake today, "there are fewer shamans, and more faith is placed in the medicines and treatments of Euro-Canadian doctors and nurses, and in Christianity" (Rogers 1962: D26). At Osnaburgh the Indian Health Service nurses have replaced traditional shamans (Bishop 1974: 88).

Many traditional medical practices continue to some extent. The use of charms and other protective devices persists, as does the pervasive belief in witchcraft. Scattered djessakid ceremonies and other cures still take place where there are active religious leaders. Yet the structure of beliefs that underpinned the traditional practices has eroded. Some Ojibwas practice a few traditional medical forms but the system of explanation and meaning has been destroyed. Furthermore, the contemporary Ojibwas perceive their present state of ill health. In southwest Ontario they say, "People were never sick in those days. They did not get sick until they commenced wearing White clothes, and men began to cut their hair" (Landes 1971: 125). The Ojibwas recognize their weakened condition but they know of no way to revive their lost traditions in order to restore their health.

RELIGIOUS LEADERSHIP

Features within Ojibwa religion, such as myths and shaking tent rites, puberty vision questing and soul journeys, helped provide Ojibwas with a sense of reality and continuity, and fostered a long and healthy life. There were within Ojibwa society certain individuals especially adept and knowledgeable in these religious aspects; indeed, it was often in the person of religious leaders that the aspects held together. Over the historical period, Ojibwa religious leadership has deteriorated, along with the other religious features.

Individual Ojibwa Autonomy and Religious Specialists

In traditional Ojibwa life every person courted and expected to receive a guardian manito who provided identity, hunting powers, and health. To a large extent each person maintained a relation with the manitos without consultation with or guidance from religious leaders. The Ojibwas spent their winters in family groups, under the leadership of the oldest male, who made practical decisions but had no authority outside the family group of perhaps thirty persons (Brown 1952: 58). In the summers no chief ruled supreme over the extended totemic gatherings. In religious as well as civil and psychological matters the Ojibwas maintained a high degree of personal autonomy (see Hallowell 1971: 135). The individual Ojibwa communicated with the manitos directly, not through intermediaries.

Despite this individuality of religious experience and power, there were religious specialists among the Ojibwas (Rousseau 1952: 185). There were no rulers responsible for maintaining relations between the manitos and the general public, but there were Ojibwas whose communication with the manitos was more frequent, more under the individual's control, and more effective than that of the ordinary person. These persons possessed extraordinary influence over the objects of Ojibwa religion, influence gained in their puberty visions. They were not full-time religious functionaries but they served the community with their abilities and led in religious ceremonies.

Religious leaders owed their powers to the blessings and protection of the manitos. They became specialists through divine intercession, not through training or payment. Djessakids and curers owed their talents to the visions granted them by their guardian manitos. Ojibwa children played at being curers but only through the choice of the manitos did one become a religious leader. Parents helped their children to become leaders by encouraging them to accept certain types of visions but the choice of leadership rested with the manitos. In a vision the manitos showed the skills and techniques necessary to perform rituals, summon the manitos, or cure the sick.

Once chosen, the visionary was only a potential specialist. Only after demonstrating abilities did one actually become a leader. Ojibwa religious leadership was charismatic. People judged their leaders by their gifts, which were blessings from the manitos. One's claim to powers served no purpose unless those powers were evident.

Furthermore, Ojibwas did not inherit religious powers (Schoolcraft 1853-1857, vol. 5: 423). There were no families of specialists; on the contrary, each extended family group contained one or more religious specialist who helped the entire group. These leaders were not people set apart from the rest of the group. Their powers were of degree, not kind. They simply were more powerful and better endowed than their fellows. Almost every Ojibwa was a visionary; the leader was the Ojibwa ideal: a highly successful visionary in a community of visionaries.

Women (Landes 1971) could be religious leaders under exceptional circumstances but in the main they took a subsidiary role to the men. Male occupations such as hunting carried a higher value than female duties like carrying loads, tanning hides, and preparing foods. When girls killed game they received no feast comparable to that given boys at the time of their first hunting kill. Girls strove for visions and success but their visions were less emphasized and considered less powerful than those of boys. Men led at ceremonies, performing the more active dances and wearing the more colorful decorations. Myths glorified male activities and leadership.

If a woman received an extraordinary vision, however, she might choose to follow her inspiration and become a religious leader. Some women took up male roles, refused to marry, and

pursued further visions to obtain curing, divining, and dancing abilities. John Tanner's adoptive mother, an Ottawa married to an Ojibwa, acted as a religious leader for her Ojibwa
community, finding game and making important decisions for
the group. Her powers resulted from her puberty vision
(James 1956: 15).

Religious Leadership Roles

The primary roles of religious leaders were curing, providing good health and long life to family members, divining,
controlling weather, finding game and leading ceremonies.
They buried the dead, admonished their fellows to uphold
morality, and passed down myths and other oral traditions.
Their chief functions lay in the area of maintaining community health. As herbal specialists, sucking doctors, djessakids
and shamans, they prevented and fought all sorts of disease,
through the powers granted them by the manitos.

Curers and other religious leaders worked individually.
There were no traditional Ojibwa medical or ceremonial socie-
ties, no associations of djessakids (Hoffman 1891: 157), no
formal means of passing down the communities' religious
knowledge, save the winter narration of myths. Generally each
leader specialized in one area of doctoring or ritual knowledge. Women were known for their herbal recipes but they
rarely acted as sucking doctors or djessakids. Each Ojibwa
stepped into a role of leadership as his or her specialization
was required by the community. Moreover, there existed no
dichotomy between civil and religious authority. Indeed, there
was no standing body of religious or political leadership
among the Ojibwa peoples. Leaders arose in specific situations
as they demonstrated their abilities.

When serving the kin community the religious leaders
received no fee. If a specialist's reputation spread beyond the
family, he or she might charge outsiders for cures. In either
case, religious leaders did not subsist on earnings from their
specializations. Each leader hunted for game in order to
survive. Rather than being a livelihood, religious leadership
was a specialized service for which one received minimal
remuneration. The specialist worked for prestige, not pay (on
the issue of fees, see Hallowell 1942: 31-33).

One of the symbols of religious leadership prestige was polygyny (Kohl 1860: 111). The specialists tended to be exceptional hunters because of their rapport with the manitos and their hunting success enabled them to support large families. Male leaders took more than one wife to help tan the hides of slain animals and perform other domestic tasks. More to the point, male leaders took extra wives to show the community their ability to support them.

The leaders' desire to show off their wealth and power indicated their character. They were fiercely proud and individualistic persons who proved their close relation with the manitos by their successes in hunting, curing, and warring. Each one, because of the favor bestowed by the manitos, considered himself (and less often, herself) superior to other humans and competed with other leaders for community status. The power struggles portrayed in Ojibwa myths (e.g., Landes 1971: 206-208), including those between Nanabozho, his brothers, and the underwater beings, reflected the rivalries among traditional religious leaders.

Because of the leaders' concern for their public image, they took easy offense to real or imagined insults. If the community slighted or mocked them, they took revenge through witchcraft, by creating the illnesses they were empowered to cure, by chasing away the game which they had the power to entice (Landes 1971: 53-59). Rival leaders attended one another's performances in order to learn each other's tricks and perhaps to expose a rival as fraudulent.

False curing activity resulted in ostracism or ridicule (James 1956: 73-74) but did not necessarily lead to a lessening of trust in religious leadership per se. Ojibwas accepted fakes for what they were and turned to the truly powerful for aid (Hilger 1936: 46-47). Because the community was on the lookout for frauds, the Ojibwa specialists had to develop their procedures and tricks and constantly add to their repertoire, in order to show increased powers. For that reason they watched each other perform, in order to learn new techniques of curing, divining, and charming (Hallowell 1942: 69-71).

The religious leaders were limited in their powers by their specializations. Some specialists performed only once a month or risked a diminution of their powers; others possessed such a limited talent that their leadership amounted to a handful of situations. One man on Berens River (reported by Hallowell

1942: 77-79) possessed power to cure a certain woman of a specific disease. When that opportunity arose, he cured her and never cured again. He used up the power allotted him in his puberty vision.

Religious leaders were also limited in their use of power by the belief that overuse of talents led to disease in the specialist's family (Kidder 1918: 85-88). Some Ojibwas were ambitious enough to sacrifice the health of their families but for the most part this belief acted as a control on the search for religious powers. Most shamans ceased their activity rather than endanger their families.

No matter how much power leaders displayed, they did not forget that their abilities and skills resulted from their relation with the manitos. The community associated the leaders with the manitos, as interpreters of their will, as wielders of their powers, but nobody considered the leaders to be rivals of the manitos. At any time the manitos might withdraw their aid and the specialists would become helpless once again, like young children who had not yet made successful vision quests. The specialists' powers were dynamic; they could increase or diminish, depending on the will of the manitos. The leaders did not control the manitos or use them as mindless powers. Neither did any one leader have the aid of all the manitos. Just as each manito held certain powers but not the totality of power, each Ojibwa received the aid of certain manitos but not the totality of manitos.

Ojibwas regarded their religious leaders with awe, respect, dependence and fear. Lahontan claimed that the Indians called their curers fools in their absence but called on them to heal the sick in times of disease (Lahontan 1703, vol. 2: 467). Ojibwas sought their leaders' opinions and ministrations but feared the very powers which made the leaders useful, since the leaders could cause as well as cure disease.

The djessakids, herbal curers, makers of charms, sucking doctors, the ceremonial leaders, all served the religious needs of their community. Not only did they tell fortunes, find lost objects, protect against witches and cure diseases, but more important, they brought the manitos closer to the Ojibwas. In the shaking tent ceremony the djessakid summoned the manitos to answer the people's questions. In curing, the sucking doctor invoked the benevolent powers of the manitos. By assigning causes for people's illnesses, the religious leaders gave meaning to existence by interpreting the will of the manitos. Specialists used their close relations with the manitos to provide game for the community; they used the knowledge provided them by the manitos to counteract the effects of witches. Each Ojibwa stood in relation to the manitos but the religious leaders provided the relational edge needed by the Ojibwas to understand and survive the often hostile world in which they lived.

White Traders, Officials, Missionaries, and the Crises of Ojibwa Leadership

Religious leaders existed by virtue of their demonstrable rapport with the manitos. If a specialist ceased to demonstrate his or her links to the objects of Ojibwa religion, the community sought a new leader. The leader was expendable. Failure meant an end to societal status and position. In the historical period Ojibwa religious leaders suffered numerous failures and lost the support of their Indian communities. The demise of Ojibwa leadership symbolized the downfall of traditional Ojibwa religion (for a study of disintegrating Ojibwa leadership, see Friedl 1950).

Early fur traders weakened the traditional Ojibwa leadership. They favored some Ojibwas over others, thereby elevating their favorites to positions of authority. The trade itself altered Ojibwa village life from kin communities to towns surrounding the trading posts. In these towns the religious leaders of each totem group came together and competed for authority, resulting in divisiveness and distrust. No longer did each leader serve relatives only. The bonds between curer and patient were weakened, along with the institution of religious leadership.

The fur traders became leaders in their own right because of their guns, wealth, and control over the lives of the Ojibwas. Traditionally Ojibwa leaders showed their power by their wealth; fur traders were wealthier than any of the Ojibwas. They possessed large amounts of tobacco, the traditional offering medium to the manitos, and in dispensing it among the Ojibwas they gained religious influence. By the nineteenth century Ojibwas were referring to traders as messengers from the supernatural. When trader Long met with Ojibwas, they promised to hunt for him, "as the great Master of Life has sent a trader to take pity on us Savages . . ." (Long 1904: 92). The

Hudson's Bay Company aimed for a situation in which its employees took advantage of their high status. It ordered its agents to remain aloof from the Indians and insist that the natives bend to the company's commands. At Fort Hope company managers took over the authority of Ojibwa communities, at the expense of native leaders (Baldwin 1957: 68, 74).

Not only fur traders but other whites in positions of authority became sources of power for the Ojibwas. The French and English in their successive regimes tried to establish an official Ojibwa leadership in military, diplomatic, and social areas which would be pliable to Western needs. They heaped gifts, medals, and honors on Ojibwas of their choice but failed to create a stable native leadership (Friedl 1950: 41-42, 68, 94). More often the European military rulers in the Ojibwa area received the Indians' reverence and the local Ojibwa leaders suffered a loss of prestige.

The United States and Canadian governments at first continued the earlier policy of developing responsive Ojibwa leadership but quickly shifted to a policy of treaties in which the white governments usurped the traditional powers of leadership until white officials exercised "legal and eventual moral control over the lives of the Chippewa people" (Keller 1972: 211).

The American governments appointed local chiefs who would agree to the decisions of the whites, thereby destroying traditional authority. The new leaders had no religious prestige in their communities, only the sanctions of the whites (Gilfillan 1901: 74). They were not links to the manitos, but rather messengers of foreign political powers.

When the whites could not gain the aid of their appointed Ojibwa leaders, they assumed the roles of leadership themselves and tried to undermine all native positions of authority. In Canada and the United States the governments provided free and compulsory health care and hospitalization, thereby taking over the curing roles of the religious leaders. Both governments focused their attacks on Ojibwa religion by discrediting the djessakids and other specialists, exposing their tricks, and competing with them. Whites outlawed polygyny among the Indians, thus undercutting the leaders' prestige. The traditional leaders were powerless to overcome white incursions; their lack of clout further diminished their status in community estimation.

Missionaries undercut Ojibwa religious leadership as much as did the governments. The preachers attacked the leaders, competed with them for control, and of course introduced a new religious outlook which conflicted with traditional views. The old leaders had rapport with the manitos; the missionaries debunked the manitos and proclaimed an omnipotent and exclusive God to whom they held the key.

When the Jesuits first railed against the Ojibwa curers, they helped strengthen the traditional leadership as a rallying point of opposition to the missions. Singly and in groups the religious leaders tried to prevent inroads by Christianity through the centuries. But most missionaries, e.g., Father Allouez, stood up to the threats of witchcraft and other reprisals from the specialists (Kellogg 1917: 102-103).

In the contempt they showed for Ojibwa manitos and the specialists who served them, the missionaries impressed many Ojibwas with their courage and power. One Catholic priest approached a fireball which had attacked an Ojibwa man and kept the Indian community at bay. "Undaunted," the priest bared his crucifix and chased the witching object. By intimidating this dangerous power, he demonstrated his own religious powers (Works Progress Administration 1936-1940; 1942, Envelope 15, "Fire Ball at Cloquet, Minn.": 1-2). Father Baraga often braved storms on Lake Superior, to the amazement of Ojibwas who feared the wrath of the Underwater Manito. His feats became the subject of Ojibwa oral traditions and helped him in gaining a position as religious leader (Works Progress Administration 1936-1940; 1942, Envelope 3).

Missionaries accrued authority through their abilities in curing Ojibwa diseases. Many of the clerics carried medicines with them and dispensed them liberally. Father Pierz administered homeopathic remedies and vaccine to many Ojibwas struck by a smallpox epidemic in 1846, so that he "supplanted the medicine men among the Christian Indians" (Seliskar 1911: 75). The cures worked by missionaries diminished the influence of the native doctors, especially when white-introduced diseases like smallpox and venereal diseases eluded Indian understanding and medicines. Djessakids and other religious specialists were hard-pressed to explain the new illnesses; the manitos offered no meaning or curative techniques. Aware of the Indians' disadvantage, missionaries recommended miraculous as well as medicinal cures in order to usurp healing powers and religious leadership among the Ojibwas (Nute 1942: 190, 239).

Preachers gained further power from traditional religious leaders by the authority granted them by Canadian and United States governments. On the Berens River the missionaries gained control through their position as distributors of the government relief rations of food and free clothing (Dunning 1959: 16-17). In the United States Grant's Peace Policy brought the Christian clergy into almost total control of Ojibwa destinies. They controlled food and clothing, and made all decisions of importance affecting their Indian charges. They mediated between the Indian factions which they helped create and selected Christian Indians as their representatives in community councils.

Christian Ojibwa Leaders

In some localities the missionaries sought out the Ojibwa youths who, in traditional times, would have been likely religious leaders: the brightest, most self-confident young men. The preachers made special attempts to convert these youths and use them as catechists, assistants, and deacons. Occasionally these Ojibwas became ordained Christian ministers; they became religious leaders to their people, but as Christians, not pagans.

The nineteenth-century Methodists and Episcopalians made the greatest efforts to train a native Ojibwa ministry, a program which has continued in the twentieth century. The earliest Methodist Ojibwa clergymen included John Sunday, Peter Marksman, Peter Jones, Peter Jacobs and George Copway.

Born in eastern Ontario in 1818, Copway was the son of a Rice Lake religious leader and curer. Rev. James Evans taught the younger Copway to read and converted him in 1830. He studied at a Methodist seminary in Illinois and spent the major part of his life trying to convert Ojibwas and other Indians to Christianity. Before his death in 1863 he had attended the Frankfurt Peace Conference in 1850, published a short-lived newspaper called *Copway's American Indian* in 1851, and translated Christian gospels into the Ojibwa language. His autobiography (Copway 1847), lectures, and writings raised funds for mission work. In his own preaching he followed his Methodist superiors' directives but achieved a formidable position of religious authority as a Christian among the Ojibwas.

In Minnesota the Episcopalians trained Ojibwa deacons at Faribault. Enmegabowh, formerly a Methodist minister, received his orders there and became the native mainstay of the Episcopalian missions in the state. Like Copway, he became a Christian religious leader of Ojibwas. He used his authority to help quell Hole in the Day's 1862 uprising and he persuaded many Ojibwas to move to White Earth when that reservation was founded in 1867 (En-me-ga-bowh 1904). He supervised the native deacons and represented Bishop Whipple on the Ojibwa reservations.

Other denominations in the nineteenth century were less eager than the Methodists and Episcopalians to support Ojibwa ministers. The Catholics were wary of rushing Ojibwas into positions of Christian leadership. Father Baraga wrote in his journal that "One should never try to form a priest of an Indian man, or a Sister from an Indian woman" (Verwyst 1900: 307), an opinion held by other Catholic clerics until after the turn of the century. It was not until 1913 that the first Ojibwa, Philip Gordon, received Catholic ordination. He served the Indian mission field until 1924, when he became a pastor of a white parish (Works Progress Administration 1936-1940; 1942, Envelope 12, No. 19). Other Ojibwas have become Catholic priests in the twentieth century, including one who gave the sermon at one of the ethnic masses — attended by some two hundred American Indians — at the forty-first International Eucharistic Congress of the Roman Catholic Church, held in Philadelphia in 1976 (*The New York Times*, 8 August 1976: 38).

Christianity often attracted interested Ojibwas when native clergy spread its message. Peter Jones was especially effective in drawing other young Ojibwa men into the Methodist fold by showing them that Ojibwas could approach the Christian God just like whites. Rev. Peter Jacobs stated that his conversion to Christianity resulted directly from his seeing Jones in a position of Christian leadership, praying directly to God (Jacobs 1855: 4). He saw a chance that he, too, could become a Christian and still be an Ojibwa religious leader.

Christianity provided a means for some women to assume positions of religious leadership. Women became active Methodist preachers in Algonkian Michigan and a few, following Jane Horn (Sister Marciana) of White Earth (Fruth 1958: 25), became Catholic sisters. In the main, however, Christianity offered no more opportunity for female religious leadership than did traditional Ojibwa religion.

All too often the Ojibwa Christians, catechists, assistants, deacons or ministers were subject to the white missionaries' authority and did not exercise independent leadership as they would have in traditional times. The letters from the Episcopalian native deacons in Minnesota to Rev. Gilfillan (Gilfillan after 1911) indicated their dependence on him and their total deference to his judgments. Gilfillan's letters to Bishop Whipple suggest that the deacons carried out very few tasks of religious import (10 March 1892 in Whipple 1833-1934, Box 22). A committee of Christian Ojibwas petitioned Whipple to ordain more native deacons as priests so they could take up leadership roles and administer communion (Whipple 1833-1934, Box 1). Beyond a score of native clergymen, the new religious leadership of the Ojibwas consisted of white Christians. It may be true that in some areas the missionaries provided the leadership necessary for Ojibwas to adjust from traditional ways of life (Baldwin 1957: 66); however, their help came at the cost of native leadership.

Ojibwa religious specialists suffered from the competition of traders, white government officials, and especially from Christian missionaries. They suffered, too, from their inability to explain the harmful changes facing the Ojibwas. The ineffectiveness with which they treated new diseases was matched by their increasing failure to locate and provide game for hunting. Animals were depleted through overhunting brought about by the fur trade and increased Ojibwa population; however, the Ojibwas blamed the lack of game partially on the inability of their leaders to locate it. They reasoned that the Owners of animals were withholding game from the Indians and the religious leaders were unable to appease the manitos. The leaders were as helpless as everyone else; consequently, they lost their prestige as links to the objects of religion.

New Forms of Native Religious Leadership

New forms of religious leadership arose in the historical period to meet the changing conditions of Ojibwa life, particularly in the areas of health and hunting subsistence. One of the most salient features of Ojibwa leadership change was the formation of associations of specialized leaders. The most famous of these associations, Midewiwin, arose in the eighteenth century. In its fullest form in the late nineteenth century it included elaborate initiations, a hierarchical priesthood, training and fees for members, and regular meetings. Other associations included the Dream (Drum) Dance, the Wabeno association, numerous prophet movements and the peyote religion.

Alanson Skinner has observed that the Plains Ojibwas adopted plains social organizations and established associations for most of the traditional specializations which were formerly practiced by individuals. They initiated associations of djessakids, sucking doctors, and other curers, including a society similar to the plains Heyoka. Skinner has also found that the easternmost group of Ojibwas, the Mississaugas, adopted a False Face society from the Iroquois for the purpose of curing disease (Skinner 1916: 500-505).

The proliferation of religious associations heightened the traditional rivalries between Ojibwa leaders. Community leadership became divided between secular and religious leaders, and the religious leaders were divided into specializations which tended toward factions. The Shawnee Prophet's followers of the early nineteenth century opposed the Midewiwin members. Midewiwin and its offshoots vied with the Wabenos and Dream Dancers for societal authority.

Each of the associations was designed to reestablish a working relation with the manitos which would benefit the Ojibwas. They all sought to regain the traditional relations with manitos which kept Ojibwas in game and in health. Traditionally, however, each leader accepted his or her revelations from the manitos as partial; no specialist claimed the only way to relate to all the manitos. Under the influence of Christian missionaries who preached a message of one God and one way to reach that God, the Ojibwa religious leaders began to emphasize the special revelation, ceremonies, and membership of their particular association as the sole way of reaching either all the manitos or the Christian God.

Even within their associations, the Ojibwa religious leaders argued over the proper ritual and doctrines. Schisms formed within the associations, leading to further factionalism. Further divisiveness resulted, for instance among the Pembina band in Minnesota, from the congealing of separate pro- and anti-Christian parties within the Ojibwa ranks, and the flourishing of ephemeral but influential prophets seeking religious prestige as messengers of God (Gilfillan 1880: 3).

The heritage of conflicting associations and movements of religious leaderships, especially in the late nineteenth and twentieth centuries, has been the increase of witchcraft accusations. Every religious association has been accused by nonmembers of fomenting witchcraft. To many Ojibwas religious leadership has come to mean religious tyranny.

A vicious cycle has formed between deteriorated leadership and increased accusations of witchcraft. As the leaders have fallen into disrepute, they have been accused more and more of witchcraft. Their failure to cure disease has made them suspect as the cause of disease. At the same time the Ojibwas have complained that witchcraft is increasing because there are no longer any powerful curers. In former times the religious leaders fought witches. Now they are powerless to do so and are accused of being the very witches that in traditional times they were expected to combat. In the twentieth century even the most respected conservative leaders like Jim Mink at Lac Court Oreilles (Casagrande 1960: 481) have found themselves regularly accused of witchcraft, their denials notwithstanding.

Decline of Ojibwa Religious Specialists

The irony of declined religious leadership among the Ojibwas is that most of the Indians desire religious leadership more than ever today, at a time when they so little respect their religious leaders. Yearning for religious leadership continues, even though Ojibwas think of their few remaining conservative leaders as potential witches.

The Ojibwas have lost much of their religious heritage. They no longer trust the traditional manitos as their ancestors did. They do not believe in the truthfulness of their once sacred myths. Their aboriginal ceremonialism has fallen into disuse, their medical powers have declined, and they no longer fast for a guardian manito. Isolated from their meaningful past, Ojibwas turn to their surviving religious leaders in order to regain contact with the sources of existence. They need them to perform the most perfunctory religious acts which in traditional times any Ojibwa could have performed, for example, animal ceremonies.

But because almost no Ojibwas today perform puberty quests for visions of guardian manitos, there is little opportunity for young Ojibwas to gain the powers necessary to become religious leaders in a traditional sense. The small numbers of specialists must travel from community to community in order to provide religious services. The situation is such that in Minnesota "one of the few remaining Chippewa shamans complains that he has too much work 'piling up' on him as a result of the failure of younger men to take up the traditional medical specialties" (Paredes, Roufs, and Pelto 1973: 161).

The average Ojibwa has been stripped of much religious knowledge through the centuries and needs a specialist to perform the most basic religious acts. He still feels a need for those religious acts because Christianity has not adequately replaced the traditional religion. Christian clergymen, Ojibwas and whites alike, have failed to deliver to the native communities the religious services once provided by aboriginal specialists. Neither Christianity nor the other religious movements — Midewiwin, the Wabeno complex, the Shawnee Prophet enthusiasm, the Dream Dance, the Ghost Dance and the peyote religion — which have touched the Ojibwas has given the Indians an enduring relation with the sources of their existence.

The past seven chapters have described the most obvious characteristics of traditional Ojibwa religion — soul beliefs, theistic beliefs, myth, ceremonials, visions, curing, and leadership — and their demise, especially during the last century under white domination. The Ojibwas did not simply give up their religion. Through the historical period they refashioned its aspects into new religious movements to be examined in the following chapters.

MIDEWIWIN

In the eighteenth century there arose among the Ojibwas a religious movement known as Midewiwin, or the Grand Medicine Society. Its characteristics included a blending of traditional and Christian elements, such as devotion to both a Supreme Being and the numerous manitos. It contained various origin myths which were recited and acted out at each meeting of the Society. Its members met at ornate, scheduled ceremonies which featured the symbolic slaying and re-vivification of initiates in specially designed lodges, using prescribed paraphernalia such as sacred seashells, animal-skin medicine bags, drums and rattles. Emphasizing the connections between morality and afterlife, a portion of its structure tried to guarantee the attainment of eternal rewards after death. The Society was also characterized by its elaborate pictographic records and hierarchical priesthood (on the identifying characteristics of Midewiwin, see Hickerson 1963: 76; Hickerson 1970: 52; Radin c.1926: n.p.).

Post-Contact Origin of the Grand Medicine Society

Present-day Ojibwas view Midewiwin, now in its decline, as their aboriginal religion; nevertheless, most evidence indicates a post-contact origin of the movement (Hickerson 1962a; Radin no date: 2; Sieber 1950: 127). Springing from traditional beliefs and practices, Midewiwin took form among the Chequamegon Ojibwas sometime after their migration to Lake Superior's southern shore in the 1690s. From there it spread with the Indians into Wisconsin, Minnesota, and southwest Ontario, and touched Ojibwa life as far as Berens River in the north and the Fort Pelly region in the west.

An indigenous Ojibwa development, it took root among the Potawatomi, Menomini, and Fox Indians, as well as the easternmost Dakota, Iowa, Winnebago, Omaha, Ponca and Kansas tribes (Radin no date). In its Ojibwa diffusion the Society underwent alterations but its basic aspects remained wherever it was practiced (map D, p. 175).

The earliest references to Ojibwa Midewiwin came in 1804, in two separate accounts from North West Company traders, Peter Grant and Thomas Conner. Grant noted its initiation

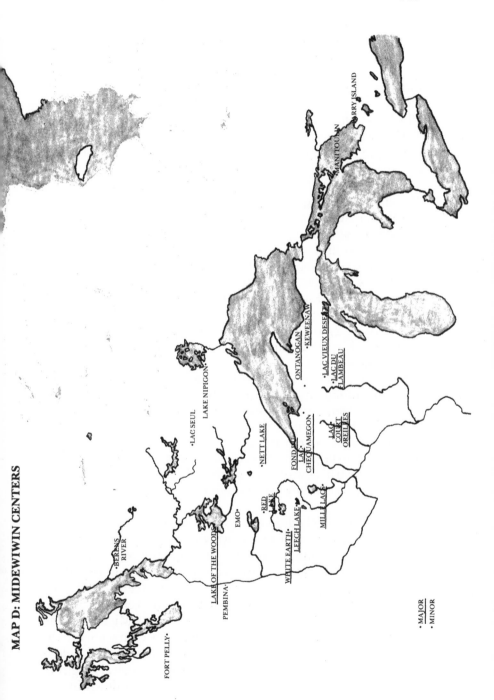

MAP D: MIDEWIWIN CENTERS

MANITOULIN

RRY ISLAND

ONTANOGAN·

·KEWEENAW

·LAC VIEUX DESERT

·LAC DU FLAMBEAU

·LAC SEUL

LAKE NIPIGON·

·NETT LAKE

LAC COURT OREILLES

FOND·

LAC· CHEQUAMEGON

·RED LAKE

MILL LACS·

·EMO

WHITE EARTH·

LEECH LAKE·

·BERENS RIVER

LAKE OF THE WOODS·

PEMBINA·

FORT PELLY·

·MAJOR

·MINOR

ceremonies in southwest Ontario but could make little sense of it, comparing it to Freemasonry (Grant 1890: 361-363). Connor reported that the Ojibwa celebrants near Cross Lake asked him for rum (which he refused them) to use in their ritual. He did not describe their ceremony but commented that it lasted all of that December day (Gates 1965: 260).

Midewiwin may not have taken identifiable shape until the late eighteenth century but two sources in the early part of that century mentioned Ojibwa practices which were central to the later movement. Lahontan described an Indian doctor as a "Quack, who being once cur'd of some dangerous Distemper, has the Presumption and Folly to fancy that he is immortal, and possessed of the Power of curing all Diseases, by speaking to the Good and Evil Spirits" (Lahontan 1703, vol. 2: 467). One of the requirements of membership in developed Midewiwin was to have been cured of a sickness. A Canadian, Antoine Denis Raudot, writing shortly after Lahontan, in 1709 or 1710, depicted a nascent Midewiwin ceremony (Kinietz 1940: 372) in which curers destroyed and revived society initiates with medicines in flamboyant displays of supernatural power.

Still, no suggestion of the full Midewiwin complex appeared until the nineteenth century. The eighteenth century contained less frequent and less intimate contacts between Ojibwas and whites than in the late seventeenth and nineteenth centuries; therefore, the movement formed in historical obscurity. When large numbers of whites entered Ojibwa lands in the nineteenth century, they found a full-blown religious movement which they assumed to have been aboriginal to the Indians.

Midewiwin surely did not exist before the first contacts with whites. The Ojibwas' closest neighbors, the Crees and Ottawas, lacked such a complex; indeed, so did many Northern Ojibwas. Those who dispersed from the Lake Superior area along the northern migration routes in the seventeenth and early eighteenth centuries did not develop the movement; neither did those who drifted south and east into Michigan and southeast Ontario. Only those Indians in contact with the Chequamegon Ojibwas adopted the ceremonies and beliefs associated with Midewiwin, indicating an historical origin of the Society (on the Chequamegon origins of Midewiwin, see Hickerson 1963: 72-75; Hickerson 1970: 57).

That myths of the origin of Midewiwin pinpointed Chequamegon as the initial center of the movement adds further
proof of the Society's relatively recent beginnings, since large
numbers of Ojibwas did not settle the area until the early
eighteenth century. Had the movement been traditional, its
myths would probably have paid closer attention to geo-
graphical locations further east.

Moreover, Midewiwin's ceremonialism and hierarchical
structure were too complex to have found support in traditional Ojibwa culture, with its relatively simple and isolated
family communities (Radin c.1926: n.p.). Ojibwa family units
had too little contact with one another to organize a priesthood such as Midewiwin's, with its lengthy and formal instruction, initiation ceremonies, esoteric knowledge and fees for
medical services. In its systematized ceremonialism, Midewiwin differed markedly from traditional rituals. In its organizational entirety, Midewiwin could not have existed among the
traditional Ojibwas (Hickerson 1970: 54).

Roots of Midewiwin in Traditional Ojibwa Religion

The Grand Medicine Society was not, however, a total
departure from Ojibwa traditions; indeed, it perpetuated
many of them (Hickerson 1962: 405-406; Hickerson 1970).
Although its members often addressed prayers to Kitche
Manito, its code of conduct insisted on homage to the old
manitos. Its origin myths often depicted Nanabozho or one of
the Four Winds as the creator of Midewiwin, and its prayers
called upon the Thunderbirds, Underwater Manito, and
other traditional manitos for guidance and aid.

At every major Grand Medicine ceremony the leaders recited the traditional Creation Myth, recounting the heroic
deeds of Nanabozho and recalling his victories over the
powers of the universe. Often the myth underwent transformations and acquired new episodes through Midewiwin influence, and there existed many — apparently contradictory
— myths of the origin of Midewiwin. Moreover, Mide members often recited the myth in summer months, contrary to
traditional practice. But in its central rite, the killing and
reviving of initiates with sacred seashells and medicine bags,
Midewiwin recreated one of the major structural themes of
the Creation Myth: the necessity of death for the continuation

and strengthening of life. In other Midewiwin rites the dancers represented Nanabozho's successful combat against the manitos of the upper and lower realms.

Furthermore, the Medicine Society carried on the hunting concern and imagery of traditional Ojibwa religion. The actions of shooting or blowing at initiates were described by the Ojibwas in terms of shooting an arrow with a bow. The initiate's heart was said to be marked like the aboriginal muzzi-neneen so that megis, the sacred seashell, would find its target (Bray and Fertey 1970: 206). A Midewiwin song described the shooting; the pictograph which represented the act showed a man shooting an arrow with a bow (Densmore 1910: 45).

The hunting connection in Midewiwin went beyond imagery. All Mides, Society members, learned hunting medicine to help themselves and their neighbors in finding game. Midewiwin prayers were for abundant game, fish, and other food, as well as for good health, long life, fair weather and community ethics (Jones 1919: 325), the concerns of traditional Ojibwas.

The Grand Medicine ceremonies incorporated the ritual components of traditional Ojibwa cult. Mides made tobacco offerings and dog sacrifices to the manitos as part of their official acts. They took ceremonial sweat baths before entering the Medicine lodges. They feasted and danced in order to commune with the objects of their organized religion, just as their ancestors did in their simpler ceremonies. Midewiwin members used mnemonic and ritual pictographs in greatly expanded form, but persisted in traditional representations. Their use of seashells, too, far outran aboriginal custom but did not diverge radically from it.

Most important in this regard, Midewiwin and traditional attitudes toward the manitos coincided. Ceremonies were not rote acts to bring the objects of religion to heel. On the contrary, they were requests — albeit by proud practitioners — for the help and blessings of the powerful manitos. Rituals changed modestly from location to location, but nowhere was Midewiwin concerned with compulsory ritual precision. The Society's members called on the manitos for pity and charity (Bray and Fertey 1970: 204), as traditional Ojibwas did in their vision quests.

The puberty vision complex found its continuation in Midewiwin in that initiates were often required to receive visions of the manitos before approaching Mides for instruction. Visions were not as important in Midewiwin as they were in traditional Ojibwa religion, but their value was recognized and respected as the first step toward Society membership and community with the manitos.

The Society devoted much of its instruction to the knowledge of medicinal herbs and other curing devices. Midewiwin's major concern was the maintenance of health, the combating of disease. Midewiwin taught its members the ways of gaining power over sickness (Bray and Fertey 1970: 199-211), just as the manitos taught traditional Ojibwas to avoid illness. In addition, Mides viewed ill health as punishment for sins against manitos and encouraged Ojibwas to lead ethical, ritually responsible lives. In keeping with traditional morality, the Society encouraged respect for all the living persons of the universe.

Midewiwin taught that every plant had a pharmaceutical use; however, each member cultivated his or her own medicinal knowledge beyond the more elementary recipes (Densmore 1928: 322-323). Midewiwin was a Society, but it was a Society of individuals who persisted in the traditional Ojibwa view that religious leaders should perform their services individually. Mides did not conduct cures as a team; they worked separately as their ancestors did. Midewiwin's initiation gave them the powers to heal and destroy but they used those powers on their own, as though they had received them from guardian manitos in private visions. The Society taught that the religious leader's proper role was to heal the sick, but Mides competed among themselves for clients and boasted of their personal talents and accomplishments. Midewiwin did not snuff out aboriginal Ojibwa pride in personal power. It continued it and many other traditional Ojibwa religious traits.

Christian Influence on Midewiwin

Christian influence played its role in the formation of Midewiwin. The concept of a Supreme God presented by the early Jesuits found its way into Ojibwa beliefs and arose in the Midewiwin complex, as the focus of the movement's worship. Nineteenth-century white observers commented that Kitche Manito's name was especially prominent in Midewiwin ceremonies (Hoffman 1891: 163; Kohl 1860: 49). The Christian God often eclipsed the Ojibwa manitos in the Society.

Most Ojibwas recognized Nanabozho as the founder of Midewiwin, but his mythic role deteriorated from that of creator to that of intercessor, mediating between Kitche Manito and Indians (Radin no date). From master of manitos, controller of the beings of the upper and lower worlds, Nanabozho assumed a subsidiary role to the Christian Supreme Being, the ultimate source of medicine in many of the Society's myths.

Midewiwin received mythic coloring from Christianity and adopted a Christian-like attitude toward its own teachings. Through its instructions to potential members, its pictographic records, and its ceremonial speeches, Midewiwin transformed its concepts into doctrines, explicit articles of belief which were necessary for admission and continued participation in the Society. The Mides gathered and arranged bodies of mythic and ethical doctrines which were very untraditional in their dogmatic assertion.

This process received impetus from the transformation of mnemonic devices into scriptural scrolls. Mides treated their birchbark records as an Indian equivalent of the Christian Bible. They used them as representations of the origin myths, charts of the movement of Ojibwas and Midewiwin, maps to heaven, guides to moral life, instructional catechisms, ceremonial guides and sacred manifestations of Kitche Manito's message (Blessing 1963: 110-111; Dewdney 1975: 21-22). The Ojibwas passed down these scrolls from teachers to students, from community to community, as embodiments of God's teachings. The Christian Bible served as model for the Midewiwin sacred scriptures.

The Medicine Society owed some of its ceremonial paraphernalia to the Christian missionaries, particularly the Christian Cross, which became an insignia for one of Midewiwin's hierarchical degrees. The French and later Canadian Jesuits, including Fathers Allouez, Dumoulin, and Provencher, carried crosses with them on their proselytizing journeys (Holand 1933: 156-159). Their instructions were to plant the Christian symbols in prominent locations in order to demonstrate Christian presence in the area.

One of the Ojibwa names for the French was "people of the waving stick," that is, those who waved crosses over their heads whenever they arrived at an Indian village (Warren 1885: 116-117). The Indians associated the French priests' crosses with the ability to communicate with the Jesuits' God, and incorporated the cruciform into their ceremonialism. In the early eighteenth century Lahontan mentioned that "the Savages never Offer Sacrifices of Living Creatures to the Kitchi Manitou; for their common Sacrifices upon that occasion are the Goods that they take from the French in exchange for Beavers" (Lahontan 1703, vol. 2: 448). When praying to the French God, the Ojibwas thought it best to offer French goods. Mides directed their cult to the Christian God and used Christian symbols to enhance its effectiveness.

Mides also incorporated Christian ethical teachings into their instructions. The Commandments of the Society in Wisconsin included the rule: to do unto others as you would have others do unto you (Works Progress Administration 1936-1940; 1942, Envelope 15, "Initiation in the Midewiwin Society": 1). In southwest Ontario James Redsky's recent Midewiwin teachings discuss the role of the rod and staff in guiding members on the path of righteousness, in order to "love thy neighbor as thyself" (Redsky 1972: 91).

Midewiwin taught that ethical living led to health, but under Christian influence the Society also emphasized the role of morality in determining one's life after death. The shift in focus to a concern for the afterlife represented a turn from traditional Ojibwa concerns.

Christianity helped in the formation of Midewiwin by its organizational example (Kinietz 1947: 175). It imparted to the Medicine Society the idea of a hierarchy in leadership, a priesthood with special duties and knowledge. Midewiwin possessed anywhere from four to sixteen degrees of membership. Almost everyone in a community belonged to the first degree, but the higher degrees constituted the religious leadership of the complex: the doctors, ceremonial leaders, holders of esoteric knowledge and speakers of archaic language. Years of detailed instruction were necessary for the higher degrees, with large tuition fees and initiations into each higher degree within the Society.

Under Christian influence Midewiwin became a type of organizational denomination. Membership enabled the Indian to communicate with Kitche Manito and the traditional Ojibwa manitos. The ability to maintain health and reach the afterworld depended on participation in Midewiwin. Mides respected the partial, personal revelation of visions but they claimed that their religious organization provided the only means to an effective relation between the Ojibwas and the objects of their religion. The Grand Medicine Society's members asserted that Midewiwin was the only means to successful hunting, health, long life and a happy afterlife. They reinterpreted sin to be a lack of participation in and respect for the movement. In the view of the Mides, Midewiwin was the only acceptable Ojibwa religion. In this respect, too, their doctrines reflected a heritage of the Christian missionary message.

Economics and Midewiwin

Midewiwin's organizational hierarchy transcended its Christian model, however, by developing a secret society within the structure of the Society (Hoffman 1891: 224). This cadre of specialists went beyond a secret language, a depth of understanding, and ceremonial knowledge separate from those of the common Ojibwas. The master Mides, those of the highest degrees whose activities were veiled from those of the lower degrees, formed a priestly class apart from the Ojibwa mainstream. They opposed the activities of the djessakids and other religious specialists. They formed an interest group unto themselves, apart from the civic leaders. Such exclusiveness and secretiveness caused alarm among some Ojibwas, charged the Mides with cryptic, hidden witchcraft. The dichotomy between religious leaders and commoners created by Midewiwin's growth resulted in increased suspicion and distrust within the ranks of Ojibwas.

The exclusiveness of Midewiwin leadership was fostered by the high cost of instruction and initiation. The fur trade provided many Ojibwas with sudden wealth. The beneficiaries of the commerce were those able to afford the fees necessary for membership and, if they were able to hold onto their wealth, their children were able to follow them into the higher ranks of Midewiwin. Kohl estimated that an Ojibwa acquaintance of his paid $30,000 in beaver pelts for his Midewiwin education (Kohl 1860: 382-383). James Redsky attended Midewiwin instruction at the cost of approximately $10,000 to his father, who took money from a school grant to see his son through to Medicine Society leadership (Dewdney 1975: 81, 177).

In keeping with the high costs of education, the Mides charged fees for their medical and other services. Their rationale was that the knowledge of Kitche Manito and the lesser manitos was valuable and should not be squandered. Putting a price tag, often an expensive one, on religious information and service derived in no small part from the Ojibwa contact with fur traders and other whites who spread their capitalistic impulses.

White traders contributed in another way to Midewiwin's development by providing large numbers of seashells to the Ojibwas. Several factories in New Jersey collected shells for Indian trade (Kohl 1860: 135-136), and Hudson's Bay Company stores distributed the shells, particularly the currency cowrie, *Cypraea moneta*, to Indians in return for furs (Dewdney 1975: 71). Seashells were always a part of Ojibwa religious paraphernalia, representing the frothing waters caused by the underwater manitos, but that Ojibwas chose a trade item, the cowrie (megis), as their central symbol of Midewiwin indicated the influence of the fur trade on that movement's development. In one of Midewiwin's creation narratives, the arrival of megis "looked as if a white man was loading a great big ship" (Dewdney 1975: 33). It was perhaps no coincidence that Mides constructed some of their special rattles from Hudson's Bay Company tobacco cans (*Stones, Bones & Skin; Ritual and Shamanic Art* 1973-1974: 81).

That Ojibwas purchased admission into Midewiwin, a Society which claimed to be the sole means of Indian relation with the objects of religion, undercut the prominence of visions as the means of establishing relations with the manitos (Benedict 1923: 73). Ojibwas could still seek puberty visions, but if they failed in their attempts they could buy their way into communication with Kitche Manito and the subsidiary manitos. Of course it was not the payment but rather the instruction which the payment bought which established contact with the manitos; nevertheless, the vision was bypassed for less traditional approaches. In some cases parents passed down their Midewiwin knowledge and materials to their children with neither visionary nor monetary prerequisites (Rogers 1974: 141-142). The result was a weakening of the puberty vision quest complex.

The Ojibwa National Religion

As a ceremony the Medicine Dance incorporated most of the traditional ritual components but transformed them into a grander, more systematized format. All central events took place inside a special, open lodge. The Midewiwin officials danced inside; the rest of the community watched from the periphery. Women took a prominent but not powerful leadership role in the proceedings. The ceremonies occurred at scheduled intervals, either once or twice a year. The rituals were precisely what traditional Ojibwa rituals were not: large, regular, lavish opportunities for the entire community to gather as a group and communicate with the objects of their organized religion.

In short, the Medicine Society Dance provided a concentrated focus for community religion. But it did more than that. Within the Southwestern Ojibwa framework and its fringes, Midewiwin served as the tribal Society which provided Ojibwas who participated in it with "national pride" (Schoolcraft 1853-1857, vol. 5: 434). During the early nineteenth century thousands of Southwestern Ojibwas congregated at Chequamegon to join in their tribal religion, to communicate with each other as a people and to communicate, as a people, with their manitos.

For that reason many of the Midewiwin scrolls documented the migrations of the Ojibwa people and their religion, from their creation by the manitos, along the trading routes of their French commercial connection, to Chequamegon and beyond, where they came together as a tribe. Their migration scrolls followed the development of Midewiwin as well as of the Ojibwa people as a tribe because the two came into being together.

The migration scrolls arose from the Algonkian tradition of drawing travel maps on birchbark shingles. In 1729 a Cree of Lake Nipigon guided the traveler Vérendrye by tracing for him a map of the route from Lake Superior to Lake Winnipeg, registering each portage and lake along the way (Burpee 1927: 53). The scrolls which recorded Midewiwin's journey showed not only the style of the Cree guide's map, but also its very path. In so doing, the charts combined theology, geography, and history. To a large degree the history of Ojibwa

contacts with whites and the history of Midewiwin's development were congruent, if not synonymous.

Midewiwin never encompassed all Ojibwas, but for those
that it did, it provided a central event, a common heritage, and
an organized leadership which helped create the Ojibwa tribe.
In the words of Harold Hickerson, "Midewiwin and its priesthood provided a mythology and a paraphernalia symbolic of a
new tribal unity which stemmed from the coming together
and integration of once discrete autonomous kindreds" (Hickerson 1962: 405). The Medicine Society was not an institution
of the relatively isolated aboriginal communities, but rather a
tribal development. Sociologically, the Society helped pull
together Ojibwa society, providing a common past and a
common cult for Ojibwas.

In this regard it is significant that Mides addressed one
another as relatives (Kohl 1860: 40-44). As totemic bonds
weakened, Midewiwin helped cohere tribal loyalties. Already
in the early nineteenth century white observers commented
that Midewiwin was the characteristic which identified Ojibwas as a people (Harper 1971: 52, 57).

Midewiwin was an organization which developed cohesive
religious leadership in the growing Ojibwa villages of Lake
Superior's south shore. Where numerous clans came together
in one location, traditional totemic authority faltered. Midewiwin provided the structure through which religious specialists could join together to make group decisions without giving
up their individual secrets and powers (Hickerson 1970: 53).
It gave young and ambitious men and women an opportunity
to join the ranks of leadership, but it maintained the means by
which old leaders could continue their sway.

Midewiwin's organization made it possible for religious
specialists, particularly curers, to share their medicines for the
good of their communities. In the face of medical crises,
Midewiwin attempted to maintain and improve Ojibwa health
through a new religious orientation. Curative concerns lay,
from Midewiwin's inception, at the heart of its purpose.

Most of the myths of Midewiwin's origin attested to the
curative nature of the movement. One accounted for the
Society's beginnings by stating that Kitche Manito and the
other manitos sent it to cure illnesses and deaths caused by a
broken taboo (Copway 1858: 163-169). Another said that the
manitos gave Midewiwin to newly created Indians to prevent

extinction caused by sickness (Hoffman 1891: 172-173). A third told how the Shell (megis) pitied Indians for their sickness and sent his messenger to Kitche Manito, who called a council and sent the messenger to teach Indians the Medicine rites (Landes 1968: 96-97). Most of the versions mirrored the myth of the origin of diseases and remedies, which stated that unbalanced or incomplete relations between humans and manitos resulted in disease. After a council, the manitos took pity on the sick humans and provided them with a cure. In Midewiwin's case, the cure derived from a reestablishment of relations with Kitche Manito and the lesser manitos.

Some of the narratives recounting Midewiwin's origin reflected the historical situation of smallpox and other epidemics which spread through the Ojibwa trading-post towns. One of the Mides' traditions stated that their rite came to them from Kitche Manito through the intercession of Nanabozho "in a time of trouble and death. . . ." Due to a great "pestilence" which killed many of them while living in "one great village," Midewiwin came about (Warren 1885: 67). The Mides claimed that the events in their myth took place while the world was new, but those events described their recent past.

Midewiwin's songs called for good health, successful cures, and long life. Its pictographs portrayed the diseases of the human body and the herbal cures for each illness. Medicine pouches and other Midewiwin paraphernalia contained roots, leaves, and other medicinal materials. The Society arose in part to systematize and improve curing. When Rev. Skolla visited Fond du Lac in 1846, he attended a Medicine Dance at which one Ojibwa spoke: "Our forefathers have faithfully kept the great medicine dance until this day because it prevents sickness and keeps our children healthy" (Verwyst 1914: 247).

Since Ojibwas associated health with correct morality, Midewiwin strove for tribal health by encouraging and enforcing tribal morality. A Mide told Frances Densmore that "the principal idea of the Midewiwin is that life is prolonged by right living, and by the use of herbs which were intended for this purpose by the Mide manido [sic]" (Densmore 1929: 86-87). Midewiwin taught that proper conduct determined one's length of healthy life.

Proper conduct in Midewiwin's terms included truthfulness, generosity, and family loyalty. Mides preached against stealing, drinking liquor, and dishonoring native women. Morality also involved respect for Midewiwin, its leaders, and for the manitos from whom it drew its authority and power. During a Medicine Dance witnessed by Rev. James Evans on the shores of Lake Superior in the early nineteenth century, the oldest man in the community exhorted his Ojibwa listeners to continue their Ojibwa religious heritage. If they did, he promised, they would attain the great age and continuing health which he enjoyed. Their hair would become as white as his (Evans 1835: 3).

Relationship between Midewiwin and Christianity

To defend and uphold their traditions, Mides criticized Christianity and encouraged Ojibwas to resist the missionaries' message. Midewiwin represented conservative elements within the native ranks which competed with the Christian preachers and their Indian sympathizers. The 1846 Mide at Fond du Lac gave a history of the Ojibwas and their relations with the manitos. He prodded his listeners to continue in their native veneration because their very existence depended on their faithfulness. He concluded: "Whereupon, my children, do not join the faith of those living men who are in black clothes and preach the Cross, but faithfully guard your household gods, as did your fathers, so that our tribe will not be scattered among other nations or utterly broken up or exterminated" (Skolla 1936: 239). The Mides made no secret of their opposition to Christianity; they increased their ceremonies and exhortations when the missionaries entered their areas.

Midewiwin's opposition to Christianity did not always take the form of hostility; nevertheless, Mides expressed their conviction that the Medicine Society was the proper, indeed the only, way for Ojibwas to enjoy relations with the manitos. A Mide from Nett Lake said of the birchbark scrolls of his Society: "When the manito spoke to the Indians, he told them to worship according to this parchment; he told the white people differently — the way they worship" (Reagan 1933: 516). Another Mide said that anyone who tried to distract the Ojibwas from practicing Midewiwin was an agent of Matchi

Manito, since the manitos gave the Society to the Indians so they could communicate with the sources of their health and life (Kinietz 1947: 179). Other Ojibwas repeated their conviction that Midewiwin's sacred scrolls held more religious knowledge and use for the Indians than did the Christian Bible.

Opposition to the missionaries and their religion did not preclude borrowing from Christianity. Midewiwin incorporated many Christian elements into its complex and redirected Ojibwa worship to the supreme God. In its desire to see its members through to a heavenly afterlife, the Society imitated Christianity.

There was the hint that Ojibwas saw Christianity as a way to attain white wealth and power; therefore, they borrowed aspects of Christianity in order to improve their worldly existence, in keeping with the nature of their traditional religion. Wealth from the fur trade helped nourish Midewiwin's flowering. Wealth may have also been one of the Society's goals, for example, when Mides danced to the song, "I have them, the goods from the whites" (Bray and Fertey 1970: 202). Mides did not always disparage white ways. Some members of the Society participated in Christian rituals as well as their native cult.

Decline of Midewiwin

Midewiwin fostered Ojibwa unity, organized religious leadership, maintained curing, upheld morality and combated Christianity, while conserving aspects of traditional religion. Moreover, it provided a new means for Ojibwas to communicate with the sources of their existence, the objects of their religion. As Ojibwas experienced crises of belief and unsatisfactory relations with the manitos, Midewiwin sought to reestablish proper relations with the traditional manitos and enter a new relationship with Kitche Manito.

In its broadest attempts Midewiwin has failed to achieve lasting success. By the end of the nineteenth century the movement was beginning to weaken. It never spread to all Ojibwas and by the 1930s its influence was receding. It disappeared from Berens River and the areas west of Lake Manitoba and was reduced to handfuls of active members along the eastern fringes of its realm in east Wisconsin. Even within its stronghold in Minnesota and southwest Ontario many modern Ojibwas have viewed it as a folly, or worse, a danger (Balikci 1956: 173; Hickerson 1970: 52; Sieber 1950: 128).

The Grand Medicine Society's decline resulted partially from the dispersion of Ojibwas throughout the nineteenth century. As they left the Chequamegon area, spread out onto the prairies, and settled around the numerous inland lakes of Minnesota and beyond, their bonds of allegiance to the tribal Midewiwin waned. Rather than congregate as a whole at Chequamegon, each village conducted its own rituals and initiated its own members. The Society changed to fit local conditions and lost its ephemeral cohesion.

Missionaries and government agents in Canada and the United States discouraged and even forbade Medicine Dances. An observer who conducted an investigation of Midewiwin concluded in 1891 that American officials would soon drive the Society underground and eventually destroy it (Hoffman 1891: 300). His predictions were not far wrong. In Canada Ojibwas gave their scrolls to museums to prevent government officials from destroying the sacred records (Cadzow 1926: 124).

Midewiwin's continuity was threatened by its own organization. That very few of the Mides knew the entirety of the movement's knowledge led to steady depletion of that knowledge as old Mides died without passing on their privileged information. When Midewiwin became defensive in response to government persecution, its priests increased their secrecy and the Society as a whole thereby lost more of its traditions through time. The gap widened between the master Mides and the members of the lowest degrees of Midewiwin, and there were fewer followers prepared to take the higher orders. Recently James Redsky sold his scrolls to the Glenbow-Alberta Institute in Calgary because he had no successor (Dewdney 1975: 4-5). Hierarchical succession was also hurt by the high fees necessary for instruction and initiation. Most Ojibwas could ill afford the cost of upper Midewiwin membership.

The breach between most Ojibwas and the few remaining active Mides has fostered distrust. In some contemporary Ojibwa villages the Mides are regarded as witches and feared for the harm they can cause. Because the Ojibwas do not know Midewiwin's secrets, they assume that the secrets are dangerous. They fear what they do not know.

A recent study of Midewiwin calls it "nearly defunct" (Vennum 1978: 753). Midewiwin has continued at Leech Lake, Mille Lacs, and other locations in Minnesota, southwest Ontario, and Wisconsin, and in the past decade has spread from there to other locations in a new efflorescence. For the most part, however, the rituals are secret and many Ojibwas know nothing of the Society's content or intent. The declining movement is closed to most Ojibwas and in most places does not function as an effective means of communication between humans and manitos. Contemporary Midewiwin holds little more currency than the traditional religion, Christianity, or the diverse religious movements in which some Ojibwas have participated over the recent centuries.

DIVERSE RELIGIOUS MOVEMENTS

Besides Midewiwin, other religious movements of diverse character touched the Ojibwas through the historical period. None of these achieved the breadth of Midewiwin among the Ojibwas, or received a wide scope of interest among white observers. As a result, a religious analysis of the movements must be considered suggestive rather than complete. Among these movements were the Wabeno complex, the Shawnee Prophet enthusiasm, the Dream Dance, the Ghost Dance and the peyote religion.

Wabeno Movement

The Wabeno movement began in the area around Lake of the Woods and along the Red River, north of Pembina, around 1796. David Thompson, who visited a North West Company post in the area two years later, reported (Tyrrell 1916: 255-258) that its rise occurred when traditional songs, dances, and other ceremonial components fell into disuse. Led by two or three men who received visionary inspiration, the Wabenos were organized into two orders, with initiations, special language forms, a dance and sacred tambours and rattles. In some areas women could neither participate in the rituals nor touch any of the special paraphernalia. Thompson observed that the complex spread, as young men purchased their admission into the society from the visionary leaders.

In Thompson's time and into the nineteenth century, the old religious leaders scorned the new religious upsurge. They ridiculed the Wabeno manitos, calling them weak. Established specialists and Mides considered the upstarts fraudulent and dangerous (James 1956: 122-123).

Wabenos showed their powers by juggling and fire displays, by taking coals and red hot stones in their hands or mouth. Some plunged their hands into boiling grease or water, or tore off their burned flesh with their teeth while singing and dancing. Others breathed fire through reeds in their mouth (Grant 1890: 363; McKenney 1827: 322-323).

At one of their major ceremonies, the Fire Dance, they tested the potency of medicines such as yarrow by placing them in pots of boiling water, while singing the Wabeno songs.

191

Then they bathed their hands in the herbal waters and attempted to hold burning objects. If their flesh did not sear, the Wabenos determined the herbs to be strong and used them against diseases (Works Progress Administration 1936-1940; 1942, "Types of Dances Practised by Chippewas of Lake Superior": 2).

Besides holding powers to cure, Wabenos served their communities by making charms for success in war, love, and especially in the hunt (Hoffman 1891: 156-157). Indeed, the key to understanding the Wabeno complex was its association with failed hunting in the late eighteenth and early nineteenth centuries. The animal population in the Lake of the Woods area in the 1790s had declined drastically and the Wabenos represented an attempt to reestablish communication with manitos to provide a resurgence of game.

The mnemonic prayerboards used by the Wabenos demonstrated the hunting purposes of the complex. They showed Nanabozho's calling all the animals together, making them subject to humans, thereby giving Indians the right to hunt. Other boards showed Nanabozho's bestowing special powers to Wabenos to control the animals through their manito Owners. The Wabenos pictured on the boards danced to thank the Culture-Hero for the powers he gave them (Burton 1909: 242-246). The fire ceremonies used by the Wabenos represented Nanabozho's theft and control of fire for the good of humans in the Creation Myth. By handling fire the Wabenos imitated Nanabozho, possibly identifying with him and sharing in his strength, all in an attempt to regain their lost hunting prowess.

The Wabenos appealed to traditional manitos and recalled the aboriginal myths. Their ceremonies used dance and song as means of religious communication, but the rituals themselves were innovations. Visionaries played prominent roles in the founding of the movement and thus continued an essential aspect of the traditional religion, as did their concern for hunting and curing (Jenness 1935: 62-63). Their leaders, however, vied with the older specialists. And when hunting did not increase, the movement vanished, leaving unassociated Wabenos in undefined positions, serving no apparent religious function and falling increasingly under the accusations of witchcraft. As a movement the Wabeno complex lasted no longer than the early twentieth century.

Shawnee Prophet Enthusiasm

An even shorter-lived attempt to right ruptured relations with divinity was the Shawnee Prophet enthusiasm, around 1808. The Prophet, brother of famed Tecumseh, sent messengers to the Ojibwas, particularly in the area of Lac Court Oreilles. These emissaries painted their faces black and performed rites at which they told the Indians that the Master of Life was finally condescending to hold relations with Indians, through the Shawnee Prophet. If the Ojibwas would return to their aboriginal customs, cease the use of steel, guns, and other white-introduced items, the Supreme Being would pity them and communicate with them. The messengers also urged the Ojibwas to cease their drinking, lying, stealing and fighting with one another. The Prophet enthusiasm competed with Midewiwin, calling it a band of witches who had strayed from the Society's initial purposes. The Prophet's followers encouraged medicine men to throw away their poisons and accept the new songs and message of the Prophet. If the Indians did these things, the Supreme Being would deliver them from dependence on the whites (on the doctrine of the Prophet, see James 1956: 144-147; Warren 1885: 320-322).

A spokesman for the Prophet invited a delegation of Ojibwas to meet with the leader at Detroit. Over 150 canoes filled with Ojibwas, including a dead child whom they hoped to be resuscitated, set off for Detroit but most turned around at Sault Ste. Marie. Those who completed the pilgrimage experienced disappointment in the Prophet and the movement faded quickly, but not before the Lac Court Oreilles Ojibwas, in their bitterness against whites, pillaged a trading post (Warren 1885: 323-324). Local Ojibwa prophets echoed the Shawnee's words and gained some followers, but none achieved a lasting influence (James 1956: 169-170, 185-190). Ojibwas did not remove themselves from whites. Neither did they enter new relations with the Master of Life which brought about any of the promised results.

Dream Dance

Of more lasting importance was the Dream Dance. Originating among the Dakotas around 1877, this religious movement spread to the Ojibwas by means of Dakota emissaries the following year. Its central feature was a circular dance, fashioned on the old Grass or Omaha Dance of the prairies and plains. But as the movement traveled among the Ojibwas, Menominis, and Potawatomis, the Fox, Iowa, Shawnee, Winnebago and Osage Indians, it took on local variations. Today it is in serious decline among the Ojibwas, but it is far from dead as a means for some Ojibwas to communicate with divinity.

According to its myth of origin, the Dream Dance began when a band of Dakotas fell to United States soldiers. An adolescent Dakota girl escaped the carnage and hid in a lake or river. She remained there for a long time, perhaps as long as ten days, until she was about to faint. Then she was lifted from the water into the air, and a voice told her not to be afraid, that she was brave and had been chosen as a recipient of an important message from the Supreme Being. She was to spread the use of a new dance (which used a distinctive drum) to her people and beyond, even to the whites. The voice promised protection from whites for all Indians, and it gave her detailed instructions for the construction and use of the ceremonial paraphernalia. She followed the command and the Dream Dance grew (for versions of the myth, see Armstrong 1892: 156-160; Barrett 1911: 256; Works Progress Administration 1936-1940; 1942, "The Origin of the Ceremonial Powwow Drum": 1-5).

The purposes of the Dream Dance movement included revitalization of community ethics and the fostering of pan-Indian friendship, two aspects of the earlier Shawnee Prophet enthusiasm. In addition, the ceremonies took over traditional religious services, such as the naming of newborn children. As a broadly-purposed movement it competed with Midewiwin and even attempted to replace the older Society, claiming that the Mides were too corrupt to communicate successfully with the Supreme Being (Reagan 1934: 36). Its members did not compete directly with Mides in the area of curing, since medicine was a minor aspect of the Dream Dance, but as a rallying point for conservative Ojibwas it duplicated many of Midewiwin's functions (Rohrl 1972: 220-223).

Like Midewiwin and the Shawnee movement, the Dream Dance directed its religious attentions to the Supreme Being and created a new mythology to explain and define the relations between the subjects and objects of religion. Like Midewiwin, it contained a fixed ritual, although the Dream

Dance ritual came directly from the Dakotas. Its ritual components — dances, feasts, songs and humor — and attitudes did not differ significantly from those of traditional Ojibwas, but the dance itself was of foreign origin.

The Dream Dance emphasized the use of distinctive paraphernalia. Besides the blue, red, and yellow drum, the Dreamers employed special calumets, pouches, and dishes, each with appointed functionaries to look after them. Like the Mides, the Dream Dancers held hierarchical positions with stated duties. Membership in the Society of Dreamers resulted from visions, purchase, or inheritance of a ceremonial item. Participation in the Dream Dance, however, was open to all, including whites.

Traditional Ojibwa dependence on visions continued in the Dream Dance movement. The complex arose from a vision, and spread because of the valid visionary experience of the founder. The ten days which she spent under the water matched the traditional length of a puberty vision quest. Moreover, the complex underwent wide changes due to visions of local members, including the appearance of the Christian Virgin Mary to a local rite founder (Howard 1960: 118-119). In another case, a teenage girl experienced a series of visions which foretold the end of the world by flood. These visions led to the local acceptance of the Christian Cross as a central ritual symbol (Barrett 1911: 326-332).

Although proponents of the Dream Dance competed with Christianity, the movement borrowed some Christian elements. The prominent role of the Virgin Mary and the Cross, and the frequent mention of Jesus Christ as well as Kitche Manito indicated the Christian influence. The spread of the movement showed the effects of Christian missionary theory and practice. Like the Shawnee Prophet adherents, and later Ghost Dancers and peyotists, Dream Dance communities preached the message of the new relations with the Supreme Being to other Indians in a way reminiscent of Christian proselytizers.

Ghost Dances, Peyote Religion, and Other Cults

The Ghost Dance came to the Ojibwas from the Dakotas, as did the Dream Dance. In 1889 a delegation of Dakotas visited White Earth, where the Ojibwas learned the dance which announced the end of the present world, the return of the dead, and the reestablishment of the aboriginal order, freeing Indians from white control.

From White Earth the dance traveled to Cass and Leech Lakes, despite the opposition of missionaries, including Rev. Gilfillan and Bishop Whipple. The Office of Indian Affairs did all it could for the "suppression of this evil" (T. J. Morgan to Whipple, 7 July 1891 in Whipple 1833-1934, Box 21), but by the summer of 1891 as many as three hundred Leech Lake Ojibwas were taking part in the dance, haranguing against whites, and threatening violence. By the following spring the Ojibwa enthusiasm for the Ghost Dance subsided (Gilfillan to Whipple, 15 July 1891, 26 April 1892 in Whipple 1833-1934, Boxes 21-22), but the legacy of anti-white sentiment played a role in the 1898 Leech Lake uprising, the last Indian battle with United States troops. Little is known about Ojibwa participation in the Ghost Dance, and its effects did not apparently continue into the twentieth century.

Leech Lake was also the scene of a small but persistent Ojibwa participation in the peyote religion, which promised to cure all diseases through the intercession of the peyote plant between Indians and the Supreme Being. Mides opposed peyote's use, as did Christian missionaries and white officials, but a core of adherents persisted in the religion and taught peyote's powers to other Ojibwas in Minnesota and Wisconsin (Blessing 1961a: 3-8). Peyote represented a new religious orientation for the few Ojibwas who took it. Peyotists claimed that the plant was the only effective means of communication between Indians and the Supreme Being. The religion bypassed the traditional Ojibwa manitos, myths, ceremonies and leadership, although it fostered an induced form of visionary experience consistent with traditional visions. It competed with the other historical religious movements but never gained as great a success among the Ojibwas as with Indians of the plains or the American Southwest.

Other dances and movements touched Ojibwas, seeking either to reestablish relations with traditional manitos or reorient Ojibwas to new religious sources. On the Berens River a local ghost dance occurred which sought to communicate with the dead, Jesus, and the Supreme Being in order to cure sickness (Hallowell 1971: 161-169). A rain dance in the Fort Pelly region tried to integrate Christian, plains, and traditional

Ojibwa religious elements into a meaningful whole (Shimpo and Williamson 1965: 217-225). The plains Sun Dance also attempted this difficult task. Midewiwin spawned a society of dancers which tried to mediate further between humans and the traditional manitos (Reagan 1934: 39). None of these movements constituted a viable new Ojibwa religion.

Today some Ojibwas look to their traditions in the hope of reviving them. Each of these movements has helped a few Ojibwas improve their relations with manitos or the Supreme Being, but none has replaced the failing traditional religion as the eminently successful means of establishing and maintaining communication between large numbers of Ojibwas and the sources of their existence.

THE LOSS OF OJIBWA RELIGION:
A CASE IN POINT

In the course of the past three centuries, the Ojibwas' traditional religion has disintegrated as they have lost their trust in their aboriginal manitos and in themselves. They have stopped telling their myths as true and meaningful accounts of a living universe, and have changed many of their religious rituals. Today they hold very few shaking tent ceremonies. In addition, the Indians have ceased their traditional puberty quest for visions of guardian manitos. The Ojibwas no longer possess the ability to find game and cure diseases through religious means, and their religious leadership has lost status, prestige, and power. In short, their traditional religion no longer exists.

In its place, some Ojibwas have turned to Christianity, Midewiwin, and other religious innovations in order to maintain their existence. But none of the religious movements has brought back abundant game; none has improved Ojibwa health. None has demonstrated the lasting strength of the traditional manitos or initiated a lasting interest in new objects of religion. Despite vestiges of their traditional religion, traces of recent religious developments, sporadic participation in Christianity and a recent renewal of interest in their past, most Ojibwas remain alienated from the traditional sources of their existence.

The loss has carried serious ramifications for the Ojibwas in their daily lives. Their religion was concerned with such vital issues as survival and ethics, and it provided them with a sense of coherency, meaning, and security. Now gone, it has taken with it the Ojibwas' firm grasp on life. Economic hardship, political impotence, environmental imbalances, and other tangible factors have helped produce the contemporary Ojibwa malaise, but in large part it also derives from their religious alienation.

Traditional Ojibwas viewed essential matters, those concerning health, subsistence, social organization and leadership, ultimately from a religious perspective. Today that perspective has been demolished, and the Ojibwas appear disoriented, having found no suitable replacement.

Much of the religious disintegration has occurred under the heavy, often brutal hand of whites. Missionary, business, and governmental policies have more often than not succeeded in eradicating Ojibwa religion. It is ironic that Western society, while undergoing its own religious alienation, has tried to impart to Ojibwas and other non-Westerners its older religious sense, but instead has served to share an intensified form of its own modern disaffection. White policies have often forcibly set the Ojibwas adrift from their ultimate moorings, without offering them alternative means of spiritual support.

The resulting Ojibwa anomie — in reservations and cities alike — evidences itself in mundane activities; however, it is even more apparent in situations of disaster. At such times, Ojibwa vulnerability and confusion brought about by religious loss seem most striking.

Grassy Narrows Ojibwas

Between 1962 and 1970 the Dryden Paper Company in Ontario dumped an estimated 20,000 pounds of mercury into the Wabigoon River, precipitating a most severe ecological, medical, and economic disaster at Grassy Narrows Indian Reserve, eighty-four miles downstream (map E, p. 200). Following the suspicious death of an Ojibwa man in 1970, exceptionally high levels of toxic mercury were discovered both in the river and in the bodies of Grassy Narrows Ojibwas.

Symptoms of mercury poisoning, including tunnel vision, loss of balance, numbness of extremities, slurred speech, loss of motor coordination, and eventual birth defects, and the similarities to the infamous Minamata tragedy in Japan brought a flurry of attention to the reserve. Books and articles documented the poisoning and the Canadian government's role in the affair (e.g., McDonald 1976; McLeod 1977; Troyer 1977). In 1978 the Canadian authorities agreed to mediate between the Ojibwas and the Ontario Provincial government which bore legal responsibility for the contamination.

In assessing the impact of the poisoning on Grassy Narrows, it was discovered (Erikson and Vecsey 1980) that the destructive force of the mercury — which toxically tainted Wabigoon fish, the Grassies' chief source of protein — was frightfully worsened by the fragile condition of the Grassy community in 1970. Weakened by decades of successive disasters brought

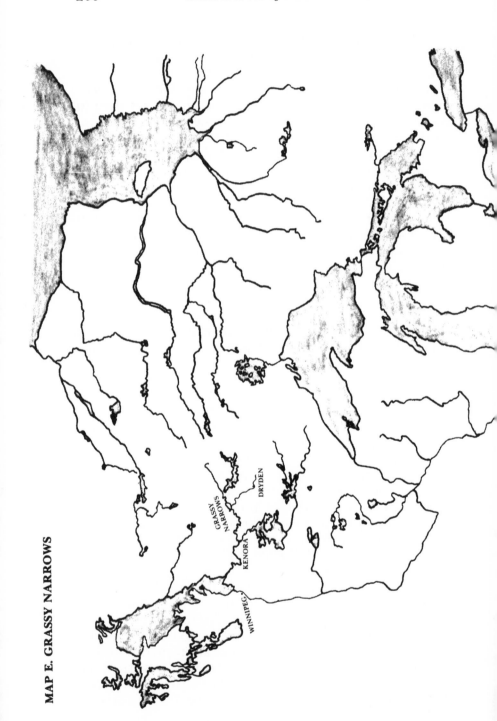

MAP E. GRASSY NARROWS

GRASSY NARROWS

DRYDEN

KENORA

WINNIPEG

about by white intrusions, the Grassy people were especially vulnerable to the bewildering devastation brought by the mercury. The Indians could make no sense of or adjustment to their dilemma. The result was societal disintegration, typified by a death rate in which over 60 percent resulted from accident, alcohol poisoning, suicide and homicide. Today 34 percent of Grassy Narrows adults are alcoholics. Statistics on crime, attempted suicide, hospitalization, school dropouts and desertion all indicate a community (or lack thereof) mired in despair (Grassy Narrows Band 1979: 16-22).

The Grassy people of today differ extensively from their ancestors of only a century ago. In 1873, when they ceded much of their land to Canada through Treaty #3, the local Ojibwas maintained most of their material and spiritual culture. After the arrival of the fur traders in the 1730s, the Ojibwas of western Ontario applied their aboriginal hunting, trapping, and fishing skills to a new economy. At the same time they secluded themselves from white influences, as the missionaries who visited them in the 1840s learned. Over 50 miles from the nearest white town, Kenora, the Grassy folk held on to their clan loyalties and political autonomy into the late nineteenth century, despite brief annual visits from Indian agents on Treaty Day. The Indians enjoyed the security of distance from white inroads.

In 1907 Grassy men helped build the Canadian Pacific Railroad, leaving the reserve and returning to it when they chose. Some traveled through Canada; others served as guides for white sportsmen. Still others adjusted to a cash economy by harvesting wild rice and fishing commercially. Into the early twentieth century the Grassy Narrows Ojibwas persisted in their freedom, while adapting old skills to new conditions.

The twentieth century brought disasters, however. In 1919 an influenza epidemic killed around 75 percent of the Grassy population, leaving about 100. The disaster not only shook the native economy and social system, but it also threw the aboriginal religion into disarray. Traditional healers, powerless to explain or combat the disease, experienced spiritual tensions. As a former Grassy chief says, "They were just buffaloed; they didn't know what to do. Some of them even blamed themselves; they didn't know anything" (Keewatin 1979). However, the epidemic did not demolish the religion; indeed, "It started right up again; everybody got into it" (Keewatin 1979).

At the same time, however, old ways were being under-
mined by coercive government attempts to deny Grassy Narrows autonomy. Treaty #3 charged the Canadian government
to provide education to the Grassy people, and the lawmakers
interpreted this to mean residential schools which forced
Ojibwa children from their families for long periods of time.
The present Grassy Narrows chief, who attended one of these
boarding schools, describes them:

> They stole the children away. The Catholics had these big schools.
> The nuns and priests got paid by the government. They took us
> away from our home life. Showed us their religion and capitalism.
> Brainwashed the children. This was the Roman Catholics' defi-
> nition of education (Fobister 1979).

In his view, the schools were intended to strip the Indians of
their language, religion, and native skills, in short, their
Ojibwa identity.

From 1907 until 1968, Grassy children were put in boarding
schools run by Oblate priests and sisters. There they were
subjected to daily routines of manual labor, performed for the
benefit of the religious authorities. They received severe
physical punishments and a steady diet of enforced acculturation, which today they recall with anger and bitterness
(Fobister 1979; Keewatin 1979; Loon and Payesh 1979). Particularly they resented the systematic attack on traditional
Ojibwa life.

Resentment against the missionaries is very strong. It is
alleged that from 1932 until 1935 they persuaded the Royal
Canadian Mounted Police to persecute Grassy religious leaders by raiding Midewiwin ceremonies, forbidding shaking tent
rites, harassing and arresting members of the Grassy population for their religious activities, thus forcing the traditional
religion underground.

The Religious Crisis

Some religions thrive under persecution, but Grassy Narrows religion, already weakened by epidemic and missionary
propaganda in residential schools, collapsed. And with it
deteriorated the Ojibwas' ability to meet future disasters. They
were losing their grounding.

Traditional Ojibwa religion did not survive the official persecution of the 1930s. One of the most respected members of the Grassy Band says that today 75 percent of the Grassies would have nothing to do with the old religion, were a revival to occur; they simply have never known the traditions. What caused the breakdown? "The church and police, especially the Catholics who were against us, using the police," they say (Keewatin 1979).

Although adults at Grassy Narrows recall the old ways with affection and nostalgia, there exist today no naming ceremonies, no shaking tent rites, no vision quests, no talk of Midewiwin. None of these religious activities has taken place since the 1940s. Old folks like John Beaver still tell traditional stories, but most young folks care little for them. Religious leadership is dying out, along with herbal and curing proficiency. There is still some talk about the manitos, but with some degree of embarrassment. For example, Pat Loon refers to such talk as "superstition" (Beaver, Loon, and Fobister 1979). Vestiges remain — tobacco thrown on stormy waters, apologies to killed animals, burial customs and stories to validate them — but there is no integration of religious elements and no fulfillment of religious hopes.

Ojibwas blame the Catholic and Anglican missionaries, as well as the Royal Canadian Mounted Police, who told the Ojibwas that their ways were sinful and illegal, that their religious leaders and Midewiwin practitioners were witches, and that they had to become Christians. If, as Ojibwas today believe, the white authorities of the 1930s "were trying to mix up the Indians" (Keewatin 1979), and were designing their educational and punitive policies to rid the Ojibwas of their identity (Beaver, Loon, and Fobister 1979), they well nigh succeeded.

They did not, however, persuade the Grassy Narrows Ojibwas to embrace Christianity as a new system of meaning, explanation, and sustenance. Very few Ojibwas at Grassy today can be called practicing, believing, or comprehending Christians. Under persecution they have lost the integrative power of the old religion, but they have not adopted a new worldview. Spiritually they are a people caught between a moribund past and a threatening present, with little hope for the future. Much of the malaise at the reserve can be traced to the ruin of the traditional religion and the failure of Christianity to provide a convincing alternative.

Rather, many Ojibwas express hostility toward Catholics, Mennonites, Anglicans, indeed, all Christians with whom they have come into contact. When asked to name the most destructive event of the past century, an Ojibwa man said, "the churches caused a lot of damage" (Keewatin 1979). Others express strong resentment. Chief Simon Fobister says of the Catholics: "They were given a corner of the Indians' road. They looked honest, like people who wouldn't hurt anyone. But the Roman Catholic Church always has been so bossy, even today. . . . Their way is disrespectful, disrespectful" (Fobister 1979).

Catholics are not currently active on the reserve; Mennonites are. But neither commands a following from the Grassy Narrows Indians. Whereas it is true that the Ojibwas there are no longer traditionalists, it is also true that they are not Christians, despite missionary and governmental coercion. They exist without a living religious tradition.

In the face of catastrophe, the Grassy Narrows Ojibwas possess no ultimate source to which they can relate. The manitos are discredited; yet the Christian deity offers no hope. The native religious leaders are dead, and the missionaries are untrustworthy. Traditional curing has no effect on mercury poisoning; neither does modern Western medicine. Old John Beaver sees an overloaded Grassy Narrows cemetery, and he knows that the reserve is potently unhealthful. He knows that when the Canadian government persuaded the Grassies to move to their present location from a nearby site in 1962 (in order to make them more accessible to white police, doctors, and teachers), there were no religious leaders alive who could consult the local manitos regarding the relocation. He knows that today there are no religious leaders to help explain the incomprehensible mercury contamination and its effects. There are no curers and no shaking tents and no vision quests, and so of course the reserve is unhealthful, destructive (Beaver, Loon, and Fobister 1979).

Most Ojibwas blame the unnaturally frequent deaths, violence, and confusion of their society on the mercury poisoning itself, along with its economic consequences — prohibition of Ojibwa commercial fishing, and the closing of nearby lodges that employed so many Grassy people. Today 95 percent of the Grassy Narrows population is unemployed, and some blame the societal disarray solely on that condition.

Upon closer examination, however, Grassy Narrows problems have a more profound cause than poison in their fish and resulting unemployment. There is among them a poison of the spirit created by religious oppression and loss of tradition. John Beaver and Chief Simon Fobister and Pat Loon and Andy Keewatin and other Ojibwas say that if traditional Ojibwa religion had not been destroyed, it would be helping today in the face of mercury fears and economic instability. In their time of crisis, Grassy Narrows Ojibwas would be turning to their religious traditions. Instead, like other Ojibwas, they are facing a world of teetering complexity without an ultimate source of existence to which they can turn.

BIBLIOGRAPHY

Abbetmeyer-Selke, Esther.
1930   "Missouri Synod's First Chippewa Mission in Minnesota," *Concordia Historical Institute Quarterly*, 3: 20-25.
Adams, Arthur T., ed.
1961   *The Explorations of Pierre Esprit Radisson* Minneapolis.
Aggassiz, Louis.
1850   *Lake Superior: Its Physical Character, Vegetation, and Animals, Compared with Those of Other and Similar Regions. With a Narrative of the Tour, by J. Elliot Cabot* Boston.
Aldrich, Vernice.
1927a   "Biographical Sketch of Rev. J. A. Gilfillan," *North Dakota Historical Quarterly*, 1: 41-44.
1927b   "Father George Antoine Belcourt, Red River Missionary," *North Dakota Historical Quarterly*, 2: 30-52.
Anderson, Charles A., ed.
1947-1948   "Frontier Mackinac Island, 1823-1834. Letters of William Montague and Amanda White Ferry," *Journal of the Presbyterian Historical Society*, 25: 199-222; 26: 101-127, 182-191.
1952   "Diaries of Peter Dougherty," *Journal of the Presbyterian Historical Society*, 30: 95-114, 175-192, 236-253.
Armstrong, Benj. G.
1892   *Early Life among the Indians* Ashland, Wisconsin.
Babcock, Willoughby M.
1940   "The Grand Medicine Society of the Chippewa Indians," Minnesota State Historical Society, Manuscripts.
Baldwin, William W.
1957   "Social Problems of the Ojibwa Indians in the Collins Area in Northwestern Ontario," *Anthropologica*, 5: 51-123.
Balikci, Asen.
1956   "Note sur le Midewiwin," *Anthropologica*, 2: 165-217.
Baraga, Frederic.
1973   *A Dictionary of the Otchipwe Language, Explained in English* Minneapolis, 2 Parts (original date of publication, 1878).
Barnouw, Victor.
1949   "The Phantasy World of a Chippewa Woman," *Psychiatry*, 12: 67-76.
1950   *Acculturation and Personality among the Wisconsin Chippewa* Menasha, Wisconsin (American Anthropological Association, Memoir 72).
1954   "Reminiscences of a Chippewa Mide Priest," *The Wisconsin Archeologist*, 35: 83-112.
1955   "A Psychological Interpretation of a Chippewa Origin Legend," *Journal of American Folklore*, 68: 73-85, 211-223, 341-355.
1960   "A Chippewa Mide Priest's Description of the Medicine Dance," *The Wisconsin Archeologist*, 41: 77-97.
1977   *Wisconsin Chippewa Myths & Tales and Their Relation to Chippewa Life* Madison, Wisconsin.
Barrett, S. A.
1911   *The Dream Dance of the Chippewa and Menominee Indians of Northern Wisconsin* Milwaukee (Bulletin of the Public Museum of the City of Milwaukee, 1).
Beard, Augustus Field.
1909   *A Crusade of Brotherhood. A History of the American Missionary Association* Boston (reprinted, 1970).

Beaver, John, Pat Loon, and Simon Fobister.
1979   Personal Interview, Grassy Narrows, Ontario, with the author.
Beaver, Robert Pierce.
1966   *Church, State, and the American Indians* Saint Louis.
Beltrami, J. C.
1828   *A Pilgrimage in Europe and America, Leading to the Discovery of the Sources of the Mississippi and Bloody River; with a Description of the Whole Course of the Former, and of the Ohio* London, 2 vols.
Benedict, Ruth Fulton.
1923   *The Concept of the Guardian Spirit in North America* Menasha, Wisconsin (American Anthropological Association, Memoir 29).
Biggar, H. P., ed.
1925   *The Works of Samuel de Champlain* Toronto, 2.
Bishop, Charles A.
1970   "The Emergence of Hunting Territories among the Northern Ojibwa," *Ethnology*, 1: 1-15.
1974   *The Northern Ojibwa and the Fur Trade: An Historical and Ecological Study* Toronto.
1976   "The Emergence of the Northern Ojibwa: Social and Economic Consequences," *American Ethnologist*, 3: 39-54.
Black, Mary B.
1977   "Ojibwa Taxonomy and Percept Ambiguity," *Ethos*, 5: 90-118.
Blackbird, Andrew J.
1887   *History of the Ottawa and Chippewa Indians of Michigan, and Grammar of Their Language* Ypsilanti, Michigan.
Blackwood, Beatrice.
1929   "Tales of the Chippewa Indians," *Folk-Lore*, 40: 315-344.
Blair, Emma Helen, ed. and trans.
1911   *The Indian Tribes of the Upper Mississippi Valley and Region of the Great Lakes as Described by Nicholas Perrot, French Commandant in the Northwest; Racqueville de la Potherie, French Royal Commissioner to Canada; Morrell Martson, American Army Officer; and Thomas Forsyth, United States Agent at Fort Armstrong* Cleveland, 2 vols. (reprinted, 1969).
Bleeker, Sonia.
1955   *The Chippewa Indians, Rice Gatherers of the Great Lakes* New York.
Blegen, Theodore C., ed.
1943   "Armistice and War on the Minnesota Frontier," *Minnesota History*, 24: 11-25.
1963   *Minnesota. A History of the State* Minneapolis.
Blessing, Fred.
1954   "A Southern Ojibway Glossary," *The Minnesota Archaeologist*, 19: 2-57.
1956   "An Exhibition of Mide Magic," *The Minnesota Archaeologist*, 20: 9-13.
1958a   "Chippewa Singing," *The Minnesota Archaeologist*, 22: 16-17.
1958b   "Field Notes for 1959 [sic]," *The Minnesota Archaeologist*, 22: 1-7.
1961a   "Discovery of a Chippewa Peyote Cult in Minnesota," *The Minnesota Archaeologist*, 23: 1-8.
1961b   "Fasting and Dreams among the Minnesota Ojibway," *The Minnesota Archaeologist*, 23: 9-11.
1961c   "A Visit to an Ojibway Dream Dance," *The Minnesota Archaeologist*, 23: 12-16.
1963   "Birchbark Mide Scrolls from Minnesota," *The Minnesota Archaeologist*, 25: 91-142.
Bloomfield, Leonard.
1957   *Eastern Ojibwa. Grammatical Sketch, Texts and Word List* Ann Arbor.

Blumensohn, Jules.
1933   "The Fast among North American Indians," *American Anthropologist*,
            35: 451-469.
Boggs, Stephen T.
1958   "Culture Change and the Personality of Ojibwa Children," *American
            Anthropologist*, 60: 47-58.
Bottineau, J. B.
1878   "Chippewa Mythology," Smithsonian Institution, Bureau of Ameri-
            can Ethnology Archives, Chippewa Manuscripts.
Braecklein, J. G.
1950   "The Midewiwin Society of the Ojibwa," *Illinois State Archaeological
            Society*, 1: 45-48.
Bray, Martha Coleman, ed. and André Fertey, trans.
1970   *The Journals of Joseph N. Nicollet. A Scientist on the Mississippi Headwaters
            with Notes on Indian Life, 1836-37* St. Paul.
Breck, (Rev.) James Lloyd.
1877   "A Sketch of Mission Work among the Chippewas," *The Church and the
            Indians* New York: 1-7.
Brinton, Daniel Garrison.
1885   "The Chief God of the Algonkins, in His Character as a Cheat and
            Liar," *The American Antiquarian*: 137-139.
Brown, Charles E.
1902-1945   "Papers," State Historical Society of Wisconsin, Manuscripts.
1944   *Winabozho, Hero-God of the Indians of the Old Northwest. Myths, Legends
            and Stories* Madison, Wisconsin.
1945   "Myths, Legends and Superstitions about Copper," *The Ancient Copper
            Mines of Northern Michigan* Detroit: 97-101.
Brown, George.
1960   "Speech, June 11, 1960, by George Brown, Chippewa Indian Chief,
            Lac du Flambeau, at the State Historical Society's Annual Meeting, on
            the Unwritten History and Folklore of the Chippewa Indians in
            Wisconsin," tape recording. The State Historical Society of Wisconsin,
            Manuscripts.
Brown, Paula.
1952   "Changes in Ojibwa Social Control," *American Anthropologist*, 54:
            57-70.
Brown, Ralph H., ed.
1942   "With Cass in the Northwest in 1820. The Journal of Charles C.
            Trowbridge," *Minnesota History*, 23: 126-148, 233-252, 328-348.
Brown, Theodore T.
1928   "The Post, Notes on Lake Chippewa History (Sawyer County)," The
            State Historical Society of Wisconsin, Manuscripts.
Burden, H. N.
1895   *Manitoulin; or, Five Years of Church Work among Ojibway Indians and
            Lumbermen, Resident upon that Island or in its Vicinity* London.
Burnford, Sheila.
1969   *Without Reserve* Boston.
Burpee, Lawrence J., ed.
1927   *Journals and Letters of Pierre Gaultier de Varennes de la Vérendrye and His
            Sons* Toronto.
Burton, Frederick R.
1909   *American Primitive Music with Especial Attention to the Songs of the Ojibways*
            New York.
Bushnell, David I., Jr.
1905   "An Ojibway Ceremony," *American Anthropologist*, 7: 69-73.

Cadieux, Lorenzo.
1959   *Au Royaume de Nanabozho* Sudbury, Ontario (La Société Historique du Nouvel-Ontario, Documents Historiques, 37).
Cadieux, Lorenzo and Ernest Comte.
1954   *Un Heros du Lac Superieur. Frédéric Baraga* Sudbury, Ontario (La Société Historique du Nouvel-Ontario, Documents Historiques, 27).
Cadzow, Donald A.
1926   "Bark Records of the Bungi Midéwin Society," *Indian Notes*, 3: 123-134.
Callender, Charles.
1962   *Social Organization of the Central Algonkian Indians* Milwaukee (Milwaukee Public Museum, Publications in Anthropology, 7).
Cameron, Duncan.
1890   "The Nipigon Country, 1804," *Les Bourgeois de la Compagnie du Nord-Ouest* Quebec, ed. L.R. Masson, 2: 229-300.
Cappel, Jeanne L'strange (Wa-be-no O-pee-chee).
1928, 1931   *Chippewa Tales* Los Angeles, 2 vols.
Carson, William.
1917   "Ojibwa Tales," *Journal of American Folklore*, 30: 491-493.
Carver, Jonathan.
1784   *Three Years Travel, through the Interior Parts of North-America for More Than Five Thousand Miles* Philadelphia.
Casagrande, Joseph B.
1952   "Ojibwa Bear Ceremonialism: The Persistence of a Ritual Attitude," *Acculturation in the Americas* Chicago, ed. Sol Tax (Proceedings and Selected Papers of the 29th International Congress of Americanists): 113-117.
1956   "The Ojibwa's Psychic Universe," *Tomorrow*, 4: 33-40.
1960   "John Mink, Ojibwa Informant," *In the Company of Man: Twenty Portraits of Anthropological Informants* New York, ed. Joseph B. Casagrande: 467-488.
Catlin, George.
1926   *North American Indians. Being Letters and Notes on Their Manners, Customs, and Conditions, Written during Eight Years' Travel amongst the Wildest Tribes of Indians in North America, 1832-1839* Edinburgh, 2 vols.
Caudill, William.
1949   "Psychological Characteristics of Acculturated Wisconsin Ojibwa Children," *American Anthropologist*, 51: 409-427.
Chamberlain, Alexander F.
1890   "The Thunder-Bird amongst the Algonkins," *American Anthropologist*, 3: 51-54.
1891   "Nanibozhu amongst the Otchipwe, Mississagas, and Other Algonkian Tribes," *Journal of American Folklore*, 4: 193-213.
1900   "Some Items of Algonkian Folk-Lore," *Journal of American Folklore*, 13: 271-277.
1906   "Cree and Ojibwa Literary Terms," *Journal of American Folklore*, 19: 346-347.
Charlevoix, Pierre de.
1761   *Journal of a Voyage to North-America* London, 2 vols. (reprinted, 1966).
Clements, William L.
1919   "Rogers's Michillimackanic Journal," *Proceedings of the American Antiquarian Society*, 28: 224-273.
Coatsworth, Emerson.
1957   *The Indians of Quetico* Toronto.

Coleman, (Sr.) M. Bernard.
1929   "Religion and Magic among Cass Lake Ojibwa," *Primitive Man*, 2: 52-55.
1937   "The Religion of the Ojibwa of Northern Minnesota," *Primitive Man*, 10: 33-57.
1947   *Decorative Designs of the Ojibwa of Northern Minnesota* Washington, D.C. (The Catholic University of America, Anthropological Series, 12).
Coleman, (Sr.) M. Bernard, Ellen Frogner, and Estelle Eich.
1962   *Ojibwa Myths and Legends* Minneapolis.
Conard, E. Lætitia Moon.
1901   *Les Idées des Indiens Algonquins Relatives a la Vie d'Outre-Tombe* Paris.
Cooper, (Rev.) John M.
1928   "Northern Algonkian Scrying and Scapulimancy," *Festschrift P.W. Schmidt* Vienna, ed. W. Koppers: 205-217.
1933   "The Cree Witiko Psychosis," *Primitive Man*, 6: 20-24.
1934   *The Northern Algonquian Supreme Being* Washington, D.C. (The Catholic University of America, Anthropological Series, 2).
1936a   *Notes on the Ethnology of the Otchipwe of Lake of the Woods and Rainy Lake* Washington, D.C. (The Catholic University of America, Anthropological Series, 3).
1936b   "Scapulimancy," *Essays in Anthropology Presented to A. L. Kroeber* Berkeley (reprinted, 1969): 29-43.
1938   *Snares, Deadfalls, and Other Traps of the Northern Algonquians and Northern Athapaskans* Washington, D.C. (The Catholic University of America, Anthropological Series, 5).
1944   "The Shaking Tent Rite among Plains and Forest Algonquians," *Primitive Man*, 17: 60-84.
1946   "The Culture of the Northeastern Indian Hunters: A Reconstructive Interpretation," *Man in Northeastern North America* Andover, Massachusetts, ed. Frederick Johnson (Papers of the Robert S. Peabody Foundation for Archaeology), 3: 272-305.
Copway, George (Kah-Ge-Ga-Gah-Bowh).
1847   *The Life, History, and Travels, of Kah-Ge-Ga-Gah-Bowh (George Copway)* Albany.
1850   *Recollections of a Forest Life* London, Edinburgh, and Dublin.
1858   *Indian Life and Indian History, by an Indian Author* Boston.
Copway's American Indian.
1851   Vol. 1 (Newspaper published by George Copway in New York, July 10, 1851).
Coues, Elliott, ed.
1895   *The Expeditions of Zebulon Montgomery Pike, to Headwaters of the Mississippi River, through Louisiana Territory, and in New Spain, during the Years 1805-6-7* New York, 3 vols.
Craker, Ruth.
1935   *First Protestant Mission in the Grand Traverse Region* Leland, Michigan.
Crouse, Nellis M.
1956   *La Verendrye. Fur Trader and Explorer* Ithaca, New York.
Culkin, William E.
1915   "Tribal Dance of the Ojibway Indians," *Minnesota History Bulletin*, 1: 83-93.
1926   *Early Protestant Missions in the Lake Superior Country* Superior, Wisconsin, 3 vols.
Cunningham, Hazel Dora.
1936   "Presbyterian and Congregational Missionary Activity in Early Wisconsin," unpublished M.A. thesis, University of Wisconsin.

Danziger, Edmund Jefferson, Jr.
1978   *The Chippewas of Lake Superior* Norman, Oklahoma (The Civilization of
            the American Indian Series, 148).
Davidson, John F.
1945   "Ojibwa Songs," *Journal of American Folklore,* 58: 303-305.
Davidson, John Nelson.
1892   "Missions on Chequamegon Bay," *Collections of the State Historical
            Society of Wisconsin,* 12: 434-452.
Delorme, David P.
1955   "History of the Turtle Mountain Band of Chippewa Indians," *North
            Dakota History,* 22: 121-134.
Densmore, Frances.
1907   "An Ojibwa Prayer Ceremony," *American Anthropologist,* 9: 443-444.
1910, 1913 *Chippewa Music* Washington, D.C., 2 vols. (Smithsonian Institution,
            Bureau of American Ethnology, Bulletins 45, 53).
1928   "Uses of Plants by the Chippewa Indians," *Bureau of American Eth-
            nology, Forty-Fourth Annual Report 1926-1927* Washington, D.C.:
            275-397.
1929   *Chippewa Customs* Washington, D.C. (Smithsonian Institution, Bureau
            of American Ethnology, Bulletin 86).
1932   "An Explanation of a Trick Performed by Indian Jugglers," *American
            Anthropologist,* 34: 310-314.
1938   "The Influence of Hymns on the Form of Indian Songs," *American
            Anthropologist,* 40: 175-177.
Dewdney, Selwyn.
1975   *The Sacred Scrolls of the Southern Ojibway* Toronto.
Dewdney, Selwyn and Kenneth E. Kidd.
1967   *Indian Rock Paintings of the Great Lakes* Toronto.
Dixon, Roland B.
1909   "The Mythology of the Central and Eastern Algonkins," *Journal of
            American Folklore,* 22: 1-9.
Dorson, Richard M.
1952   *Bloodstoppers & Bearwalkers. Folk Traditions of the Upper Peninsula* Cam-
            bridge, Massachusetts.
Ducatel, I. I.
1877   "A Fortnight among the Chippewas of Lake Superior," *The Indian
            Miscellany* Albany, ed. William Wallace Beach (original date of pub-
            lication, 1846): 361-378.
Dunning, R. W.
1959   *Social and Economic Change among the Northern Ojibwa* Toronto.
Dusenberry, Verne.
1962   *The Montana Cree. A Study in Religious Persistence* Stockholm (Stock-
            holm Studies in Comparative Religion, 3).
Eastman, Charles A. (Ohiyesa)
1911   "A Canoe Trip among the Northern Ojibways," *The Red Man,* 3:
            236-244.
Eliza, the Indian Sorceress.
1835   New York (American Tract Society, 293).
Elliott, Richard R.
1896   "The Chippewas of Lake Superior," *The American Catholic Quarterly
            Review,* 21: 354-373.
1897   "The Chippewas and Ottawas: Father Baraga's Books in Their Lan-
            guage," *The American Catholic Quarterly Review,* 22: 18-46.
En-me-gah-bowh (John Johnson).
1904   *An Account of the Disturbances of the Chippewa Indians at Gull Lake in 1857
            and 1862 and Their Removal in 1868* Minneapolis.

Erikson, Kai T. and Christopher Vecsey.
1980   "A Report to the People of Grassy Narrows," *American Indian Environments. Ecological Issues in Native American History* Syracuse, eds. Christopher Vecsey and Robert W. Venables: 152-161.
Evans, (Rev.) James.
1835   "Conjuror's Great Feast or Medai Kech-E-We-Goon-De-Win," *Christian Guardian*: 45-46 (copied by Frank A. Myers in 1955). Smithsonian Institution, Bureau of American Ethnology Archives, Chippewa Manuscripts.
Farb, Peter.
1968   *Man's Rise to Civilization as Shown by the Indians of North America from Primeval Times to the Coming of the Industrial State* New York.
Ferry, (Rev.) William M.
1834   *Notices of Chippeway Converts* Boston (American Board of Commissioners for Foreign Missions, Missionary Paper 7).
Fiero, Charles and Norman Quill.
1967   *Ojibwa Assimilation* Loman, Minnesota.
Fisher, John and Christopher Vecsey.
1975   "Two Approaches to an Understanding of the Ojibwa Creation Myth." Unpublished paper presented at the American Academy of Religion Annual Meeting, 31 October 1975.
Fisher, Margaret W.
1946   "The Mythology of the Northern and Northeastern Algonkians in Reference to Algonkian Mythology as a Whole," *Man in Northeastern North America* Andover, Massachusetts, ed. Frederick Johnson (Papers of the Robert S. Peabody Foundation for Archaeology), 3: 226-262.
Fitting, James E. and Charles E. Cleland.
1969   "Late Prehistoric Settlement Patterns in the Upper Great Lakes," *Ethnohistory*, 16: 289-302.
Flandrau, Charles E.
1905   "The Work of Bishop Whipple in Missions for the Indians," *Collections of the Minnesota Historical Society*, 10: 691-696.
Flannery, Regina.
1940   "The Cultural Position of the Spanish River Indians," *Primitive Man*, 13: 1-25.
1946   "The Culture of the Northeastern Indian Hunters: A Descriptive Analysis," *Man in Northeastern North America* Andover, Massachusetts, ed. Frederick Johnson (Papers of the Robert S. Peabody Foundation for Archaeology), 3: 263-271.
Fobister, Simon.
1979   Personal Interviews, Grassy Narrows, Ontario, with the author.
Foster, (Rev.) Frank Hugh.
1892   "The Oberlin Ojibway Mission," *Papers of the Ohio Church History Society*, 2: 1-25.
Fowke, Gerard.
no date   "The Ground House Indians," Smithsonian Institution, Bureau of American Ethnology Archives, Chippewa Manuscripts.
Friedl, Ernestine.
1950   "An Attempt at Directed Culture Change. Leadership among the Chippewa, 1640-1948," unpublished Ph.D. dissertation, Columbia University.
1956   "Persistence in Chippewa Culture and Personality," *American Anthropologist*, 58: 814-825.
Frost, (Rev.) Frederick.
1904   *Sketches of Indian Life* Toronto.

Fruth, (Rev.) Alban.
1958   *A Century of Missionary Work among the Red Lake Chippewa Indians 1858-1958* Redlake, Minnesota.
Furlan, William P.
1952   *In Charity Unfeigned. The Life of Father Francis Xavier Pierz* St. Cloud, Minnesota.
Gabaoosa, George.
1900   "Story of Nanabosho's Mother," Smithsonian Institution, Bureau of American Ethnology Archives, Chippewa Manuscripts.
1921   "Nanabosho Myth, with Occasional Notes by J.N.B. Hewitt," Smithsonian Institution, Bureau of American Ethnology Archives, Chippewa Manuscripts.
1925   "The Myth of the Daymaker," 2 Parts, Smithsonian Institution, Bureau of American Ethnology Archives, Chippewa Manuscripts.
Gates, Charles M., ed.
1965   *Five Fur Traders of the Northwest. Being the Narrative of Peter Pond and the Diaries of John Macdonell, Archibald N. McLeod, Hugh Faries, and Thomas Conner* St. Paul.
Gatschet, Albert S.
1889   "Ojibwe (Ojibwa) Texts, from Ka'spash, at Turtle Mountain Reservation, N.D.," Smithsonian Institution, Bureau of American Ethnology Archives, Chippewa Manuscripts.
Gilfillan, (Rev.) Joseph Alexander.
1873   *The Church and the Indians. Fruits of Christian Work among the Chippewas* New York.
1880   *Domestic Missions. The Indian Deacons at White Earth* no place of publication.
1901   "The Ojibways in Minnesota," *Collections of the Minnesota Historical Society,* 9: 55-128.
1908-1909   "Ojibway (Chippewa) Legends," Smithsonian Institution, Bureau of American Ethnology Archives, Chippewa Manuscripts.
c.1911   "Miscellaneous Lot of Notes," Smithsonian Institution, Bureau of American Ethnology Archives, Chippewa Manuscripts.
after 1911 "Letters in Chippewa from Rev. George B. Morgan and Rev. Mark Hart, both Deacons in the Episcopal Church," Smithsonian Institution, Bureau of American Ethnology Archives, Chippewa Manuscripts.
1927   "A Trip through the Red River Valley in 1864," *North Dakota Historical Quarterly,* 1: 37-40.
Gillin, John.
1942   "Acquired Drives in Culture Contact," *American Anthropologist,* 44: 545-554.
Gillin, John and Victor Raimy.
1940   "Acculturation and Personality," *American Sociological Review,* 5: 371-380.
Graham, Elizabeth.
1975   *Medicine Man to Missionary. Missionaries as Agents of Change among the Indians of Southern Ontario* Toronto.
Grant, Peter.
1890   "The Sauteux Indians, about 1804," *Les Bourgeois de la Compagnie Nord-Ouest* Quebec, ed. L.R. Masson, 2: 303-366.
Grassy Narrows Band.
1979   "Presentation of the Grassy Narrows Band to the Governments of Canada and Ontario at the Opening Session of the Mediation Process," unpublished ms.

Gregorich, Joseph.
1932   *The Apostle of the Chippewas. The Life Story of The Most Rev. Frederick Baraga, D.D. the First Bishop of Marquette* Chicago.
Grey Owl (Wa-Sha-Quon-Asin).
1935   *Pilgrims of the Wild* New York.
Hagan, Lois D.
1938   *A Parish in the Pines* Caldwell, Idaho.
Hale, Edward E.
1893-1894   "Eliot's Bible and the Ojibway Language," *Proceedings of the American Antiquarian Society,* 9: 314-319.
Hallowell, A. Irving.
1923-1928   "Correspondence with Franz Boas," American Philosophical Society Library Archives.
1926   "Bear Ceremonialism in the Northern Hemisphere," *American Anthropologist,* 28: 1-175.
1931   "Letters to Frank G. Speck," American Philosophical Society Library Archives, Frank G. Speck Papers.
1934   "Some Empirical Aspects of Northern Saulteaux Religion," *American Anthropologist,* 36: 389-404.
1936   "The Passing of the Midewiwin in the Lake Winnipeg Region," *American Anthropologist,* 38: 32-51.
1938a   "Freudian Symbolism in the Dream of a Saulteaux Indian," *Man,* 38: 47-48.
1938b   "The Incidence, Character, and Decline of Polygyny among the Lake Winnipeg Cree and Saulteaux," *American Anthropologist,* 40: 235-256.
1939a   "Sin, Sex and Sickness in Saulteaux Belief," *The British Journal of Medical Psychology,* 18: 191-197.
1939b   "Some European Folktales of the Berens River Saulteaux," *Journal of American Folklore,* 52: 155-179.
1942   *The Role of Conjuring in Saulteaux Society* Philadelphia (Publications of the Philadelphia Anthropological Society, 2).
1946   "Concordance of Ojibwa Narratives in the Published Works of Henry R. Schoolcraft," *Journal of American Folklore,* 59: 136-153.
1947   "Myth, Culture and Personality," *American Anthropologist,* 49: 544-556.
1960   "Ojibwa Ontology, Behavior, and World View," *Culture in History: Essays in Honor of Paul Radin* New York, ed. Stanley Diamond: 19-52.
1971   *Culture and Experience* New York (original date of publication, 1955).
Hamilton, James Cleland.
1898-1899   "Famous Algonquins; Algic Legends," *Transactions of the Canadian Institute,* 6: 285-312.
1903   "The Algonquin Manabozho and Hiawatha," *Journal of American Folklore,* 16: 229-233.
Harper, J. Russell, ed.
1971   *Paul Kane's Frontier, Including "Wanderings of an Artist among the Indians of North America" by Paul Kane* Fort Worth, Texas.
Harrington, Mark Raymond.
1960   "An Ojibwa Medicine Bundle," *The Masterkey,* 34: 37.
Hart, Irving Harlow.
1928   "The Story of Beengwa, Daughter of a Chippewa Warrior," *Minnesota History,* 9: 319-330.
Hawkins, Lucy Rogers.
1927   "A Chippewa Indian Idol," *The Wisconsin Archeologist,* 6: 83-85.
Hay, Thomas H.
1977   "The Development of Some Aspects of the Ojibwa Self and Its Behavioral Environment," *Ethos,* 5: 71-89.

Hennepin, (Rev.) Louis.
1880   *A Description of Louisiana* New York, trans. John Gilmary Shea (original date of publication, 1683, reprinted 1966).
Henry, Alexander.
1809   *Travels and Adventures in Canada and the Indian Territories, between the Years 1760 and 1776* New York (reprinted, 1966).
Hewitt, J. N. B.
1926   "Ethnological Researches among the Iroquois and Chippewa," *Explorations and Field-Work of the Smithsonian Institution in 1925* Washington, D.C. (Smithsonian Miscellaneous Collections, 78, No. 1): 114-117.
no date a   "Notes & Discussion of the Myth of the Mudjikewis or Inabiozio'," Smithsonian Institution, Bureau of American Ethnology Archives, Chippewa Manuscripts.
no date b   "Transliteration of Nanabosho Myth into the B.A.E. Alphabet of Chippewa Text, No. 1637," Smithsonian Institution, Bureau of American Ethnology Archives, Chippewa Manuscripts.
Hickerson, Harold.
1956   "The Genesis of a Trading Post Band: The Pembina Chippewa," *Ethnohistory*, 3: 289-345.
1959   "Journal of Charles Jean Baptiste Chaboillez," *Ethnohistory*, 6: 265-316.
1960   "The Feast of the Dead among the Seventeenth Century Algonkians of the Upper Great Lakes," *American Anthropologist*, 62: 81-107.
1962a   "Notes on the Post-Contact Origin of the Midewiwin," *Ethnohistory*, 9: 404-426.
1962b   *The Southwestern Chippewa: An Ethnohistorical Study* Menasha, Wisconsin (American Anthropological Association, Memoir 92).
1963   "The Sociohistorical Significance of Two Chippewa Ceremonials," *American Anthropologist*, 65: 67-85.
1965   "William T. Boutwell of the American Board and the Pillager Chippewa: The History of a Failure," *Ethnohistory*, 12: 1-29.
1966   "The Genesis of Bilaterality among Two Divisions of Chippewa," *American Anthropologist*, 68: 1-26.
1970   *The Chippewa and Their Neighbors: A Study in Ethnohistory* New York.
Hilger, (Sr.) M. Inez (Agnes).
1936a   "Letters and Documents of Bishop Baraga Extant in the Chippewa Country," *Records of the American Catholic Historical Society of Philadelphia*, 47: 292-302.
1936b   "In the Early Days of Wisconsin. An Amalgamation of Chippewa and European Cultures," *The Wisconsin Archeologist*, 16: 32-49.
1937   "Chippewa Interpretations of Natural Phenomena," *Scientific Monthly*, 45: 178-179.
1939   *A Social Study of One Hundred Fifty Chippewa Indian Families of the White Earth Reservation of Minnesota* Washington, D.C.
1944   "Chippewa Burial and Mourning Customs," *American Anthropologist*, 46: 564-568.
1951   *Chippewa Child Life and Its Cultural Background* Washington, D.C. (Smithsonian Institution, Bureau of American Ethnology, Bulletin 146).
1958   "Naming a Chippewa Indian Child," *The Wisconsin Archeologist*, 39: 120-126.
Hiller, Wesley R.
1937   "A Discourse on Chippewa Medicine," *The Minnesota Archaeologist*, 3: 1-8.
Hindley, (Rev.) John I.
1885   *Indian Legends. Nanabush, the Ojibbeway Saviour* no place of publication.

Hinsdale, W. B.
1926 "Religion at the Algonquian Level," *Papers of the Michigan Academy of Science Arts and Letters,* 5: 15-27.
1935 "The Midewiwin," *Indians at Work,* 3: 21.
Hoffman, Bernard G.
1961 "The Codex Canadiensis: An Important Document for Great Lakes Ethnography," *Ethnohistory,* 8: 382-400.
Hoffman, Walter J.
1886 "Letter to Henry Phillips," American Philosophical Society Library Archives.
1888 "Pictography and Shamanistic Rites of the Ojibwa," *American Anthropologist,* old series, 1: 209-229.
1889 "Notes on Ojibwa Folk-Lore," *American Anthropologist,* old series, 2: 215-223.
1890 "Remarks on Ojibwa Ball Play," *American Anthropologist,* old series, 3: 133-135.
1891 "The Midě'wiwin or 'Grand Medicine Society' of the Ojibwa," *Bureau of Ethnology, Seventh Annual Report, 1885-'86* Washington, D.C.: 143-300.
Hofsinde, Bob (Graywolf).
1934 "The 21 Precepts or Moral Commandments of the Ottawa and Chippewa Indians by Which They Were Governed in Their Primitive State, before Coming in Contact with the White Races in Their Country, translated from the Ottawa tongue by Andrew J. Blackbird," Smithsonian Institution, Bureau of American Ethnology Archives, Chippewa Manuscripts.
Holand, Hjalmar R.
1933 "The Sign of the Cross," *The Wisconsin Magazine of History,* 17: 155-167.
Holdich, Joseph.
1839 *The Wesleyan Student; or Memoirs of Aaron Haynes Hurd, Late a Member of the Wesleyan University, Middletown, Conn.* Middletown.
Howard, James H.
1961 "The Identity and Demography of the Plains-Ojibwa," *Plains Anthropologist,* 6: 171-178.
1966 "The Henry Davis Drum Rite: An Unusual Drum Religion Variant of the Minnesota Ojibwa," *Plains Anthropologist,* 11: 117-126.
Hugolin, R. P.
1907 "L'Idée Spiritualiste et l'Idée Morale chez les Chippewas," *Congrès International des Américanistes, XVe Session Tenue à Québec en 1906* Quebec: 329-335.
Hultkrantz, Åke.
1953 *Conceptions of the Soul among North American Indians* Stockholm (The Ethnographical Museum of Sweden, Monograph Series, 1).
1957 *The North American Indian Orpheus Tradition* Stockholm (The Ethnographical Museum of Sweden, Monograph Series, 2).
1967 "Spirit Lodge, a North American Shamanistic Séance," *Studies in Shamanism* Stockholm, ed. Carl-Martin Edsman (Scripta Instituti Donneriani Aboensis, 1): 32-68.
Hyde, George E.
1962 *Indians of the Woodlands from Prehistoric Times to 1725* Norman (The Civilization of the American Indian Series, 64).
Jacobs, (Rev.) Peter (Pah-tah-se-ga).
1855 *Journal from Rice Lake to Hudson's Bay Territory, and Returning. Commencing May, 1852* New York.
James, Bernard J.
1954 "Some Critical Observations concerning Analyses of Chippewa

'Atomism' and Chippewa Personality," *American Anthropologist*, 56: 283-286.

1961   "Social-Psychological Dimensions of Ojibwa Acculturation," *American Anthropologist*, 63: 721-746.

1970   "Continuity and Emergence in Indian Poverty Culture," *Current Anthropology*, 11: 435-452.

James, Edwin, ed.

1956   *A Narrative of the Captivity and Adventures of John Tanner (U.S. Interpreter at the Saut de Ste. Marie) during Thirty Years Residence among the Indians in the Interior of North America* Minneapolis (original date of publication, 1830).

Jenks, Albert Ernest.

1900   "The Wild Rice Gatherers of the Upper Great Lakes. A Study in American Primitive Economics," *Bureau of American Ethnology, Nineteenth Annual Report, 1897-98* Washington, D.C., Part 2: 1013-1137.

1902   "The Bear-Maiden an Ojibway Folk-Tale from Lac Courte Oreille Reservation, Wisconsin," *Journal of American Folklore*, 15: 33-35.

Jenness, Diamond.

1935   *The Ojibwa Indians of Parry Island, Their Social and Religious Life* Ottawa (Canada Department of Mines, Bulletin 78, Anthropological Series, 17).

Johnson, Frederick.

1929   "Notes on the Ojibwa and Potawatomi of the Parry Island Reservation, Ontario," *Indian Notes*, 6: 193-216.

Johnston, Basil.

1976   *Ojibway Heritage* New York.

Johnston, William.

1909-1910   "Letters on the Fur Trade," ed. John Sharpless Fox, *Historical Collections of the Michigan Pioneer and Historical Society*, 37: 132-207.

Jones, (Rev.) Peter (Kahkewaquonaby).

1861   *History of the Ojebway Indians; with Especial Reference to Their Conversion to Christianity* London.

Jones, William.

1903-1907   "Correspondence with Franz Boas," American Philosophical Society Library Archives.

1917, 1919   *Ojibwa Texts* Leyden, New York, ed. Truman Michelson (Publications of the American Ethnological Society, 7, Parts 1, 2).

Josephy, Alvin M., Jr.

1968   *The Indian Heritage of America* New York.

Josselin de Jong, J. P. B. de.

1912   "A Few Otchipwe-Songs," *Internationales Archiv für Ethnographie*, 20: 189-190.

1913   "Original Odžibwe-Texts," *Beiträge zur Völkerkunde* Leipzig (Herausgegeben aus Mitteln des Baessler-Instituts, 5): 1-54.

Keating, William H.

1824   *Narrative of an Expedition to the Source of St. Peter's River, Lake Winnepeek, Lake of the Woods, &c. &c. Performed in the Year 1823* Philadelphia, 2 vols.

Keewatin, Andy.

1979   Personal Interviews, Grassy Narrows, Ontario, with the author.

Keller, Robert H., Jr.

1972   "On Teaching Indian History: Legal Jurisdiction in Chippewa Treaties," *Ethnohistory*, 19: 209-218.

1978   "An Economic History of Indian Treaties in the Great Lakes Region," *American Indian Journal*, 1: 2-20.

Kellogg, Louise Phelps, ed.
1917   *Early Narratives of the Northwest 1634-1639* New York.
1925   *The French Régime in Wisconsin and the Northwest* Madison.
Kennedy, J. H.
1950   *Jesuit and Savage in New France* New Haven.
Ke-Wa-Ze-Zhig.
1861   *An Address, Delivered in Allston Hall, Boston, February 26th, 1861, before a Convention Met to Devise Ways and Means to Elevate and Improve the Condition of the Indians in the United States* Boston.
Kidder, Homer Huntington.
1898   "Letter to A. Kidder," American Philosophical Society Library Archives.
1918   "Ojibwa Myths & Halfbreed Tales Related by Charles and Charlotte Kobawgam and Jacques le Pique 1893-1895," American Philosophical Society Library Archives.
Killy, Monroe.
1948   "Modern Burial Customs of the Chippewa," *The Minnesota Archaeologist,* 14: 55-61.
Kinietz, W. Vernon.
1939   "Birch Bark Records among the Chippewa," *Proceedings of the Indiana Academy of Science,* 49: 38-40.
1940   *The Indians of the Western Great Lakes 1615-1760* Ann Arbor (Occasional Contributions from the Museum of Anthropology of the University of Michigan, 10).
1947   *Chippewa Village, the Story of Katikitegon* Bloomfield Hills, Michigan.
Kinnaman, J. O.
1910a   "Chippewa Legends," *The American Antiquarian,* 32: 96-102, 137-144.
1910b   "History of the Chippewa Nation as Told by Themselves and Catholic Documents," *The American Antiquarian,* 32: 183-190.
Kinsey, Mabel C.
1933   "An Ojibwa Song," *Journal of American Folklore,* 46: 416-417.
Knight, Julia.
1913   "Ojibwa Tales from Sault Ste. Marie, Mich.," *Journal of American Folklore,* 26: 91-96.
Kohl, J. G.
1860   *Kitchi-Gami. Wanderings round Lake Superior* London, ed. and trans. Lascelles Wraxall.
Kurath, Gertrude Prokosch.
1946   *Michigan Indian Festivals* Ann Arbor.
1954   "Chippewa Sacred Songs in Religious Metamorphosis," *Scientific Monthly,* 79: 311-317.
1957a   "Catholic Hymns of Michigan Indians," *Anthropological Quarterly,* 30: 31-44.
1957b   "Pan-Indianism in Great Lakes Tribal Festivals," *Journal of American Folklore,* 70: 179-182.
1959   "Blackrobe and Shaman: The Christianization of Michigan Algonquians," *Papers of the Michigan Academy of Science, Arts, and Letters,* 44: 209-215.
Kurath, Gertrude Prokosch, Jane Ettawageshik, and Fred Ettawageshik.
1955   "Religious Customs of Modern Michigan Algonquians," American Philosophical Society Library Archives.
Lafleur, Laurence J.
1940   "On the Midé of the Ojibway," *American Anthropologist,* 42: 706-708.

Lahontan, Baron de.
1905   *New Voyages to North-America* Chicago, ed. Reuben Gold Thwaites, 2
            vols. (original date of publication, 1703).
Laidlaw, Geo. E.
1914-1925   "Certain Ojibwa Myths" and "Ojibwa Myths and Tales," Ontario
            Annual Archaeological Report, 26: 77-79; 27: 71-90; 28: 84-92; 30:
            74-110; 32: 66-85; 33: 84-99; 35: 34-80.
1922   "Ojibwa Myths and Tales," *The Wisconsin Archeologist*, 1: 28-38.
Landes, Ruth.
1937   *Ojibwa Sociology* New York.
1938   "The Abnormal among the Ojibwa Indians," *The Journal of Abnormal
            and Social Psychology*, 33: 14-33.
1967   "The Ojibwa of Canada," *Cooperation and Competition among Primitive
            Peoples* Boston, ed. Margaret Mead (original date of publication,
            1937): 87-126.
1968   *Ojibwa Religion and the Midéwiwin* Madison.
1971   *The Ojibwa Woman* New York.
Landon, R. Horace, ed.
1964   "Letters of Early Missionary Days," *The Minnesota Archaeologist*, 26:
            55-63.
Lathrop, (Rev.) Stanley Edwards.
1905   *A Historical Sketch of the "Old Mission," and Its Missionaries to the Ojibway
            Indians, on Madeline Island, Lake Superior, Wisconsin* Ashland,
            Wisconsin.
League of Women Voters of Minnesota.
1971   *Indians in Minnesota* St. Paul.
Leary, James Russell.
1960   "Cultural Variation, Personality, and Values among the Chippewa,"
            unpublished Ph.D. dissertation, Harvard University.
Leekley, Thomas B.
1965   *The World of Manabozho. Tales of the Chippewa Indians* New York.
Levi, (Sr.) M. Carolissa.
1956   *Chippewa Indians of Yesterday and Today* New York.
Lindquist, G. E. E.
1952   *Indians of Minnesota. A Survey of Social and Religious Conditions among
            Tribes in Transition* New York.
Long, John.
1904   *Voyages and Travels of an Indian Interpreter and Trader, 1768-1782*
            Cleveland, ed. Reuben Gold Thwaites (Early Western Travels,
            1746-1846, 2).
Loon, Steve and Tom Payesh.
1979   Personal Interview, Grassy Narrows, Ontario, with the author.
Luckhard, Charles F.
1952   *Faith in the Forest* Sebewaing, Michigan.
Lurie, Nancy Oestreich.
1962   "Comments on Bernard J. James's Analysis of Ojibwa Accultur-
            ation," *American Anthropologist*, 64: 826-833.
1969   "Wisconsin: A Natural Laboratory for North American Indian Stud-
            ies," *Wisconsin Magazine of History,* 53: 3-20.
"The Mackinac Register"
1910   *Collections of the State Historical Society of Wisconsin*, 19: 1-162.
Maeder, (Rev.) Tobias.
1962   "St. John's among the Chippewa," *The Scriptorium,*" 21: 57-73.
Majerus, Yvette.
1967   *Le Journal du Père Dominique du Ranquet, S.J.* Sudbury, Ontario (Le

Société Historique du Nouvel-Ontario, Documents Historiques, 49-50).

Makarius, Laura.
1973   "The Crime of Manabozo," *American Anthropologist*, 75: 663-675.
Mallery, Garrick.
1972   *Picture-writing of the American Indians* New York, 2 vols. (original date of publication, 1893).
McClintock, Walter.
1941-1942   "The Thunderbird Myth," *The Masterkey*, 15: 164-168; 224-227; 16:16-18.
McDonald, (Sr.) Grace.
1929   "Father Francis Pierz, Missionary," *Minnesota History*, 10: 107-125.
McDonald, Marci.
1976   "Horrors of Minamata Haunt Canadian Indians," *Audubon*, 78, No. 2: 125-129.
McGee, W. J.
1898   "Ojibwa Feather Symbolism," *American Anthropologist*, old series, 11: 177-180.
McKenney, Thomas L.
1827   *Sketches of a Tour to the Lakes, of the Character and Customs of the Chippeway Indians, and of Incidents Connected with the Treaty of Fond du Lac* Baltimore.
McKenney, Thomas L. and James Hall.
1933-1934   *The Indian Tribes of North America with Biographical Sketches and Anecdotes of the Principal Chiefs* Edinburgh, 3 vols., ed. Frederick Webb Hodge and David I. Bushnell, Jr.
McKern, W. C.
1946   "A Cultural Perspective of Northeastern Area Archaeology," *Man in Northeastern North America* Andover, Massachusetts, ed. Frederick Johnson (Papers of the Robert S. Peabody Foundation for Archaeology, 3): 33-36.
McLean, John.
1891   *The Hero of the Saskatchewan. Life among the Ojibway and Cree Indians in Canada* Barrie, Ontario.
McLeod, Joseph.
1977   *And the Rivers Our Blood* Toronto.
Means, Philip Ainsworth.
1917   *Preliminary Survey of the Remains of the Chippewa Settlements on La Pointe Island, Wisconsin* Washington, D.C. (Smithsonian Miscellaneous Collections, 66, No. 14).
Michelson, Truman.
1911   "Ojibwa Tales," *Journal of American Folklore*, 24: 249-250.
1916   "Nanabosho Swallowed by the Sturgeon," Smithsonian Institution, Bureau of American Ethnology Archives, Chippewa Manuscripts.
1923   "On the Origin of the So-Called Dream Dance of the Central Algonkians," *American Anthropologist*, 25: 277-278.
1924   "Further Remarks on the Origin of the So-Called Dream Dance of the Central Algonkians," *American Anthropologist*, 26: 293-294.
1925   "Chippewa Ethnology, Legends, Physical Anthropology and Linguistics," Smithsonian Institution, Bureau of American Ethnology Archives, Chippewa Manuscripts.
1926a   "Final Notes on the Central Algonquian Dream Dance," *American Anthropologist*, 28: 573-576.
1926b   "Studies of the Fox and Ojibwa Indians," *Explorations and Field-Work of the Smithsonian Institution in 1925* Washington, D.C. (Smithsonian Miscellaneous Collections, 78, No. 1): 111-113.

1934   "Maiden Sacrifice among the Ojibwa," *American Anthropologist*, 36: 628-629.
no date a   "Chippewa and Ottawa Ethnology, Linguistics and Physical Anthropology," Smithsonian Institution, Bureau of American Ethnology Archives, Chippewa Manuscripts.
no date b   "Chippewa and Potawatomi Linguistics, Ethnology, and Physical Anthropology," Smithsonian Institution, Bureau of American Ethnology Archives, Chippewa Manuscripts.
no date c   "Chippewa Legend and Ethnology," Smithsonian Institution, Bureau of American Ethnology Archives, Chippewa Manuscripts.
no date d   "Chippewa Linguistics and Ethnology," Smithsonian Institution, Bureau of American Ethnology Archives, Chippewa Manuscripts.
The Minnesota Historical Records Survey Project.
1941   *Report of the Chippewa Mission Archaeological Investigation* St. Paul.
Miscogeon, John L.
1900a   "The Legend of Nanabozho," Smithsonian Institution, Bureau of American Ethnology Archives, Chippewa Manuscripts.
1900b   "Ojibwa (Ottawa) Text; Note, Correction and Occasional Translation by J.N.B. Hewitt," Smithsonian Institution, Bureau of American Ethnology Archives, Chippewa Manuscripts.
1900c   "Story of Nanabozho's Mother," Smithsonian Institution, Bureau of American Ethnology Archives, Chippewa Manuscripts.
1900d   "The Story of the South (Summer) and the North (Winter) in Ojibwa (or Ottawa) Text," Smithsonian Institution, Bureau of American Ethnology Archives, Chippewa Manuscripts.
Miscogeon, John L. and George Gabaoosa.
1900   "A Visit to Skyland, in Ojibwa (or Ottawa) Text," Smithsonian Institution, Bureau of American Ethnology Archives, Chippewa Manuscripts.
Mittelholtz, Erwin F.
1957   *Historical Review of the Red Lake Indian Reservation* Bemidji, Minnesota.
Morriseau, Norval.
1965   *Legends of My People* Toronto, ed. Selwyn Dewdney.
Morse, Richard E.
1857   "The Chippewas of Lake Superior," *Collections of the State Historical Society of Wisconsin*, 3: 338-369.
Moyne, Ernest J.
1965   "Manabozho, Tarenyawagon, and Hiawatha," *Southern Folklore Quarterly*, 29: 195-203.
Müller, Werner.
1954   *Die Blaue Hütte. Zum Sinnbild der Perle bei Nordamerikanischen Indianern* Wiesbaden (Studien zur Kulturkunde, 12).
1956   *Die Religionen der Waldlandindianer Nordamerikas* Berlin.
1969   "North America," *Pre-Columbian American Religions* New York, Walter Krickeberg et al., trans. Stanley Davis: 147-229.
Neill, Edward Duffield.
1885   "History of the Ojibways, and Their Connection with Fur Traders, Based upon Official and Other Records," *Collections of the Minnesota Historical Society*, 5: 395-510.
no date   "Memoir of William T. Boutwell, the First Christian Minister Resident among the Indians of Minnesota," *Macalester College Contributions* no place of publication (Department of History, Literature and Political Science, 2nd Series, 1).
Nelson, J. Raleigh.
1965   *Lady Unafraid* Calumet, Michigan.

Nichols, Francis S.
1954   *Index to Schoolcraft's "Indian Tribes of the United States"* Washington,
            D.C. (Smithsonian Institution, Bureau of American Ethnology,
            Bulletin 152).
Nohl, William G.
no date   "Reminiscences," The State Historical Society of Wisconsin,
            Manuscripts.
Norton, (Sr.) Mary Aquinas.
1930   *Catholic Missionary Activities in the Northwest, 1818-1864* Washington,
            D.C.
Nute, Grace Lee, ed.
1930   *Documents Relating to Northwest Missions 1815-1827* St. Paul.
1944   *Lake Superior* Indianapolis.
Old Schusco
no date   no place of publication (American Tract Society, Narrative 4).
O'Meara, (Rev.) Frederick A., et al.
1847-1848   "Letters, Missions to the Ojibwa Indians," New York Public Library,
            Manuscripts.
Order of St. Benedict.
1887   *Schools for the Chippewa Indians* St. Paul.
Osborn, Chase S. and Stellanova Osborn.
1942   *Schoolcraft — Longfellow — Hiawatha* Lancaster, Pennsylvania.
Osgood, Phillips Endecott.
1958   *Straight Tongue. A Story of Henry Benjamin Whipple First Episcopal
            Bishop of Minnesota* Minneapolis.
Paredes, J. Anthony.
1971   "Toward a Reconceptualization of American Indian Urbanization:
            A Chippewa Case," *Anthropological Quarterly*, 44: 256-271.
Paredes, J. Anthony, Timothy G. Roufs, and Gretel H. Pelto
1973   "On James's 'Continuity and Emergence in Indian Poverty Cul-
            ture,' " *Current Anthropology*, 14: 158-167.
Parker, Seymour.
1960   "The Wiitiko Psychosis in the Context of Ojibwa Personality and
            Culture," *American Anthropologist*, 62: 603-623.
1962   "Motives in Eskimo and Ojibwa Mythology," *Ethnology*, 1: 516-523.
Parkman, Francis.
1901   *The Jesuits in North America in the Seventeenth Century* Boston, 2 vols.
            (Francis Parkman's Works, Frontenac Edition, 3, 4).
Peabody, B.O.
1877   "The Early Jesuit Missionaries of the North Western Territories,"
            The Indian Miscellany Albany, ed. William Wallace Beach: 102-119.
Perrault, Jean Baptiste.
1909-1910   "Narrative of the Travels and Adventures of a Merchant Voyageur
            in the Savage Territories of Northern America Leaving Montreal the
            28th of May 1783 (to 1820)," ed. John Sharpless Fox, *Historical
            Collections of the Michigan Pioneer and Historical Society*, 37: 508-619.
Pierz, (Rev.) Francis.
1947-1948   "The Indians of North America," trans. Eugene Hagerdorn, *Social
            Justice Review*, 40: 24-27, 59-62, 96-98, 130-133, 167-170, 207-209,
            243-245, 279-282, 316-318, 353-355, 388-390; 41: 24-27, 60-64,
            97-100, 132-134, 168-170 (original date of publication, 1855).
Pitezel, John H.
1860   *Lights and Shades of Missionary Life* Cincinnati.
1901   *Life of Rev. Peter Marksman. An Ojibwa Missionary. Illustrating the
            Triumphs of the Gospel among the Ojibwa Indians* Cincinnati.

Polack, W. G.
1928   *Bringing Christ to the Ojibways in Michigan. A Story of the Mission Work of E.R. Baierlein* New York.
Prindle, (Rev.) Cyrus.
1842   *Memoir of the Rev. Daniel Meeker Chandler: for Several Years Missionary among the Indians, at Ke-wa-we-non, and Sault de St. Marie, Lake Superior* Middlebury, Vermont.
Quimby, George Irving.
1960   *Indian Life in the Upper Great Lakes, 11,000 B.C. to A.D. 1800* Chicago.
1966   *Indian Culture and European Trade Goods* Madison.
Radin, Paul.
1913   "On Ojibwa Work in Southeastern Ontario, 1912," *Summary Report of the Geological Survey, Canada* (Anthropological Division, Sessional Paper 26): 482-483.
1914a   "An Introductive Enquiry in the Study of Ojibwa Religion," *Ontario Historical Society Papers and Records,* 12: 210-218.
1914b   *Some Aspects of Puberty Fasting among the Ojibwa* Ottawa (Canada Department of Mines, Geological Survey, Museum Bulletin 2, Anthropological Series, 2).
1914c   *Some Myths and Tales of the Ojibwa of Southeastern Ontario* Ottawa (Canada Department of Mines, Geological Survey, Memoir 48, Anthropological Series, 2).
1914d   "On Ojibwa Work, 1913," *Summary Report of the Geological Survey, Canada* (Anthropological Division, Sessional Paper 26): 374.
1924   "Ojibwa Ethnological Chit-Chat," *American Anthropologist,* 26: 491-530.
c.1926   "Ojibwa and Ottawa Indians, Notes," American Philosophical Society Library Archives.
1928   "Ethnological Notes on the Ojibwa of Southeastern Ontario," *American Anthropologist,* 30: 659-668.
1936   "Ojibwa and Ottawa Puberty Dreams," *Essays in Anthropology Presented to A.L. Kroeber* Berkeley (reprinted, 1969): 233-264.
no date   "Medicine Dance," American Philosophical Society Library Archives.
Radin, Paul and Albert B. Reagan.
1928   "Ojibwa Myths and Tales," *Journal of American Folklore,* 41: 61-146.
Reagan, Albert B.
1921a   "The Flood Myth of the Chippewas," *Proceedings of the Indiana Academy of Science 1919*: 347-352.
1921b   "Some Chippewa Medicinal Receipts," *American Anthropologist,* 23: 246-249.
1922   "Medicine Songs of George Farmer," *American Anthropologist,* 24: 332-369.
1924   "The Bois Fort Chippewa," *The Wisconsin Archeologist,* 3: 101-132.
1927   "Picture Writings of the Chippewa Indians," *The Wisconsin Archeologist,* 6: 80-83.
1928   "The Magic Pots," *The Wisconsin Archeologist,* 7: 227-228.
1933   "Some Notes on the Grand Medicine Society of the Bois Fort Ojibwa," *Americana,* 27: 502-519.
1934   "The Society of Dreamers and the O-ge-che-dah, or Head-Men Dance of the Bois Fort (Ojibwe) Indians of Nett Lake, Minnesota," *The Wisconsin Archeologist,* 13: 35-43.
1935   "A Ritual Parchment and Certain Historical Charts of the Bois Fort Ojibwa of Minnesota," *Americana,* 29: 228-244.

Redsky, James (Equekisik).
1972   *Great Leader of the Ojibway: Mis-quona-queb* Toronto, ed. James R. Stevens.
Reid, Dorothy M.
1963   *Tales of Nanabozho* New York.
Riggs, (Rev.) Stephen R.
1894   "Protestant Missions in the Northwest," *Collections of the Minnesota Historical Society,* 6: 117-188.
Ritzenthaler, Robert E.
1945a   "Ceremonial Destruction of Sickness by the Wisconsin Chippewa," *American Anthropologist,* 47: 320-322.
1945b   "Totemic Insult among the Wisconsin Chippewa," *American Anthropologist,* 47: 322-324.
1953   "Chippewa Preoccupation with Health; Change in a Traditional Attitude Resulting from Modern Health Problems," *Bulletin of the Public Museum of the City of Milwaukee,* 19: 175-258.
Ritzenthaler, Robert E. and Pat Ritzenthaler.
1970   *The Woodland Indians of the Western Great Lakes* Garden City, New York.
Rogers, Edward S.
1962   *The Round Lake Ojibwa* Toronto (Royal Ontario Museum — University of Toronto, Art and Archaeology Division, Occasional Paper 5).
Rogers, John (Chief Snow Cloud).
1974   *Red World and White. Memories of a Chippewa Boyhood* Norman (original date of publication, 1957).
Róhrl, Vivian.
1972   "Some Observations on the Drum Society of Chippewa Indians," *Ethnohistory,* 19: 219-225.
Roufs, Tim.
1974   "Myth in Method: More on Ojibwa Culture," *Current Anthropology,* 15: 307-310.
1975   *The Anishinabe of the Minnesota Chippewa Tribe* Phoenix.
Rousseau, Jacques.
1952   "Persistances Païennes chez les Amérindiens de la Forêt Boréale," *Les Cahiers des Dix,* 17: 183-208.
Ruffee, C.A.
1875   *Report of the Chippewas of Minnesota* St. Paul.
Schell, (Rev.) James Peery.
1911   *In the Ojibway Country. A Story of Early Missions on the Minnesota Frontier* Walhalla, North Dakota.
Schmidt, Wilhelm.
1948   "The Central-Algonkin Floodmyth," *Actes du XXVIII' Congrès International des Americanistes, Paris 1947* Paris: 317-319.
Schoolcraft, Henry Rowe.
1839   *Algic Researches, Comprising Inquiries Respecting the Mental Characteristics of the North American Indians* New York, 2 vols.
1848   *The Indian in His Wigwam, or Characteristics of the Red Race of America* New York.
1853-1857   *Information, Respecting the History, Condition and Prospects of the Indian Tribes of the United States: Collected and Prepared under the Direction of the Bureau of Indian Affairs, per Act of Congress of March 3d, 1847* Philadelphia, 6 vols.
1953   *Narrative Journal of Travels through the Northwestern Regions of the United States Extending from Detroit through the Great Chain of American Lakes to the Sources of the Mississippi River in the Year 1820* East Lansing, ed. Mentor L. Williams (original date of publication, 1821).

Scott, Hugh L., ed.
1919-1931   "Reports and Correspondence from Chippewa Agency, Minnesota,"
             Smithsonian Institution, Bureau of American Ethnology Archives,
             Chippewa Manuscripts.
Seliskar, John.
1911   "The Reverend Francis Pirec, Indian Missionary," *Acta et Dicta*, 3:
             66-90.
Shimpo, Mitsuru and Robert Williamson.
1965   *Socio-cultural Disintegration among the Fringe Saulteaux* Saskatoon,
             Saskatchewan.
Sieber, S. A.
1950   *The Saulteaux Indians* Techny, Illinois.
Skinner, Alanson.
1912   "Notes on the Eastern Cree and Northern Saulteaux," *Anthro-
             pological Papers of the American Museum of Natural History*, 9, Part 1:
             119-177.
1914a   "The Algonkin and the Thunderbird," *The American Museum Jour-
             nal*, 14: 71-72.
1914b   "The Cultural Position of the Plains Ojibway," *American Anthro-
             pologist*, 16: 314-318.
1914c   "Some Aspects of the Folk-Lore of the Central Algonkin," *Journal of
             American Folklore*, 27: 97-100.
1916a   "European Tales from the Plains Ojibwa," *Journal of American Folk-
             lore*, 29: 330-340.
1916b   "Political and Ceremonial Organization of the Plains-Ojibway," *An-
             thropological Papers of the American Museum of Natural History*, 11:
             475-511.
1919   "Plains Ojibwa Tales," *Journal of American Folklore*, 32: 280-305.
1920   *Medicine Ceremony of the Menomini, Iowa, and Wahpeton Dakota, with
             Notes on the Ceremony among the Ponca, Bungi Ojibwa, and Potawatomi*
             New York (Museum of the American Indian, Heye Foundation,
             Indian Notes and Monographs, 4).
1921   "The Sun Dance of the Plains-Ojibway," *Sun Dance of the Plains
             Indians* New York, ed. Clark Wissler (Anthropological Papers of the
             American Museum of Natural History, 16): 311-315.
1923   "A Further Note on the Origin of the Dream Dance of the Central
             Algonkian and Southern Siouan Indians," *American Anthropologist*,
             25: 427-428.
Skolla, (Rev.) Otto.
1936   "Father Skolla's Report on His Indian Missions," trans. Thomas J.
             Shanahan, *Acta et Dicta*, 7: 217-268.
Smith, G. Hubert.
1946   "The Form and Function of the Midewiwin," *The Minnesota Archae-
             ologist*, 12: 22-37.
Smith, Harlan I.
1894   "Ojibwa Legends," Smithsonian Institution, Bureau of American
             Ethnology Archives, Chippewa Manuscripts.
1896   "Certain Shamanistic Ceremonies among the Ojibwas," *The Ameri-
             can Antiquarian and Oriental Journal*, 18: 282-284.
1897   "The Monster in the Tree: An Ojibwa Myth," *Journal of American
             Folklore*, 10: 324-325.
1906   "Some Ojibwa Myths and Traditions," *Journal of American Folklore*,
             19: 215-230.
Smith, Huron H.
1932   "Ethnobotany of the Ojibwe Indians," *Bulletin of the Public Museum of
             the City of Milwaukee*, 4: 327-525.

Smith, James G. E.
1973   *Leadership among the Southwestern Ojibwa* Ottawa (National Museum
               of Man, Publications in Ethnology, 7).
Smith, John.
1919   *Being the Life History of Chief John Smith, as Narrated by Himself and
               Interpreted by His Adopted Son, Thomas E. Smith* Walker, Minnesota.
Speck, Frank G.
1915   *Myths and Folk-Lore of the Timiskamins Algonquin Timagami Ojibwa*
               Ottawa (Canada Department of Mines, Geological Survey, Memoir
               71, Anthropological Series, 9).
Spindler, George D.
1958   "Research Design and Ojibwa Personality Persistence," *American
               Anthropologist,* 60: 934-937.
Steinbring, J.
1965   "Culture Change among the Northern Ojibwa," *Transactions of the
               Historical and Scientific Society of Manitoba,* 3, No. 21: 13-24.
Stevens, Michael E.
1974-1975   "Catholic and Protestant Missionaries among Wisconsin Indians:
               The Territorial Period," *Wisconsin Magazine of History,* 58: 140-148.
Stones, Bones & Skin: Ritual and Shamanic Art.
1973-1974   (*artscanada,* Nos. 184-187).
Stromberg, Jerome S.
1963   "Some Problems in Minnesota Chippewa Acculturation," *Pro-
               ceedings of Minnesota Academy of Science,* 31: 18-23.
Teicher, Morton I.
1960   *Windigo Psychosis: A Study of a Relationship between Belief and Behavior
               among the Indians of Northeastern Canada* Seattle (Proceedings of the
               American Ethnological Society, 1960 Annual Spring Meeting).
Tennelly, J. B.
1935   "Father Pierz, Missionary and Colonizer," *Acta et Dicta,* 7: 104-130.
Thayer, R. W.
1962   " 'Mong,' the Loon," *The Minnesota Archaeologist,* 24: 84-85.
"Thunderbird Legend of the Post."
1930   *The Wisconsin Archaeologist,* 9: 128-129.
Thwaites, Reuben Gold, ed.
1896-1901   *The Jesuit Relations and Allied Documents. Travels and Explorations of the
               Jesuit Missionaries in New France 1610-1791* Cleveland, 73 vols.
Troyer, Warner.
1977   *No Safe Place* Toronto.
Tuttle, Sarah.
1838   *Letters on the Mission to the Ojibwa Indians* Boston.
Tyrrell, J. B., ed.
1916   *David Thompson's Narrative of His Explorations in Western America:
               1784-1812* Toronto.
Vecsey, Christopher.
1971   "Christian Missions to American Indians," unpublished M.A. thesis,
               Northwestern University.
Vennum, Thomas, Jr.
1978   "Ojibwa Origin-Migration Songs of the *mitewiwin,*" *Journal of Ameri-
               can Folklore,* 91: 753-791.
Verwyst, (Rev.) Chrysostom.
1886   *Missionary Labors of Fathers Marquette, Menard and Allouez, in the Lake
               Superior Region* Milwaukee.
1900   *Life and Labors of Rt. Rev. Frederic Baraga, First Bishop of Marquette,
               Mich.* Milwaukee.

1914   "A Short Account of the Fond du Lac Indian Mission," *Acta et Dicta,* 3: 236-252.

1971   *Chippewa Exercises, Being a Practical Introduction into the Study of the Chippewa Language* Minneapolis (original date of publication, 1901).

no date a "Notes on Chequamegon Bay, Including Several Indian Legends," The State Historical Society of Wisconsin, Manuscripts.

no date b "Some Peculiarities of the Chippewa Language," Smithsonian Institution, Bureau of American Ethnology Archives, Chippewa Manuscripts.

no date c "Tchissakiwin, or Indian Jugglery," The State Historical Society of Wisconsin, Manuscripts.

Vizenor, Gerald.

1972   *The Everlasting Sky. New Voices from the People Named the Chippewa* New York.

Voegelin, Erminie W.

1942   "Notes on Ojibwa-Ottawa Pictography," *Proceedings of the Indiana Academy of Science,* 51: 44-47.

Vogel, Virgil J.

1967   "The Missionary as Acculturation Agent: Peter Dougherty and the Indians of Grand Traverse," *Michigan History,* 51: 185-201.

Wagner, Henry R.

1955   *Peter Pond. Fur Trader & Explorer* New Haven.

Wahla, Edward J.

1957   "Religious Beliefs of Early Great Lakes Indians," *The Totem Pole,* 40: 2-5.

Walker, Louise Jean.

1959   *Legends of Green Sky Hill* Grand Rapids, Michigan.

1961   *Red Indian Legends. Tribal Tales of the Great Lakes* London.

1964   *Woodland Wigwams* Hillsdale, Michigan.

Warren, William Whipple.

1885   "History of the Ojibways, Based upon Traditions and Oral Statements," *Collections of the Minnesota Historical Society,* 5: 21-394.

Warren Family.

1756-1907 "Papers," The State Historical Society of Wisconsin, Manuscripts.

Whipple, Henry Benjamin.

1833-1934 "Papers," Minnesota State Historical Society, Manuscripts.

1899   *Lights and Shadows of a Long Episcopate* New York.

1901a "Civilization and Christianization of the Ojibways in Minnesota," *Minnesota Historical Society Collections,* 9: 129-142.

1901b "Recollections of Persons and Events in the History of Minnesota," *Collections of the Minnesota Historical Society,* 9: 576-586.

White Wolf.

1957   *Reminiscences* Sault Ste. Marie, Michigan.

Wilford, Loyd.

1951   "History of the Chippewa," *The Minnesota Archaeologist,* 17: 3-10.

Williams, Mentor L., ed.

1956   *Schoolcraft's Indian Legends* East Lansing, Michigan.

Wilson, (Rev.) Edward F.

1886   *Missionary Work among the Ojebway Indians* London.

Winchell, N. H.

1911   *The Aborigines of Minnesota. A Report Based on the Collections of Jacob V. Brower, and on the Field Surveys and Notes of Alfred J. Hill and Theodore H. Lewis, 1906-1911* St. Paul.

"Winneboujou."

1930   *The Wisconsin Archeologist,* 9: 130.

Wisdom, Charles.
1936   "Report on the Great Lakes Chippewa," U.S. Office of Indian
            Affairs, Applied Anthropology Unit.
Woolworth, Nancy L.
1965   "The Great Portage Mission: 1731-1965," Minnesota History, 39:
            301-310.
Works Progress Administration.
1936-1940; "Chippewa Indian Historical Project Records," The State Historical
1942   Society of Wisconsin, Manuscripts.
Works Progress Administration Writers' Project.
1849-1942   "Minnesota Papers," Minnesota State Historical Society,
            Manuscripts.
Wright, J. V.
1965   "A Regional Examination of Ojibwa Culture History," Anthro-
            pologica, 7: 189-227.
Wright, Robert C.
1907   Indian Masonry Ann Arbor, Michigan.
Wright, Robert H.
1927   Legends of the Chippewas Munsing, Michigan.
Wright, (Rev.) Sela G.
1894   "Words, Phrases and Sentences in Printed Outline, J. W. Powell,
            Introduction to the Study of Indian Languages with Words, Phrases and
            Sentences to Be Collected (Washington, D.C.: 1880)." Smithsonian
            Institution, Bureau of American Ethnology Archives, Chippewa
            Manuscripts.
Yarnell, Richard Asa.
1964   Aboriginal Relationships between Culture and Plant Life in the Upper Great
            Lakes Region Ann Arbor (Museum of Anthropology, University of
            Michigan, Anthropological Papers, 23).
Young, Egerton R.
1895   Oowikapun; or How the Gospel Reached the Nelson River Indians
            Toronto.
1897   On the Indian Trail and Other Stories of Missionary Work among the Cree
            and Saulteaux Indians London.
1899   The Apostle of the North, Rev. James Evans London.
1903   Algonquin Indian Tales New York.
no date a   Indian Life in the Great North-West Toronto.
no date b   Stories from Indian Wigwams and Northern Campfires Toronto.
Zaplotnik, (Rev.) J. L.
1917   "A Lecture Delivered by Bishop Baraga, 1863," Acta et Dicta, 5:
            99-110.
1934   "Rev. Lawrence Lautishar in Minnesota," Acta et Dicta, 6: 258-287.

INDEX

CPSIA information can be obtained
at www.ICGtesting.com
Printed in the USA
LVHW032220221221
706957LV00003B/275